LATIN AMERICAN POLITICAL, ECONOMIC, AND SECURITY ISSUES

CENTRAL AMERICA: PROFILES AND U.S. RELATIONS

LATIN AMERICAN POLITICAL, ECONOMIC, AND SECURITY ISSUES

Additional books in this series can be found on Nova's website
under the Series tab.

Additional E-books in this series can be found on Nova's website
under the E-books tab.

LATIN AMERICAN POLITICAL, ECONOMIC, AND SECURITY ISSUES

CENTRAL AMERICA: PROFILES AND U.S. RELATIONS

BRIAN J. DURHAM
EDITOR

Nova Science Publishers, Inc.
New York

Copyright © 2011 by Nova Science Publishers, Inc.

All rights reserved. No part of this book may be reproduced, stored in a retrieval system or transmitted in any form or by any means: electronic, electrostatic, magnetic, tape, mechanical photocopying, recording or otherwise without the written permission of the Publisher.

For permission to use material from this book please contact us:
Telephone 631-231-7269; Fax 631-231-8175
Web Site: http://www.novapublishers.com

NOTICE TO THE READER

The Publisher has taken reasonable care in the preparation of this book, but makes no expressed or implied warranty of any kind and assumes no responsibility for any errors or omissions. No liability is assumed for incidental or consequential damages in connection with or arising out of information contained in this book. The Publisher shall not be liable for any special, consequential, or exemplary damages resulting, in whole or in part, from the readers' use of, or reliance upon, this material. Any parts of this book based on government reports are so indicated and copyright is claimed for those parts to the extent applicable to compilations of such works.

Independent verification should be sought for any data, advice or recommendations contained in this book. In addition, no responsibility is assumed by the publisher for any injury and/or damage to persons or property arising from any methods, products, instructions, ideas or otherwise contained in this publication.

This publication is designed to provide accurate and authoritative information with regard to the subject matter covered herein. It is sold with the clear understanding that the Publisher is not engaged in rendering legal or any other professional services. If legal or any other expert assistance is required, the services of a competent person should be sought. FROM A DECLARATION OF PARTICIPANTS JOINTLY ADOPTED BY A COMMITTEE OF THE AMERICAN BAR ASSOCIATION AND A COMMITTEE OF PUBLISHERS.

Additional color graphics may be available in the e-book version of this book.

Library of Congress Cataloging-in-Publication Data

Central America : profiles and U.S. relations / editor, Brian J. Durham.
    p. cm.
  Includes bibliographical references and index.
  ISBN 978-1-61470-122-4 (hardcover : alk. paper) 1. Central America--History--1979- 2. Central America--Foreign relations--1979- 3. Central America--Foreign relations--United States. 4. United States--Foreign relations--Central America. 5. United States--Foreign relations--1945-1989. 6. United States--Foreign relations--1989- I. Durham, Brian J.
  F1439.5.C4565 2011
  972.8--dc23
                              2011019864

Published by Nova Science Publishers, Inc. † New York

CONTENTS

Preface		**vii**
Chapter 1	Belize Profile *U.S. Department of State*	**1**
Chapter 2	Costa Rica Profile *U.S. Department of State*	**11**
Chapter 3	Costa Rica: Background and U.S. Relations *Peter J. Meyer*	**21**
Chapter 4	El Salvador Profile *U.S. Department of State*	**35**
Chapter 5	El Salvador: Political, Economic, and Social Conditions and U.S. Relations *Clare Ribando Seelke*	**45**
Chapter 6	Guatemala Profile *U.S. Department of State*	**57**
Chapter 7	Honduras Profile *U.S. Department of State*	**69**
Chapter 8	Honduran-U.S. Relations *Peter J. Meyer*	**81**
Chapter 9	Honduran Political Crisis, June 2009 - January 2010 *Peter J. Meyer*	**105**
Chapter 10	Nicaragua Profile *U.S. Department of State*	**125**
Chapter 11	Nicaragua: Political Situation and U.S. Relations *Clare Ribando Seelke*	**137**
Chapter 12	Panama Profile *U.S. Department of State*	**145**

Chapter 13	Panama: Political and Economic Conditions and U.S. Relations *Mark P. Sullivan*	**155**
Index		**183**

PREFACE

This book profiles the countries of Central America. Discussed are the political, economic and social conditions of these countries, as well as their relations with the United States. Highlighted are the countries of Belize, Costa Rica, El Salvador, Guatemala, Honduras, Nicaragua and Panama.

Chapter 1- Belize is the most sparsely populated nation in Central America. It is larger than El Salvador and compares in size to the State of Massachusetts. Slightly more than half of the population lives in rural areas. About one-fourth live in Belize City, the principal port, commercial center, and former capital. More than one-third of the population is comprised of persons younger than 14 years of age.

Chapter 2- Unlike many of their Central American neighbors, present-day Costa Ricans are largely of European rather than mestizo descent; Spain was the primary country of origin. However, an estimated 10% to 15% of the population is Nicaraguan, of fairly recent arrival and primarily of mestizo origin. Descendants of 19th-century Jamaican immigrant workers constitute an English-speaking minority and--at 3% of the population--number about 119,000. Few of the native Indians survived European contact; the indigenous population today numbers about 29,000 or less than 1% of the population.

Chapter 3- Costa Rica is a politically stable Central American nation with a relatively well-developed economy. Former president (1986-1990) and Nobel-laureate Oscar Arias of the historically center-left National Liberation Party was elected President in 2006. Throughout his term, Arias has advanced so-called "third-way" policies, embracing his party's traditional support for social welfare programs while rejecting state-led development in favor of market-oriented economic policies. Considerable economic growth and social protection programs have provided Costa Rica's citizens with a relatively high standard of living, however, conditions have deteriorated recently as a result of the global financial crisis and U.S. recession. Although Costa Rica's economy contracted and poverty increased in 2009, analysts believe President Arias' ambitious fiscal stimulus and social protection plan and improving global economic conditions should aid recovery in 2010.

Chapter 4- El Salvador's population numbers about 7.2 million. Almost 90% is of mixed Indian and Spanish extraction. About 1% is indigenous; very few Indians have retained their customs and traditions. The country's people are largely Roman Catholic and Protestant. Spanish is the language spoken by virtually all inhabitants. The capital city of San Salvador has about 1.6 million people; an estimated 37.3% of El Salvador's population lives in rural areas.

Chapter 5- Throughout the last few decades, the United States has maintained a strong interest in El Salvador, a small Central American country with a population of 7.2 million. During the 1980s, El Salvador was the largest recipient of U.S. aid in Latin America as its government struggled against the Farabundo Marti National Liberation Front (FMLN) insurgency during a 12-year civil war. A peace accord negotiated in 1992 brought the war to an end and formally assimilated the FMLN into the political process as a political party. After the peace accords were signed, U.S. involvement shifted toward helping the government rebuild democracy and implement market- friendly economic reforms.

Chapter 6- More than half of Guatemalans are descendants of indigenous Mayan peoples. Westernized Mayans and mestizos (mixed European and indigenous ancestry) are known as Ladinos. Most of Guatemala's population is rural, though urbanization is accelerating. The predominant religion is Roman Catholicism, into which many indigenous Guatemalans have incorporated traditional forms of worship. Protestantism and traditional Mayan religions are practiced by an estimated 40% and 1% of the population, respectively. Though the official language is Spanish, it is not universally understood among the indigenous population. The peace accords signed in December 1996 provide for the translation of some official documents and voting materials into several indigenous languages.

Chapter 7- About 90% of the population is mestizo. There also are small minorities of European, African, Asian, Arab, and indigenous Indian descent. A majority of Hondurans are Roman Catholic, but Protestant churches are growing in number. While Spanish is the predominant language, some English is spoken along the northern coast and is prevalent on the Caribbean Bay Islands. Several indigenous Indian languages and Garífuna (a mixture of Afro-indigenous languages) are also spoken. The restored Mayan ruins near the Guatemalan border in Copan reflect the great Mayan culture that flourished there for hundreds of years until the early 9th century. Columbus landed at mainland Honduras (Trujillo) in 1502, and named the area "Honduras" (meaning "depths") for the deep water off the coast. Spaniard Hernan Cortes arrived in 1524.

Chapter 8- On January 27, 2010, Porfirio "Pepe" Lobo Sosa was inaugurated President of Honduras, assuming power after seven months of domestic political crisis and international isolation that had resulted from the June 28, 2009, ouster of President Manuel Zelaya. While the strength of Lobo's National Party in the legislature has enabled the government to secure passage of much of its policy agenda, the Lobo Administration has made only limited progress in addressing the challenges inherited as a result of the political crisis. Several efforts to foster political reconciliation, including the creation of a truth commission and the passage of a measure to enable constitutional reform, have done little to lesson domestic polarization. Moreover, human rights abuses have continued, and the country has failed to secure recognition from some sectors of the international community.

Chapter 9- On June 28, 2009, the Honduran military detained President Manuel Zelaya and flew him to exile in Costa Rica, ending 27 years of uninterrupted democratic, constitutional governance. Honduran governmental institutions had become increasingly polarized in the preceding months as a result of Zelaya's intention to hold a non-binding referendum and eventually amend the constitution. After the ouster, the Honduran Supreme Court asserted that an arrest warrant had been issued for Zelaya as a result of his noncompliance with judicial decisions that had declared the non-binding referendum unconstitutional. However, the military's actions halted the judicial process before a trial could be held. The Honduran National Congress then adopted a resolution to replace Zelaya with the President of Congress, Roberto Micheletti.

Chapter 10- Most Nicaraguans are of both European and indigenous ancestry, and the culture of the country reflects the mixed Ibero-European and indigenous heritage of its people. Only the indigenous of the eastern half of the country remain ethnically distinct and retain their tribal customs and languages. A large black minority, of Afro-Caribbean origin, is concentrated along the Caribbean coast. In the mid-1980s, the central government divided the eastern half of the country--the former department of Zelaya--into two autonomous regions and granted the people of the region limited self-rule under an elected regional council of 45 deputies and an indirectly-elected governor.

Chapter 11- Nicaragua, the second poorest country in Latin America after Haiti, has had a difficult path to democracy, characterized by ongoing struggles between rival caudillos (strongmen), generations of dictatorial rule, and civil war. Since 1990, Nicaragua has been developing democratic institutions and a framework for economic development. Nonetheless, the country remains extremely poor and its institutions are weak. Former revolutionary Sandinista leader, Daniel Ortega, was inaugurated to a new five-year presidential term in January 2007 and appears to be governing generally democratically and implementing market-friendly economic policies. The United States, though concerned about Ortega's ties to Venezuela and Iran and his authoritarian tendencies, has remained actively engaged with the Ortega Administration. The two countries are working together to implement the U.S.-Dominican Republic-Central America Free Trade Agreement (CAFTA-DR), control narcotics and crime, and promote economic development through the Millennium Challenge Account (MCA). Nicaragua is receiving some $28.6 million in U.S. assistance in FY2008 and could benefit from the proposed Mérida Initiative for Mexico and Central America.

Chapter 12- Panamanians' culture, customs, and language are predominantly Caribbean Spanish. The majority of the population is ethnically mestizo or mixed Spanish, indigenous, Chinese, and West Indian. Spanish is the official and dominant language; English is a common second language spoken by the West Indians and by many businesspeople and professionals. More than half the population lives in the Panama City-Colon metropolitan corridor.

Chapter 13- With five successive elected civilian governments, the Central American nation of Panama has made notable political and economic progress since the 1989 U.S. military intervention that ousted the regime of General Manuel Noriega from power. Current President Ricardo Martinelli of the center-right Democratic Change (CD) party was elected in May 2009, defeating the ruling center-left Democratic Revolutionary Party (PRD) in a landslide. Martinelli was inaugurated to a five-year term on July 1, 2009. Martinelli's Alliance for Change coalition also captured a majority of seats in Panama's National Assembly. Panama's service-based economy has been booming in recent years, largely because of the ongoing Panama Canal expansion project (slated for completion in 2014), but economic growth slowed in 2009 because of the global financial crisis and U.S. economic recession. Nevertheless, the economy rebounded in 2010, with a growth rate approaching 7%, and strong growth is continuing in 2011.

In: Central America: Profiles and U.S. Relations
Editor: Brian J. Durham
ISBN: 978-1-61470-122-4
© 2011 Nova Science Publishers, Inc.

Chapter 1

BELIZE PROFILE

U.S. Department of State

GEOGRAPHY

Area: 22,966 sq. km. (8,867 sq. mi.); slightly larger than Massachusetts.
Cities: *Capital*--Belmopan (June 2008 pop. est. 18,100). *Other cities and towns*--Belize City (65,200), Corozal (9,300), Orange Walk (16,300), San Ignacio and Santa Elena (19,100), Dangriga (12,000), Punta Gorda (5,400), and San Pedro (11,600).
Terrain: Flat and swampy coastline, low mountains in interior.
Climate: Subtropical (dry and wet seasons). Hot and humid. Rainfall ranges from 60 inches in the north to 200 inches in the south annually.

Flag of Belize

PEOPLE

Nationality: *Noun and adjective*--Belizean(s).
Population (July 2010 est.): 307,899.
Annual population growth rate (2010 est.): 2.154%.
Ethnic groups: Creole, Garifuna, mestizo, Mayan.
Religions: Roman Catholic, Anglican, Methodist, Mennonite, other Protestant, Muslim, Hindu, and Buddhist.
Languages: English (official), Creole, Spanish, Garifuna, Mayan.
Education: *Years compulsory*--9. *Attendance* (2006 est.)--90% primary; 38% secondary. *Literacy* (2006 est.)--76.5%.
Health (2009): *Infant mortality rate*--23.07/1,000 live births. *Life expectancy*--68.2 years.
Work force (2009, 122,300): *Services*--71.7%. *Agriculture, hunting, forestry, and fishing*--10.2%. *Industry and commerce*--18.1%.

GOVERNMENT

Type: Parliamentary democracy.
Independence: September 21, 1981.
Constitution: September 21, 1981.
Branches: *Executive*--Queen Elizabeth II (head of state), represented by a governor general; prime minister (head of government, 5-year term). *Legislative*--bicameral National Assembly. *Judicial*--Court of Appeal, Supreme Court, district magistrates.
Subdivisions: Six districts.
Political parties: United Democratic Party (UDP), People's United Party (PUP), National Alliance for Belizean Rights (NABR), National Reform Party (NRP), Vision Inspired By the People (VIP), People's National Party (PNP), We the People Reform Movement (WTP).
Suffrage: Universal adult.

ECONOMY

GDP (current market prices, 2009): $2.534 billion.
Real annual growth rate (2009): -1.5%; (2008): 2.1%.
Per capita income (2009): $8,200.
Avg. inflation rate (2009 est.): 0.3%.
Natural resources: Arable land, timber, seafood, minerals.
Primary sectors (10.2% of GDP, 2009): Agriculture, forestry, fishing, and mining.

Secondary sectors (18.1% of GDP, 2009): Manufacturing, electricity and water supply, and construction.

Tertiary sectors (54.1% of GDP, 2009): Hotels and restaurants, financial intermediation, trade, and transport and communication.

Trade: *Exports* (2009 est.)--$395 million: cane sugar, citrus concentrate, marine products, bananas, clothing, molasses, and crude oil. *Major markets*--U.S. (36.9%), U.K., CARICOM.

Imports (2009 est.)--$616 million: food, consumer goods, machinery and transportation equipment, chemicals, pharmaceuticals, tobacco, mineral fuels, and lubricants. *Major suppliers*--U.S. (38%), Central America, Mexico, and China.

Official exchange rate: Since 1976 Belizean banks have bought U.S. dollars at the rate of 2.0175 and sold them at 1.9825, making for an effective fixed rate of Belize $2=U.S. $1.

PEOPLE

Belize is the most sparsely populated nation in Central America. It is larger than El Salvador and compares in size to the State of Massachusetts. Slightly more than half of the population lives in rural areas. About one-fourth live in Belize City, the principal port, commercial center, and former capital. More than one-third of the population is comprised of persons younger than 14 years of age.

Most Belizeans are of multiracial descent. About 43.7% of the population is of mixed Mayan and European descent (mestizo); 29.8% are of African and Afro-European (Creole) ancestry; about 11.0% are Mayan; and about 6.6% are Afro-Amerindian (Garifuna). The remainder, about 8.9%, includes European, East Indian, Chinese, Middle Eastern, and North American groups.

English, the official language, is spoken by virtually all except the refugees who arrived during the past decade. Spanish is the native tongue of about 50% of the people and is spoken as a second language by another 20%. The various Mayan groups still speak their indigenous languages, and an English-Creole dialect similar to the Creole dialects of the English-speaking Caribbean Islands is spoken by most. The rate of functional literacy is 76%. About 50% of the population is Roman Catholic; the Anglican Church and other Protestant Christian groups account for most of the remaining 50%. Mennonite settlers number about 8,500.

HISTORY

The Mayan civilization spread into the area of Belize between 1500 BC and AD 300 and flourished until about AD 1200. Several major archeological sites--notably Caracol, Lamanai, Lubaantun, Altun Ha, and Xunantunich--reflect the advanced civilization and much denser population of that period. European contact began in 1502 when Christopher Columbus sailed along the coast. The first recorded European settlement was established by shipwrecked English seamen in 1638. Over the next 150 years, more English settlements were established. This period also was marked by piracy, indiscriminate logging, and sporadic attacks by Indians and neighboring Spanish settlers.

Great Britain first sent an official representative to the area in the late 18th century, but Belize was not formally termed the "Colony of British Honduras" until 1840. It became a crown colony in 1862. Subsequently, several constitutional changes were enacted to expand representative government. Full internal self-government under a ministerial system was granted in January 1964. The official name of the territory was changed from British Honduras to Belize in June 1973, and full independence was granted on September 21, 1981.

GOVERNMENT

Belize is a parliamentary democracy based on the Westminster model and is a member of the Commonwealth. Queen Elizabeth II is head of state and is represented in the country by Governor General Colville N. Young, Sr., a Belizean and Belize's second governor general. The primary executive organ of government is the cabinet, led by a prime minister (head of government). Cabinet ministers are members of the majority political party in parliament and usually hold elected seats in the National Assembly concurrently with their cabinet positions.

The National Assembly consists of a House of Representatives and a Senate. The 31 members of the House are popularly elected to a maximum 5-year term. The governor general appoints the Senate's 12 members. Six are appointed in accordance with the advice of the prime minister, 3 with the advice of the leader of the opposition. The Belize Council of Churches and the Evangelical Association of Churches, the Belize Chamber of Commerce and Industry and the Belize Business Bureau, and the National Trade Union Congress and the Civil Society Steering Committee each advise the Governor General on the appointment of one senator each. (A majority of Belizeans who decided to participate in the referendum held along with the national elections on February 7, 2008 voted in favor of a change from the current appointed Senate to an elected one. This change will take effect during the next general election, which is slated to take place by early 2013.) The Senate is headed by a president, who is a non-voting member appointed by the governing party.

Members of the independent judiciary are appointed. The judicial system includes local magistrates, the Supreme Court, and the Court of Appeal. Cases may, under certain circumstances, be appealed to the Privy Council in London. However, in 2001 Belize joined with most members of the Caribbean Common Market (CARICOM) to establish a "Caribbean Court of Justice," which was inaugurated on April 16, 2005. The country is divided into six districts: Corozal, Orange Walk, Belize, Cayo, Stann Creek, and Toledo.

POLITICAL CONDITIONS

In national elections on February 7, 2008, the United Democratic Party (UDP) prevailed over the incumbent People's United Party (PUP). The UDP won 25 of the 31 seats in the House of Representatives, while the PUP won the other six seats. UDP leader Dean Barrow replaced PUP leader Said Musa as Prime Minister. The PUP governed Belize from 1998-2008; the UDP from 1993-98; the PUP from 1989-1993; and the UDP from 1984-89. Before 1984, the PUP had dominated the electoral scene for more than 30 years and was the party in power when Belize became independent in 1981. Third-party alternatives to the two-party system have arisen in the recent years, but these parties garnered less than 2% of the vote in the February 2008 elections.

The UDP is responding to concerns of an unsustainable foreign debt, high unemployment, growing involvement in the South American drug trade, high crime rates, and increasing incidents of HIV/AIDS through a four-pillar approach: social investment through poverty alleviation; job creation through public sector investment; improving access to credit; and combating crime and violence. As of February 2010, Belize's total national debt (both external and domestic) was U.S. $1.173 billion (public external debt was U.S. $1.0095 billion and domestic debt was $163.8 million), an amount that is equivalent to approximately 72.1% of GDP. On January 31, 2007 the Government of Belize officially announced that the holders of Belize's public external commercial debt had agreed to exchange their existing claims against the country for new bonds to be issued by Belize, maturing in 2029. Belize traditionally maintains a deep interest in the environment and sustainable development. A lack of government resources seriously hampers progress toward these goals. On other fronts, the government is working to improve its law enforcement capabilities. A longstanding territorial dispute with Guatemala continues, although cooperation between the two countries has increased in recent years across a wide spectrum of common interests, including trade and environment. Seeing itself as a bridge, Belize is actively involved with the Caribbean nations of CARICOM, and also has taken steps to work more closely with its Central American neighbors as a member of SICA (Central American Integration System).

Principal Government Officials

Head of State--Queen Elizabeth II
Governor General--Colville N. Young, Sr.
Prime Minister and Minister of Finance--Dean Barrow
Deputy Prime Minister and Minister of Natural Resources and the Environment--Gaspar Vega
Minister of Foreign Affairs and Foreign Trade--Wilfred Elrington
Minister of Economic Development, Commerce, Industry and Consumer Protection--Erwin Contreras
Minister of Defense--Carlos Perdomo
Minister of Labor, Local Government and Rural Development--Gabriel Martinez
Ambassador to the United States--Nestor Mendez
Ambassador to the OAS--Nestor Mendez
Ambassador to the United Nations--Janine Coye-Felson
Belize maintains an embassy in the United States at 2535 Massachusetts Avenue NW, Washington, DC 20008 (tel: 202-332-9636; fax: 202-332-6888; website: http://www.embassyofbelize.org/) and a consulate in Los Angeles. Belize travel information office in New York City: 800-624-0686.

ECONOMY

Forestry was the only economic activity of any consequence in Belize until well into the 20th century, when the supply of accessible timber began to dwindle. Cane sugar then became the principal export. Exports were augmented by expanded production of citrus, bananas, seafood, and apparel. The agricultural sector suffered from damage resulting from hurricanes that struck Belize in late 2007 and heavy flooding in mid-June and October of 2008. The farm shrimp industry, a chief export earner until 2005, continues to decline. The service sector and nascent petroleum sector lead Belize's economic growth.

The country has about 809,000 hectares of arable land, only a small fraction of which is under cultivation. To curb land speculation, the government enacted legislation in 1973 that requires non-Belizeans to complete a development plan on land they purchase before obtaining title to plots of more than 10 acres of rural land or more than one-half acre of urban land.

Domestic industry is limited, constrained by relatively high-cost labor and energy and a small domestic market. Some 185 U.S. companies have operations in Belize, including Archer Daniels Midland, Texaco, and Esso. Tourism attracts the most foreign direct investment, although significant U.S. investment also is found in the telecommunications and agriculture sectors.

A combination of natural factors--climate, the longest barrier reef in the Western Hemisphere, numerous islands, excellent fishing, safe waters for boating, jungle wildlife, and Mayan ruins--support the thriving tourist industry. Development costs are high, but the Government of Belize has designated tourism as one of its major development priorities. However, although in 2006 tourist arrivals in Belize totaled 958,813 (about 70% from the United States), tourist arrivals were down 2.5% in 2008 alone. This decline is primarily the result of the global economic crisis.

Belize's investment policy is codified in the Belize Investment Guide, which sets out the development priorities for the country. A **Country Commercial Guide** for Belize is available from the U.S. Embassy's Economic/Commercial section and on the Internet at: http://belize.usembassy.gov/investing_in_belize2.html.

Infrastructure

A major constraint on the economic development of Belize continues to be the scarcity of infrastructure investments. As part of its financial austerity measures started in late 2004, the government froze expenditures on several capital projects. Although electricity, telephone, and water utilities are all relatively good, Belize has the most expensive electricity in the region. Large tracts of land, which would be suitable for development, are inaccessible due to lack of roads. Some roads, including sections of major highways, are subject to damage or closure during the rainy season. Ports in Belize City, Dangriga, and Big Creek handle regularly scheduled shipping from the United States and the United Kingdom, although draft is limited to a maximum of 10 feet in Belize City and 15 feet in southern ports. American Airlines, Continental Airlines, U.S. Air, Delta Airlines, and TACA provide international air service to gateways in Dallas, Houston, Miami, Charlotte, Atlanta, and San Salvador.

Trade

Belize's economic performance is highly susceptible to external market changes, a fact that was reflected in the rise of its real growth rate from 1.2% in 2007 to 2.1% in 2008. The global slowdown hit Belize hard, and in 2009, growth decreased to -1.5%. World commodity price fluctuations and continuation of preferential trading agreements, especially with the United States and the European Union (cane sugar) and the United Kingdom (bananas), greatly impact Belize's economic performance.

Belize continues to rely heavily on foreign trade. Imports at June 2009 totaled $616 million, while total exports were $395 million. The United States continues to be Belize's number-one trading partner. Through 2009, the United States provided 38.0% of all Belizean imports and accounted for 37% of Belize's total exports. Other major trading partners include Mexico, the United Kingdom, European Union, Central America, and the CARICOM member states. In 2006-2007, Taiwan and Japan emerged as new trading partners with Belize.

Belize aims to stimulate the growth of commercial agriculture through CARICOM. However, Belizean trade with the rest of the Caribbean is small compared to that with the United States and Europe. The country is a beneficiary of the Central American Regional Security Initiative (CARSI), through which the U.S. Government seeks to strengthen the capacities of the governments of Central America to confront and disrupt criminal organizations operating into, through, and within the region. U.S. trade preferences allowing for duty-free re-import of finished apparel cut from U.S. textiles have significantly expanded the apparel industry. European Union (EU) and U.K. preferences also have been vital for the expansion and prosperity of the sugar and banana industries.

NATIONAL SECURITY

The Belize Defense Force (BDF), established in January 1973, is comprised of a light infantry force of regulars and reservists along with small air and maritime wings. The BDF, currently under the command of Brigadier General Dario Tapa, assumed total defense responsibility from British Forces Belize (BFB) on January 1, 1994. The United Kingdom continues to maintain the British Army Training Support Unit Belize (BATSUB) to assist in the administration of the Belize Jungle School. The BDF receives military assistance from the United States and the United Kingdom.

FOREIGN RELATIONS

Belize's principal external concern has been the dispute involving the Guatemalan claim to Belizean territory. This dispute originated in Imperial Spain's claim to all "New World" territories west of the line established in the Treaty of Tordesillas in 1494. Nineteenth-century efforts to resolve the problems led to later differences over interpretation and implementation of an 1859 treaty intended to establish the boundaries between Guatemala and Belize, then named British Honduras. Guatemala contends that the 1859 treaty is void because the British failed to comply with all its economic assistance clauses. Neither Spain nor Guatemala ever exercised effective sovereignty over the area.

Negotiations have been underway for many years, including one period in the 1960s in which the U.S. Government sought unsuccessfully to mediate. A 1981 trilateral (Belize, Guatemala, and the United Kingdom) "Heads of Agreement" was not implemented due to continued contentions. Belize became independent on September 21, 1981, with the territorial dispute unresolved. Significant negotiations between Belize and Guatemala, with the United Kingdom as an observer, resumed in 1988. Guatemala recognized Belize's independence in 1991, and diplomatic relations were established.

Eventually, on November 8, 2000, the two parties agreed to respect an "adjacency zone" extending one kilometer east and west from the border. Around this time, the Government of Guatemala insisted that the territorial claim was a legal one and that the only possibility for a resolution was to submit the case to the International Court of Justice (ICJ). However, the Government of Belize felt that taking the case to the ICJ or to arbitration represented an unnecessary expenditure of time and money. So the Belizean Government proposed an alternate process, one under the auspices of the Organization of American States (OAS).

Since then, despite efforts by the OAS to jumpstart the process, movement has been limited to confidence-building measures between the parties. In November 2007, the Secretary General of the OAS recommended that the dispute be referred to the International Court of Justice. Currently Belize and Guatemala are preparing for a referendum, to be held simultaneously in both countries, on whether this dispute will move forward to the ICJ. No date for the referendum has been set.

In order to strengthen its potential for economic and political development, Belize has sought to build closer ties with the Spanish-speaking countries of Central America to complement its historical ties to the English-speaking Caribbean states. In 2005 Belize joined other Central American countries participating in the Cooperating Nations Information Exchange System (CNIES), which assists in locating, identifying, tracking, and intercepting civil aircraft in Belize's airspace. Belize and other Central American countries signed the Conjunta Centroamerica-USA (CONCAUSA) agreement on regional sustainable development. Belize held the presidency of the Central American Integration System (SICA) for a 6-month period in 2007. Belize is a member of CARICOM, which was founded in 1973, and held the chairmanship of CARICOM for a 6-month period in 2008. Belize became a member of the OAS in 1990.

U.S.-BELIZEAN RELATIONS

The United States and Belize traditionally have had close and cordial relations. The United States is Belize's principal trading partner and major source of investment funds. It is also home to the largest Belizean community outside Belize, estimated to be 70,000 strong. Because Belize's economic growth and accompanying democratic political stability are important U.S. objectives, Belize benefits from the Central American Regional Security Initiative (CARSI), through which the U.S. Government seeks to strengthen citizen safety and improve the government's capacity to confront and disrupt criminal organizations.

International crime issues dominate the agenda of bilateral relations between the United States and Belize. The United States is working closely with the Government of Belize to fight illicit narcotics trafficking, and in 2008 Belize began to receive funding under the Merida Initiative, now called CARSI. Both governments also seek to control the flow of illegal migrants to the United States through Belize. Belize and the United States brought into force a Stolen Vehicle Treaty, an Extradition Treaty, and a Mutual Legal Assistance Treaty between 2001 and 2003.

The United States is one of the largest providers of economic assistance to Belize, contributing $3.5 million in various bilateral economic and military aid programs to Belize in FY 2008. The U.S. military has a diverse and growing assistance program in Belize that has included the construction and renovation of several schools and youth hostels, medical assistance programs, and drug reduction programs. The U.S. Military Liaison Office (MLO), in conjunction with the Belize Defense Force, also worked to establish the Belize National Coast Guard. The U.S. Agency for International Development (USAID) closed its Belize office in August 1996 after a 13-year program during which USAID provided $110 million worth of development assistance to Belize. Belize still benefits from USAID regional programs. In addition, during the past 42 years, almost 2,000 Peace Corps volunteers have served in Belize. As of October 2010, the Peace Corps had 75 volunteers working in Belize. Private North American investors continue to play a key role in Belize's economy, particularly in the tourism sector.

Chapter 2

COSTA RICA PROFILE

U.S. Department of State

Official Name: Republic of Costa Rica

GEOGRAPHY

Area: 51,100 sq. km (19,730 sq. mi.) about the size of the states of Vermont and New Hampshire combined.

Cities: *Capital*--San Jose (greater metropolitan area pop. 2.1 million, the greater metropolitan area as defined by the Ministry of Planning and Economic Policy includes the cities of Alajuela, Cartago, and Heredia). *Other major cities outside the San Jose capital area*--Puntarenas, Limon, and Liberia.

Terrain: A rugged, central range separates the eastern and western coastal plains.

Climate: Mild in the central highlands, tropical and subtropical in coastal areas.

Flag of Costa Rica

PEOPLE

Nationality: *Noun and adjective*--Costa Rican(s).
Population (2010): 4.516 million.
Annual population growth rate (2010 est.): 1.347%.
Ethnic groups: European and some mestizo 94%, African origin 3%, Chinese 1%, Amerindian 1%, other 1%.
Religion: Roman Catholic 76.3%, Evangelical Protestant 13.7%, other 4.8%, none 3.2%.
Languages: Spanish, with a southwestern Caribbean Creole dialect of English spoken around the Limon area.
Education: *Years compulsory*--9. *Attendance*--99% grades 1-6; 71% grades 7-9. *Literacy*--96%.
Health: *Infant mortality rate*--9.45/1,000. *Life expectancy*--men 74.61 yrs., women 79.94 yrs.
Work force (2009 est.): 2.05 million; this official estimate excludes Nicaraguans living in Costa Rica legally and illegally.

GOVERNMENT

Type: Democratic republic.
Independence: September 15, 1821.
Constitution: November 7, 1949.
Branches: *Executive*--president (head of government and chief of state) elected for one 4-year term, two vice presidents, Cabinet (22 ministers, two of whom are also vice presidents). *Legislative*--57-deputy unicameral Legislative Assembly elected at 4-year intervals. *Judicial*--Supreme Court of Justice (22 magistrates elected by Legislative Assembly for renewable 8-year terms). The offices of the Ombudsman, Comptroller General, and Procurator General assert autonomous oversight of the government.
Subdivisions: Seven provinces, divided into 81 cantons, subdivided into 421 districts.
Political parties: National Liberation Party (PLN), Citizen's Action Party (PAC), Libertarian Movement Party (PML), Social Christian Unity Party (PUSC), and other smaller parties.
Suffrage: Universal and compulsory at age 18.

ECONOMY

GDP (2010): $38.27 billion.

GDP PPP (2009 est.): $48.19 billion.

Inflation (2010 est.): 6.9%.

Real growth rate (2010 est.): 3.6%.

Per capita income: (2009) $6,900; (2010 est., PPP) $10,569.

Unemployment (2010 est.): 6.7%.

Currency: Costa Rica Colon (CRC).

Natural resources: Hydroelectric power, forest products, fisheries products.

Agriculture (6.5% of GDP): *Products*--bananas, pineapples, coffee, beef, sugar, rice, dairy products, vegetables, fruits, ornamental plants, corn, beans, potatoes, timber.

Industry (25.5% of GDP): *Types*--electronic components, medical equipment, textiles and apparel, tires, food processing, construction materials, fertilizer, plastic products.

Commerce, tourism, and services (68% of GDP): Hotels, restaurants, tourist services, banks, and insurance.

Trade (2010 est.): *Exports*--$10.01 billion: integrated circuits, medical equipment, bananas, pineapples, coffee, melons, ornamental plants, sugar, textiles, electronic components, medical equipment. *Major markets* (2009)--U.S. 32.61%, Netherlands 12.82%, China 11.81%, Mexico 4.2%. *Imports*--$13.32 billion: raw materials, consumer goods, capital equipment, petroleum. *Major suppliers* (2009)--U.S. 44.72%, Mexico 7.65%, Venezuela 5.56%, China 5.15%, Japan 4.36%

PEOPLE

Unlike many of their Central American neighbors, present-day Costa Ricans are largely of European rather than mestizo descent; Spain was the primary country of origin. However, an estimated 10% to 15% of the population is Nicaraguan, of fairly recent arrival and primarily of mestizo origin. Descendants of 19th-century Jamaican immigrant workers constitute an English-speaking minority and--at 3% of the population--number about 119,000. Few of the native Indians survived European contact; the indigenous population today numbers about 29,000 or less than 1% of the population.

HISTORY

In 1502, on his fourth and last voyage to the New World, Christopher Columbus made the first European landfall in the area. Settlement of Costa Rica began in 1522. For nearly 3 centuries, Spain administered the region as part of the Captaincy General of Guatemala under a military governor. The Spanish optimistically called the country "Rich Coast." Finding little gold or other valuable minerals in Costa Rica, however, the Spanish turned to agriculture.

The small landowners' relative poverty, the lack of a large indigenous labor force, the population's ethnic and linguistic homogeneity, and Costa Rica's isolation from the Spanish colonial centers in Mexico and the Andes all contributed to the development of an autonomous and individualistic agrarian society. An egalitarian tradition also arose. This tradition survived the widened class distinctions brought on by the 19th-century introduction of banana and coffee cultivation and consequent accumulations of local wealth.

Costa Rica joined other Central American provinces in 1821 in a joint declaration of independence from Spain. Although the newly independent provinces formed a Federation, border disputes broke out among them, adding to the region's turbulent history and conditions. Costa Rica's northern Guanacaste Province was annexed from Nicaragua in one such regional dispute. In 1838, long after the Central American Federation ceased to function in practice, Costa Rica formally withdrew and proclaimed itself sovereign.

An era of peaceful democracy in Costa Rica began in 1899 with elections considered the first truly free and honest ones in the country's history. This began a trend that continued until today with only two lapses: in 1917-19, Federico Tinoco ruled as a dictator, and, in 1948, Jose Figueres led an armed uprising in the wake of a disputed presidential election.

With more than 2,000 dead, the 44-day civil war resulting from this uprising was the bloodiest event in 20th-century Costa Rican history, but the victorious junta drafted a constitution guaranteeing free elections with universal suffrage and the abolition of the military. Figueres became a national hero, winning the first election under the new constitution in 1953. Since then, Costa Rica has held 15 presidential elections, the latest in 2010.

GOVERNMENT

Costa Rica is a democratic republic with a very strong system of constitutional checks and balances. Executive responsibilities are vested in a president, who is the country's center of power. There also are two vice presidents and a 20-plus member cabinet. The president and 57 Legislative Assembly deputies are elected for 4-year terms. In April 2003, the Costa Rican Constitutional Court annulled a 1969 constitutional reform which had barred presidents from running for reelection. As a result, the law reverted back to the 1949 Constitution, which permits ex-presidents to run for reelection after they have been out of office for two presidential terms, or 8 years. Deputies may run for reelection after sitting out one term, or 4 years.

The electoral process is supervised by an independent Supreme Electoral Tribunal--a commission of three principal magistrates and six alternates selected by the Supreme Court of Justice. Judicial power is exercised by the Supreme Court of Justice, composed of 22 magistrates selected for renewable 8-year terms by the Legislative Assembly, and subsidiary courts. A Constitutional Chamber of the Supreme Court (Sala IV), established in 1989, reviews the constitutionality of legislation and executive decrees and all habeas corpus warrants. The last national elections took place in February 2010.

The offices of the Comptroller General of the Republic, the Solicitor General, and the Ombudsman exercise oversight of the government. The Comptroller General's office has a statutory responsibility to scrutinize all but the smallest public sector contracts and strictly enforces procedural requirements. Along with the Sala IV, these institutions are playing an increasingly prominent role in governing Costa Rica.

There are provincial boundaries for administrative purposes, but no elected provincial officials. Costa Rica held its first mayoral elections in December 2002, whereby mayors were elected to 4-year terms by popular vote through general elections. Prior to 2002, the office of mayor did not exist, and the president of each municipal council was responsible for the administration of his/her municipality. The most recent nationwide mayoral elections took place in December 2010.

Costa Rica's insurance, telecommunications, electricity distribution, petroleum distribution, potable water, sewage, and railroad transportation industries are currently state monopolies. However, with the Central America-Dominican Republic-United States Free Trade Agreement (CAFTA-DR), Costa Rica accords substantial market access in a wide range of services, subject to very few exceptions. The wireless telephony, data telecommunications, and insurance markets opened to market competition in 2010. As part of the implementing agenda for CAFTA-DR, Costa Rica intends to strengthen and modernize the state monopoly telecommunications provider (ICE) so that it can remain competitive with new companies entering the market.

Costa Rica has no military and maintains only domestic police and security forces. A professional Coast Guard was established in 2000.

Principal Government Officials

President--Laura CHINCHILLA Miranda
Vice Presidents--Alfio PIVA and Luis LIBERMAN
Foreign Minister--Rene CASTRO Salazar
Ambassador to the United States--Muni FIGUERES Boggs
Ambassador to the Organization of American States--Jose Enrique CASTILLO Barrantes
Ambassador to the United Nations--Jairo HERNANDEZ Milian

Costa Rica maintains an **embassy** in the United States at 2114 S Street NW, Washington, DC 20008 (tel. 202-234-2945 and 202-234-2946).

POLITICAL CONDITIONS

Costa Rica has long emphasized the development of democracy and respect for human rights. The country's political system has steadily developed, maintaining democratic institutions and an orderly, constitutional scheme for government succession. Several factors have contributed to this trend, including enlightened leadership, comparative prosperity, flexible class lines, educational opportunities that have created a stable middle class, and high social indicators. Also, because Costa Rica has no armed forces, it has avoided military involvement in political affairs, unlike other countries in the region.

On May 8, 2010 Laura Chinchilla, of the National Liberation Party (PLN), was sworn in as President of the Republic of Costa Rica. Throughout her campaign, Chinchilla's primary message was strengthening security; her platform also included improvement of the country's infrastructure, creation of a progressive income tax and expanding jobs through a "green jobs" initiative, better living conditions for children and senior citizens, and supporting women's issues. Immediately upon assuming office, Chinchilla signed four decrees, two involving citizen security and two in the social and environmental field. Following the 2010 elections, the 57-member unicameral Legislative Assembly fragmented into several parties, with no faction having a plurality--the PLN won 23 seats, the PAC 12 seats, ML 9 seats, and the Social Christian Unity Party (PUSC) 6 seats, with the remaining seats split among lesser known parties.

ECONOMY

After experiencing positive growth over the previous several years, the Costa Rican economy shrank slightly in 2009 (-2.5%) due to the global economic crisis. The services sector--around 68% of GDP--was the most affected, with tourism falling by 8%. The economy experienced a rebound in 2010 with a 3.6% GDP growth rate. Costa Rica enjoys the region's highest standard of living, with a per capita income of about U.S. $10,569, and an unemployment rate of 6.7%. Consumer price inflation is high but relatively constant at about a 10% annual rate in the last decade. Both the central government and the overall public sector ran fiscal surpluses in 2007.

Costa Rica's major economic resources are its fertile land and frequent rainfall, its well-educated population, and its location in the Central American isthmus, which provides easy access to North and South American markets and direct ocean access to the European and Asian continents. Costa Rica is known worldwide for its conservation efforts with more than 26% of its land under protection, thus safeguarding more than 5% of the entire world's biodiversity. The country's top economic priorities include passing fiscal reform, pursuing responsible monetary policy, and creating opportunities for inclusive economic growth. Significant legislative hurdles slow down passage of new laws and present challenges for the country's economic policymakers.

Costa Rica used to be known principally as a producer of bananas and coffee, but pineapples have surpassed coffee as the number two agricultural export. Manufacturing and industry's contribution to GDP overtook agriculture in the 1990s, led by foreign investment in Costa Rica's free trade zone. Well over half of that investment has come from the United States. Del Monte, Dole, and Chiquita have a large presence in the banana and pineapple industries. In recent years, Costa Rica has successfully attracted important investments by such companies as Intel Corporation, which employs 3,200 people at its $1.996 billion microprocessor plant; Procter and Gamble, which employs about 1,200 people in its administrative center for the Western Hemisphere; and Boston Scientific, Allergan, Hospira, and Baxter Healthcare from the health care products industry. Two-way trade between the U.S. and Costa Rica exceeded $10.3 billion in 2010. Costa Rica was the United States' 37th largest goods export market in 2009.

The country is rich with renewable energy. It gets about 99% of all its electrical energy from clean sources, and it is aiming to become carbon neutral by 2021. Costa Rica has oil deposits off its Atlantic Coast, but the Pacheco administration (2002-2006) decided not to develop the deposits for environmental reasons. The Arias administration (2006-2010) reaffirmed this policy. The country's mountainous terrain and abundant rainfall have permitted the construction of a dozen hydroelectric power plants, making it largely self-sufficient in electricity, but it is completely reliant on imports for liquid fuels. Costa Rica has the potential to become a major electricity exporter if plans for new generating plants and a regional distribution grid are realized. Its mild climate and trade winds make neither heating nor cooling necessary, particularly in the highland cities and towns where some 90% of the population lives.

Costa Rica ranked 121st out of 183 countries in the 2010 World Bank's Ease of Doing Business Index. This hampers the flow of investment and resources badly needed to repair and rebuild the country's public infrastructure, which has deteriorated from a lack of maintenance and new investment. Most parts of the country are accessible through an extensive road system of more than 30,000 kilometers, although much of the system has fallen into disrepair. Contamination in rivers, beaches, and aquifers is a matter of rising concern. Although Costa Rica has made significant progress in the past decade in expanding access to water supplies and sanitation, just 3.5% of the country's sewage is managed in sewage treatment facilities, and the Water and Sewage Institute (AyA) estimates that perhaps 50% of septic systems function. In 2007, Costa Rica experienced nationwide blackouts resulting from a severe dry season (which limited hydroelectric resources) and the state electricity monopoly's inadequate investment in maintenance and capacity increases.

Costa Rica has sought to widen its economic and trade ties within and outside the region. The country signed a bilateral trade agreement with Mexico in 1994, which was later amended to cover a wider range of products. Costa Rica also has signed trade agreements with Canada, Chile, the Dominican Republic, Panama, and several Caribbean Community countries. In March 1998, it joined other Central American countries and the Dominican Republic in establishing a Trade and Investment Council with the United States. Following a 2007 public referendum, Costa Rica ratified the U.S.-Central American-Dominican Republic Free Trade Agreement (CAFTA-DR), which entered into force in January 2009. The country was an active participant in the negotiation of the hemispheric Free Trade Area of the Americas and is active in the Cairns Group, which is pursuing global agricultural trade liberalization within the World Trade Organization.

In October 2007, Costa Rica began negotiating a regional Central American-European Union (EU) trade agreement. Together with El Salvador, Guatemala, Honduras, Nicaragua, and Panama, its free trade agreement with the EU came into force in January 2011. In April 2010 Costa Rica signed free trade agreements with China and Singapore. Additionally, Costa Rica is looking to join the Asia-Pacific Economic Cooperation (APEC) forum.

FOREIGN RELATIONS

Costa Rica is an active member of the international community and proclaimed its permanent neutrality in 1993. Its record on the environment and human rights and advocacy of peaceful settlement of disputes give it a weight in world affairs far beyond its size. The country lobbied aggressively for the establishment of the UN High Commissioner for Human Rights and became the first nation to recognize the jurisdiction of the Inter-American Human Rights Court, based in San Jose. Costa Rica has been a strong proponent of regional arms limitation agreements. In 2009, Costa Rica finished its third term as a non-permanent member of the United Nations Security Council.

During the tumultuous 1980s, then-President Oscar Arias authored a regional peace plan that served as the basis for the Esquipulas Peace Agreement. Arias' efforts earned him the 1987 Nobel Peace Prize. Subsequent agreements, supported by the United States, led to the

Nicaraguan election of 1990 and the end of civil war in Nicaragua. Costa Rica also hosted several rounds of negotiations between the Salvadoran Government and the Farabundo Marti National Liberation Front (FMLN), aiding El Salvador's efforts to emerge from civil war and culminating in that country's 1994 free and fair elections.

In 2007 Costa Rica established diplomatic ties with China, ending nearly 60 years of diplomatic relations with Taiwan. In 2008, Costa Rica established diplomatic relations with "The State of Palestine," and in 2009 Costa Rica reopened formal relations with Cuba. In 2009, then-President Arias acted as mediator in the Honduran constitutional crisis, working closely with ousted President Manuel Zelaya and the interim Honduran government. Costa Rica formally recognized Porfirio "Pepe" Lobo as the winner of the 2009 Honduran elections and the President of Honduras. In October 2010, Costa Rica accused Nicaragua of invading its territory and claimed Nicaragua's dredging of the San Juan River was causing irreparable environmental damage. The case is currently pending at the International Court of Justice, which is considering Costa Rica's request for provisional measures.

U.S.-Costa Rican Relations

The United States and Costa Rica have a history of close and friendly relations based on respect for democratic government, human freedoms, free trade, and other shared values. The country generally supports the U.S. in international fora, especially in the areas of democracy and human rights.

The United States is Costa Rica's most important trading partner. The U.S. accounts for almost half of Costa Rica's exports, imports, and tourism, and more than two-thirds of its foreign investment. The two countries share growing concerns for the environment and want to preserve Costa Rica's important tropical resources and prevent environmental degradation. In October 2010, the U.S. and Costa Rican Governments, the Central Bank of Costa Rica, and The Nature Conservancy concluded agreements that will provide more than $27 million over 15 years for tropical forest conservation in Costa Rica. The agreements were made possible by the Tropical Forest Conservation Act of 1998 (TFCA). Together with a previous TFCA program established in 2007, these agreements make Costa Rica, one of the most biologically diverse countries on earth, the largest beneficiary under the TFCA, with more than $50 million generated for the conservation, restoration, and protection of tropical forests.

The United States responded to Costa Rica's economic needs in the 1980s with significant economic and development assistance programs. Through provision of more than $1.1 billion in assistance, the U.S. Agency for International Development (USAID) supported Costa Rican efforts to stabilize its economy and broaden and accelerate economic growth through policy reforms and trade liberalization. Assistance initiatives in the 1990s concentrated on democratic policies, modernizing the administration of justice, and sustainable development. Once the country had graduated from most forms of U.S. assistance, the USAID Mission in Costa Rica closed in 1996. However, USAID completed a $9 million project in 2000-2001 to support refugees of Hurricane Mitch residing in Costa Rica. Additionally, Costa Rica benefits from regional USAID development programs.

For decades, Peace Corps volunteers have provided technical assistance in the areas of environmental education, natural resources, management, small business development, microfinance, basic business education, urban youth, and community education. In 2007, the Costa Rica Multilingue initiative approached the Peace Corps with a request for a new project focused on teaching English as a foreign language (TEFL). The first group of 25 Peace Corp trainees under the TEFL project arrived in October 2010.

Over 50,000 private American citizens, including many retirees, reside in the country and more than 700,000 American citizens visit Costa Rica annually. A few vexing expropriation and U.S. citizen investment disputes have hurt Costa Rica's investment climate and have occasionally produced bilateral friction.

The U.S.-Costa Rica Maritime Cooperation Agreement, the first of its kind in Central America, entered into force in late 1999. The agreement, which facilitates cooperation between the Coast Guard of Costa Rica and the U.S. Coast Guard, has resulted in a growing number of narcotics seizures, illegal migrant rescues, illegal fishing seizures, and search-and-rescue missions. Bilateral Costa Rican law enforcement cooperation, particularly against narcotrafficking, has been exemplary.

In: Central America: Profiles and U.S. Relations
Editor: Brian J. Durham

ISBN: 978-1-61470-122-4
© 2011 Nova Science Publishers, Inc.

Chapter 3

COSTA RICA: BACKGROUND AND U.S. RELATIONS

Peter J. Meyer

SUMMARY

Costa Rica is a politically stable Central American nation with a relatively well-developed economy. Former president (1986-1990) and Nobel-laureate Oscar Arias of the historically center-left National Liberation Party was elected President in 2006. Throughout his term, Arias has advanced so-called "third-way" policies, embracing his party's traditional support for social welfare programs while rejecting state-led development in favor of market-oriented economic policies. Considerable economic growth and social protection programs have provided Costa Rica's citizens with a relatively high standard of living, however, conditions have deteriorated recently as a result of the global financial crisis and U.S. recession. Although Costa Rica's economy contracted and poverty increased in 2009, analysts believe President Arias' ambitious fiscal stimulus and social protection plan and improving global economic conditions should aid recovery in 2010.

On February 7, 2010, former Vice President Laura Chinchilla (2006-2008) of the ruling National Liberation Party was elected president, easily defeating her competitors. Chinchilla, who is closely tied to President Arias and the centrist faction of her party, will be Costa Rica's first female president. Throughout the campaign, Chinchilla pledged to maintain the Arias Administration's economic and social welfare policies while improving public security. She will need to form cross-party alliances to implement her policy agenda, however, as her party will lack a majority in Costa Rica's unicameral National Assembly. Chinchilla and the new legislature are scheduled to take office in May 2010.

Successive Costa Rican administrations have sought to address extensive deforestation and environmental degradation that resulted from decades of logging and agricultural expansion. The country's strong conservation system and innovative policies have done much to restore Costa Rica's environment and ecotourism has provided a significant source of economic growth. Costa Rica's efforts also have led many observers to recognize it as a world leader in environmental protection and have enabled the country to play an outsized role in the formulation of global environmental policies. Nonetheless, some maintain that a number of environmental problems in Costa Rica remain unaddressed.

The United States and Costa Rica have long enjoyed close relations as a result of the countries' shared commitments to strengthening democracy, improving human rights, and advancing free trade. The countries have also maintained strong commercial ties, which are likely to become even more extensive as a result of President Arias' efforts to secure ratification and implementation of CAFTA-DR. On April 28, 2009, the House of Representatives passed H.Res. 76 (Burton), which mourns the loss of life in Costa Rica and Guatemala that resulted from natural disasters that occurred in January 2009. The resolution also expresses the senses of the House, that the U.S. government should continue providing technical assistance relating to disaster preparedness to Central American governments.

POLITICAL AND ECONOMIC SITUATION

Background

Costa Rica is a politically stable Central American country of 4.3 million people with a relatively well-developed economy. The country gained its independence from Spain in 1821 as a part of the Central American Union, and became a sovereign nation following the union's dissolution in 1838. Costa Rica has enjoyed continuous civilian democratic rule since the end of a 1948 civil war, the longest period of unbroken democracy in Latin America. The civil war led to the creation of a new constitution, the abolition of the military, and the foundation of one of the first welfare states in the region. Although Costa Rica pursued state-led development throughout much of the 20th century, over the past several decades, it has implemented market-oriented economic policies designed to attract foreign direct investment (FDI), develop the country's export sector, and diversify what was once a predominantly agricultural economy.[1] The World Bank now classifies Costa Rica as an upper-middle-income country with a 2008 per capita income of $6,060.[2]

Public fatigue with politics has grown in recent years as a result of corruption scandals that have implicated three former presidents from the two traditional ruling parties: Rafael Angel Calderón (1990-1994) and Miguel Angel Rodríguez (1998-2002) of the center-right Social Christian Unity Party (PUSC) and José María Figueres (1994-1998) of the traditionally center-left National Liberation Party (PLN). This disillusionment has contributed to a rise in voter abstention, from just 19% in 1994 to 35% in 2006. It has also contributed to a fragmentation of Costa Rica's political party system. The PUSC has collapsed and newer parties—such as the conservative Libertarian Movement (ML) and the center-left Citizen Action Party (PAC)—have grown considerably.[3]

Arias Administration

Oscar Arias, a former president (1986-1990) and Nobel-laureate, was elected president in February 2006.[4] Arias won 41% of the vote to narrowly defeat his closest rival, the PAC's Ottón Solís, who had served as Minister for National Planning and Economic Policy during

Arias' first administration.[5] Throughout his term, President Arias has advanced so-called "third-way" policies, embracing his party's traditional support for social welfare programs while rejecting state-led development in favor of market-oriented economic policies. Arias also has pursued an active foreign policy. Although Arias' PLN is the largest of the nine parties represented in the unicameral National Assembly, it holds just 25 of the 57 seats, which has made cross-party alliances necessary to pass legislation.[6]

Economic and Social Welfare Policies

President Arias has maintained the market-friendly economic policies that Costa Rican administrations from both traditional governing parties have pursued since the 1980s. Between 2006 and 2008, economic growth averaged 6.5%, fueled in large part by export growth and increased investment.[7] Export earnings grew over 36% between 2005 and 2008 to $9.7 billion while FDI grew over 134% to $2 billion during the same time period.[8] Much of the FDI has been invested in high technology sectors, often located in free trade zones. High-tech products—such as integrated circuits and medical equipment—now account for 45% of Costa Rican exports.[9] Arias also has pursued a number of free trade agreements (FTAs) during his current term. He won ratification of CAFTA-DR through a national referendum in 2007 and secured its implementation in January 2009 despite strong opposition from the PAC and labor unions.[10] Additionally, he concluded an agreement with Panama, has completed FTA negotiations with China and Singapore, and is engaged in ongoing FTA talks with the European Union along with the other member nations of the Central American Integration System (SICA).

Source: Map Resources. Adapted by CRS Graphics.

Figure 1. Map of Costa Rica.

Arias has sought to complement Costa Rica's considerable economic growth with moderate social welfare programs. He has doubled welfare pensions, created new centers for primary healthcare services, and increased education funding.[11] President Arias also introduced *Avancemos*, a conditional cash transfer program that provides monthly stipends to the families of 140,000 poor students as long as the children remain in school and receive annual medical care. [12] *Avancemos* is modeled after successful social protection programs that have been implemented elsewhere in Latin America, such as *Oportunidades* in Mexico and *Bolsa Familia* in Brazil, and is designed to alleviate poverty in the near-term while fostering long-term reductions in the poverty rate through increased educational attainment. Costa Rica now invests the equivalent of 17.3% of its gross domestic product (GDP) in public health, education, and social welfare, the highest percentage of any nation in Central America and the fifth highest in all of Latin America.[13] These social investments, combined with substantial economic growth, have provided Costa Rica's citizens with a relatively high standard of living. According to the United Nations' 2009 Human Development Report, Costa Rica has the highest level of human development in Central America with a life expectancy at birth of 79 years and an adult literacy rate of 96%.

Economic and social conditions have deteriorated recently, however, as a result of the global financial crisis and U.S. recession. The Costa Rican economy grew by just 2.6% in 2008 and experienced its first contraction in 27 years in 2009. GDP contracted by 1.3% as investment, export demand, and tourism declined. [14] Likewise, the poverty rate climbed nearly two points over the course of 2008 and 2009 to 18.5%, and unemployment increased almost three points in 2009 alone to 7.8%.[15] President Arias has sought to counter the economic downturn with a $2.5 billion (8% of GDP) economic stimulus and social protection plan known as *Plan Escudo*. Among other provisions, the plan recapitalizes state banks, provides support to small and medium-sized enterprises, increases labor flexibility, invests in infrastructure projects, provides grants to workers in the worst-affected sectors, and increases the number of students eligible for the *Avancemos* program. The majority of *Plan Escudo* is financed through new loans from international financial institutions. Analysts assert that Costa Rica's economy showed signs of recovery in late 2009, and expect the country to rebound in 2010 with GDP growth of 3.3%.[16]

Foreign Policy

President Arias has pursued an active foreign policy throughout his term. He established diplomatic ties with China in 2007, ending Costa Rica's 60-year relationship with Taiwan.[17] Arias also established formal ties with the Palestinians, recognizing Palestine as an independent state in February 2008. Costa Rica had previously moved its embassy in Israel from Jerusalem to Tel Aviv.[18] In March 2009, Arias reestablished diplomatic relations with Cuba, 48 years after Costa Rica suspended ties with the nation. Costa Rica was one of the last countries in Latin America to reestablish ties with Cuba.[19]

Arias also has sought to reassume the leadership role that he held in Latin America during his first administration when he received the Nobel Peace Prize (1987) for his efforts to end the conflicts in Central America. Following the June 2009 ouster of Honduran President Manuel Zelaya, Arias offered to mediate between the parties involved. The so-called "San José Accord" that Arias proposed provided the framework for several rounds of negotiations to end the political crisis in Honduras, though it ultimately failed to restore Zelaya to office.[20] Arias has seized on the Honduran crisis to reiterate his long-held belief that

Latin America possesses a dangerous combination of powerful militaries and fragile democracies. He maintains that countries in the region should focus their resources on economic development and democratic institutions rather than military expenditures.[21]

2010 Elections

Results

Elections for the presidency and all 57 seats in the unicameral National Assembly were held in Costa Rica on February 7, 2010. Former Vice President and Minister of Justice Laura Chinchilla (2006-2008) of the ruling PLN was elected president with 46.9% of the vote, well above the 40% needed to avoid a second-round runoff. Chinchilla easily defeated her closest competitors Ottón Solís of the center-left PAC and Otto Guevara of the right-wing ML, who took 25.1% and 20.9% of the vote, respectively.[22] In legislative elections, Chinchilla's PLN won a plurality with 23 seats.

The PAC will be the principal opposition party with 12 seats, followed by the ML with 9 seats, the PUSC with 6 seats, and several smaller parties with a combined 7 seats.[23]

According to many analysts, Chinchilla benefitted the fragmentation of Costa Rica's political party system. They assert that Costa Ricans view the PLN as the country's only credible governing party due to the PUSC's effective collapse as a result of corruption scandals, the PAC's lack of direction after failing to block CAFTA-DR, and the ML's recent history outside the mainstream of Costa Rican politics.[24] Consequently, Chinchilla won by over 20 points despite a considerable decline in public support for the Arias Administration and late polling that showed Guevara forcing Chinchilla into a close second-round runoff vote.[25]

Prospects for the Chinchilla Administration

Chinchilla is closely tied to President Arias' centrist faction of the PLN and is expected to largely continue the Arias Administration's policies. She will likely maintain Costa Rica's market- oriented economic policies, pushing for ratification of pending free trade agreements with China and Singapore, while strengthening the country's social welfare programs. Throughout much of the electoral campaign, Chinchilla focused on improving public security. Among other policies, she proposed increasing the size of the police force, improving protection and support for victims and witnesses, and increasing government security spending by as much as 50% (currently 0.6% of GDP). Moreover, analysts expect Chinchilla to implement policies designed to meet President Arias' goal of making Costa Rica carbon neutral by 2021 and take socially conservative stands on issues such as abortion, homosexual marriage, and church-state relations.[26]

Costa Rica's unicameral National Assembly will present Chinchilla with considerable challenges in implementing her policy agenda. Chinchilla's PLN will control just 23 of the 57 seats, making cross-party alliances necessary to pass any legislation. The PLN will likely form ad hoc alliances with varying parties dependent on the issue.[27] Even if Chinchilla and the PLN are able to cobble together a working majority, however, a group of 10 members of the National Assembly may appeal the constitutionality of any bill to the Supreme Court and significantly slow legislative progress.[28]

ENVIRONMENTAL LEADERSHIP

Successive Costa Rican administrations have sought to address extensive deforestation and environmental degradation that resulted from decades of logging and agricultural expansion. The country's strong conservation system and innovative policies have done much to restore Costa Rica's environment and ecotourism has provided a significant source of economic growth. Costa Rica's efforts also have led many observers to recognize it as a world leader in environmental protection and have enabled the country to play an outsized role in the formulation of global environmental policies. Despite these accomplishments, some maintain that there are a number of environmental problems that must still be addressed by the country.

Environmental Policies

Although observers have long admired the country's tropical forests, it is only relatively recently that Costa Rica has placed much emphasis on environmental protection. Approximately 75% of Costa Rican territory was forest covered in the 1940s, however, just 21% remained covered in 1987 as a result of logging and agricultural expansion.[29] Alarmed at the pace of deforestation and the extent of environmental degradation, the Costa Rican government began implementing a variety of conservation programs. Among these programs is the National System of Conservation Areas (SINAC), which was founded in the 1960s but has been significantly expanded in recent decades. SINAC now provides formal protection for over 26% of Costa Rica's land and 16.5% of its waters.[30]

Costa Rica has built upon the success of SINAC with a number of innovative environmental protection policies. Since 1997, Costa Rica has imposed a 3.5% "carbon tax" on fossil fuels. A portion of the funds generated by the tax are directed to the so-called "Payment for Environmental Services" (PSA) program, which pays private property owners to practice sustainable development and forest conservation.[31] Some 11% of Costa Rica's national territory is protected by the program.[32] Costa Rica also imposes a tax on water pollution to penalize homes and businesses that dump sewage, agricultural chemicals, and other pollutants into waterways. In 2009, the government expected the water pollution tax to generate some $8 million, which was to be used to improve the water treatment system, monitor pollution, and promote environmentally- friendly practices.[33] Moreover, Costa Rica generates 76% of its energy from hydro, geo-thermal, and wind power,[34] and President Arias has opposed exploitation of the country's discovered oil reserves in order to maintain incentives to further develop alternative energies.[35]

The country's environmental policies have been relatively successful, both in ecological and economic terms. Costa Rica has experienced a substantial increase in forest conservation and reforestation. Since 1997, the percentage of the nation covered by forest has expanded an average of 0.66% annually,[36] and over 50% of Costa Rican territory now falls under forest cover.[37] This has provided crucial habitat, as Costa Rica is home to a disproportionately high percentage of the earth's biological diversity with 5% of the planet's plant and animal species.[38] Environmental protection has also been a significant source of economic growth for Costa Rica, which is now one of the world's premier destinations for ecotourism. More than one million people visit Costa Rica's environmental attractions each year, generating $1.1 billion in foreign exchange.[39]

Global Role

Costa Rica's domestic success has allowed it to play an outsized role in formulating global environmental policies. In the lead up to the 2009 United Nations Climate Change Conference in Copenhagen, Denmark, President Arias asserted that developed nations, which "achieved their development poisoning the environment," should be most responsible for reducing global greenhouse gasses.[40] He proposed that such countries cut their carbon emissions by 45%.[41] Arias also pushed for technological exchange, financial assistance for mitigation and adaptation programs, and "debt-for-nature" swaps.[42] Nonetheless, Arias has asserted that developing nations must reduce their green house gas emissions as well. In 2008, Costa Rica announced its intention to become carbon-neutral by 2021, the first developing nation to make such a pledge. Additionally, Costa Rica has sought to export its successful environmental policies—such as the PSA program—to other developing nations.[43]

Criticism

Despite its considerable achievements and global recognition, some observers assert there are still a number of environmental problems that Costa Rica must address. According to a recent SINAC study, Costa Rica lacks adequate protection for coastal and marine biological diversity. The study of 35 sites of ecological importance found that less than 10% of the areas examined are currently protected.[44] Another recent study, conducted by the country's state universities with support from private and public institutions, highlighted a number of other environmental problems in Costa Rica, including continued water pollution, overexploitation of marine resources, and a notable decline in the rate of reforestation.[45] The U.N. Ozone Secretariat has also highlighted environmental shortcomings in Costa Rica, noting that the country has led Latin America in per capita importation of ozone depleting substances since 2004.[46]

U.S.-COSTA RICAN RELATIONS

Relations between the United States and Costa Rica traditionally have been strong as a result of common commitments to democracy, free trade, and human rights. U.S. intervention in Central America during the 1980s, however, slightly strained the relationship. President Arias responded to the various conflicts in the region by crafting a peace plan during his first administration, which excluded the involvement of extra-regional powers. As a result of his efforts, Arias was awarded the Nobel Peace Prize in 1987. U.S. policy in Iraq also strained relations between Costa Rica and the United States. Although then President Pacheco (2002-2006) supported the U.S. invasion, Costa Rica's Constitutional Court ruled that listing the country as a member of the "coalition of the willing" violated the country's constitutionally mandated neutrality. President Arias has questioned the priorities of the United States for spending substantial funds in Iraq while allocating comparatively little to assist allies in Central America.[47]

Current relations between the United States and Costa Rica could be characterized as friendly. Costa Rica finally implemented CAFTA-DR in January 2009. The agreement will likely strengthen Costa-Rica's already significant trade relationship with the United States. Vice President Biden visited Costa Rica during his first trip to Central America, leading the Arias Administration to describe the meeting as "a clear recognition of the trajectory of Costa Rica as the United States' strategic partner in the region."[48] Additionally, President Arias criticized the anti-Americanism of some of his fellow Latin American leaders at the Fifth Summit of the Americas, and the United States strongly supported President Arias' role as mediator in the political crisis in Honduras.[49]

U.S. Assistance

For more than a decade, Costa Rica has not been a large recipient of U.S. assistance as a result of its relatively high level of development; however, this is likely to change somewhat as a result of the "Mérida Initiative" and its successor program, the Central America Regional Security Initiative (CARSI). The Peace Corps has been operating in Costa Rica since 1963 and generally has been the largest source of U.S. assistance to the country since the U.S. Agency for International Development mission closed in 1996. In recent years, Costa Rica has also received U.S. assistance through the "International Narcotics Control and Law Enforcement" (INCLE), "International Military Education and Training" (IMET), and "Foreign Military Financing" (FMF) accounts. Costa Rica received $364,000 in regular U.S. assistance in FY2009 and is scheduled to receive an estimated $705,000 in FY2010. The Obama Administration has requested $750,000 for Costa Rica for FY2011.

In 2007, Costa Rica signed one of the largest ever debt-for-nature swaps with the U.S. government. Authorized by the Tropical Forest Conservation Act of 1998 (P.L. 105-214), the agreement reduced Costa Rica's debt payments by $26 million over 16 years. In exchange, the Costa Rican Central Bank agreed to use the funds to support grants to non-governmental organizations and other groups committed to protecting and restoring the country's tropical forests. In order to fund the agreement, the U.S. government contributed $12.6 million and Conservation International and the Nature Conservancy contributed a combined donation of more than $2.5 million.[50]

Mérida Initiative & Central America Regional Security Initiative (CARSI)[51]

Costa Rica historically has not experienced significant problems as a result of the regional drug trade, however, crime and violence have surged in recent years as Colombian and Mexican cartels have increased their operations throughout Central America.[52] Costa Rica's murder rate nearly doubled between 2004 and 2008, from 6 per 100,000 to 11 per 100,000 residents.[53] Although Costa Rica's murder rate remains significantly lower than those of the "northern triangle" countries of Guatemala, El Salvador, and Honduras, the surge in organized crime has presented the Costa Rican government with a considerable security challenge.

In October 2007, the United States and Mexico announced the Mérida Initiative, a multi-year proposal to provide U.S. assistance to Mexico and Central America aimed at combating drug trafficking and organized crime. Congress appropriated some $165 million for Central America under the Mérida Initiative—a portion of which was to go to Costa Rica—through the FY2008 Supplemental Appropriations Act (P.L. 110-252) and the F2009 Omnibus Appropriations Act (P.L. 111-8). The FY2010 Consolidated Appropriations Act (P.L. 111-117) split Central America from the Mérida Initiative, and appropriated $83 million under a new Central America Regional Security Initiative (CARSI). The Obama Administration has requested $100 million for CARSI in FY2011.

Costa Rica received an initial $1.1 million in Mérida/CARSI funds in June 2009, after Costa Rica and the United States signed a letter of agreement implementing the initiative. The initial funds were to be used to finance the Central American Fingerprint Exchange, improved policing and equipment, improved prison management, maritime interdiction support, border assistance and inspection equipment, and a number of regional training programs.[54] President Arias has praised the security initiative as a "step in the right direction,"[55] but maintains that the U.S. funding of the program in Central America—and Costa Rica in particular—is "insufficient."[56]

International Military Education and Training

Although Costa Rica has no military, it receives IMET assistance to train its public security forces. These funds have been used to improve the counterdrug, rule of law, and military operations capabilities of the Costa Rican Coast Guard and law enforcement services. Costa Rica was prohibited from receiving IMET assistance in FY2004, FY2005, and FY2006 as a result of its refusal to sign an Article 98 agreement exempting U.S. personnel from the jurisdiction of the International Criminal Court. In October 2006, President Bush waived FY2006 IMET restrictions for a number of countries—including Costa Rica—and signed the John Warner National Defense Authorization Act for Fiscal Year 2007 into law (P.L. 109-364), a provision of which ended Article 98 sanctions on IMET funds.[57] Costa Rica began receiving IMET funds again in FY2007.

In January 2009, Security Minister Janina del Vecchio revealed that Costa Rica would once again send police officers to the Western Hemisphere Institute for Security Cooperation (WHINSEC, formerly known as the School of the Americas) in Fort Benning, GA.[58] The decision to resume training came just a year and a half after President Arias, following a meeting with opponents of WHINSEC, announced that Costa Rica would withdraw its students from the school.[59] WHINSEC, which has trained tens of thousands of military and police personnel from throughout Latin America—including 2,600 Costa Ricans, has been criticized for the human rights abuses committed by some of its graduates.[60] Supporters of the school maintain that WHINSEC emphasizes democratic values and respect for human rights, develops camaraderie between U.S. military officers and military and police personnel from other countries in the hemisphere, and is crucial to developing military partners capable of effective combined operations.[61]

A provision of the Omnibus Appropriations Act of 2009 (P.L. 111-8) directs the Department of State to provide a report of the names, ranks, countries of origin, and years of attendance of all students and instructors at WHINSEC for fiscal years 2005, 2006, and 2007. The Latin American Military Training Review Act (H.R. 2567, McGovern), which was introduced in the House in May 2009, would suspend all operations at WHINSEC, establish a joint congressional task force to assess the types of training that are appropriate to provide Latin American militaries, and establish a commission to investigate activities at WHINSEC and its predecessor.

Free Trade Agreement

In August 2004, the United States Trade Representative (USTR) and the trade ministers from the Dominican Republic, Costa Rica, El Salvador, Guatemala, Honduras, and Nicaragua signed the Dominican Republic-Central America-United States Free Trade Agreement (CAFTA-DR). [62] CAFTA-DR liberalizes trade in goods, services, government procurement, intellectual property, and investment, immediately providing duty-free status to a number of commercial and farm goods while phasing out tariffs on other trade over five to twenty years. Prior to the agreement, the countries of Central America all had tariff-free access to the U.S. market on approximately three-quarters of their products through the Caribbean Basin Trade Partnership Act (P.L. 106-200, Title II).[63] The CAFTA-DR agreement makes the arrangement permanent and reciprocal. Although CAFTA-DR is a regional agreement under which all parties are subject to the same obligations and commitments, each country defines its own market access schedule with the United States.

Ratification

Following the August 2004 signature of CAFTA-DR, the agreement had to be approved by the legislatures of all of the countries involved. In Costa Rica, a qualified congressional majority (38 of 57 legislators) was needed to ratify the agreement. Although Costa Rican leaders across the political spectrum support liberalized trade, there has been intense internal debate concerning the benefits of CAFTA-DR. While the Arias Administration was able to create a cross-party alliance of 38 deputies, the PAC opponents of the agreement were able to block ratification through various delaying tactics. In order to avoid missing the ratification deadline, President Arias asked the TSE for a binding referendum on CAFTA-DR.

The referendum was held in October 2007 and reflected the polarization of the issue among the Costa Rican electorate. Trade unions, students, a variety of social movements, and the PAC opposed the ratification of CAFTA-DR, while business groups and each of the other major political parties were in favor of the agreement. The referendum campaign was often contentious. Just two weeks before the vote, Arias' Second Vice President was forced to resign after authoring a memorandum recommending that the Administration link the anti-CAFTA-DR forces to Presidents Castro of Cuba and Chávez of Venezuela and play up the possible consequences of a failed referendum.[64] Then, days before the referendum, Costa Rican media published statements by members of the Bush Administration saying it was unlikely that the United States would renegotiate the agreement or maintain the unilateral trade preferences Costa Rica received under the Caribbean Basin Initiative should the country vote against CAFTA-DR.[65] In the end, 51.6% of Costa Ricans voted in favor of CAFTA-DR while 48.4% voted against the agreement. Referendum turnout was just over 60%, well above the 40% minimum necessary for it to be binding.[66]

Implementation

After the approval of CAFTA-DR by referendum, the Costa Rican legislature still had to pass 13 laws in order to implement the agreement. These included a variety of intellectual property law reforms, an opening of the insurance and telecommunications sectors, reform of the criminal code, an anti-corruption law, and a law protecting agents of foreign firms.[67] Costa Rica's consensus-seeking tradition and the ability of PAC legislators to challenge the constitutionality of the proposed legislation in the Constitutional Chamber slowed the implementation of CAFTA-DR significantly. As of the original February 2008 deadline for implementation, Costa Rica had only passed five of the necessary reforms.[68] Then, prior to the extended deadline of October 2008, the Constitutional Chamber ruled that the intellectual property legislation was unconstitutional as a result of the Arias Administration's failure to meet with indigenous and tribal groups about the bill before sending it to the legislature.[69] After obtaining a second extension, Costa Rica passed all of the necessary reforms and implemented CAFTA-DR on January 1, 2009.[70]

Prior to the implementation of CAFTA-DR, the United States was already Costa Rica's largest trading partner as the destination of about 36% of Costa Rican exports and the origin of about 38% of its imports. Despite the global financial crisis and U.S. recession, U.S. trade with Costa Rica increased by over 7% in 2009. U.S. exports to Costa Rica amounted to about $4.7 billion and U.S. imports from Costa Rica amounted to about $5.6 billion. Electrical and heavy machinery and oil accounted for the majority of the exports while machinery parts, medical instruments, and fruit accounted for the majority of the imports.[71]

End Notes

[1] A regional recession in the 1980s led Costa Rica to borrow heavily and eventually default on its foreign debt in 1983. Following the economic collapse, Costa Rica sought assistance from the International Monetary Fund (IMF) and other international financial institutions, which required the country to implement structural adjustment programs that liberalized the country's economy and privatized the majority of its state-owned enterprises. Tom Barry, *Costa Rica: A Country Guide* (Albuquerque, NM: Inter-Hemispheric Education Resource Center, 1991).

[2] World Bank, *World Development Report*, 2010.

[3] "Costa Rica: Elections end in dead heat," *Oxford Analytica*, February 8, 2006. "Country Profile: Costa Rica," *Economist Intelligence Unit*, 2008.

[4] In 2003, a controversial ruling by Costa Rica's Supreme Court annulled the country's prohibition on presidential reelection. The ruling allows former leaders to run for a second term after eight years out of office. "Costa Rican court says ex-presidents can seek re-election," *Associated Press*, April 4, 2003.

[5] "Costa Rica: Arias Finally Wins It," *Latin American Regional Report: Caribbean & Central America*, March 2006.

[6] "Costa Rica: Elections end in dead heat," *Oxford Analytica*, February 8, 2006; "Costa Rica: Arias Finally Wins It," *Latin American Regional Report: Caribbean & Central America*, March 2006; "Country Profile: Costa Rica," *Economist Intelligence Unit*, 2008.

[7] "Country Profile: Costa Rica," *Economist Intelligence Unit*, 2008.

[8] Costa Rican National Institute of Statistics and Census trade data presented by *Global Trade Atlas*, 2009; U.N. Economic Commission for Latin America and the Caribbean, *Foreign Investment in Latin American and the Caribbean, 2008*, July 2009.

[9] "Economic Overview: Costa Rica," *Latin American Regional Report: Caribbean & Central America*, October 2009.

[10] For additional information on CAFTA-DR, see CRS Report RL3 1870, *The Dominican Republic-Central America- United States Free Trade Agreement (CAFTA-DR)*, by J. F. Hornbeck.

[11] "Country Profile: Costa Rica," *Economist Intelligence Unit*, 2008.

[12] Gillian Gillers, "Dr. 's Visit Now Required To Get Cash Benefits," *Tico Times*, February 1, 2008.

[13] Costa Rica trails Argentina, Brazil, Chile, and Uruguay in social expenditure as a percentage of GDP. "Costa Rica: Signs of a Pick Up," *Latin American Economy & Business*, July 2009.

[14] "Country Report: Costa Rica," *Economist Intelligence Unit*, December 2009; "Costa Rica economy suffers first contraction in 27 Yrs," *Reuters*, January 28, 2010.

[15] "Pobreza y el desempleo siguen agobiando en Costa Rica (sondeo oficial)," *Agence France Presse*, October 29, 2009.

[16] "Clearer signs of recovery in Costa Rica – IMF," *Reuters*, November 12, 2009; "Country Report: Costa Rica," *Economist Intelligence Unit*, February 2009 & December 2009.

[17] "China y Costa Rica establecen relaciones diplomáticas a nivel de embajador," *Xinhua*, June 7, 2007.

[18] "Costa Rica se alía a Palestina," *La Nación* (Costa Rica), February 6, 2008.

[19] "Costa Rica reopens formal relations with Cuba," *Reuters*, March 18, 2009.

[20] Álvaro Murillo, "Arias sigue como mediador en Honduras," *La Nación* (Costa Rica), September 23, 2009. For more information on the political crisis in Honduras, see CRS Report RL34027, *Honduran-U.S. Relations*.

[21] Oscar Arias, "Fuel for a Coup; The Perils of Latin America's Oversized Militaries," *Washington Post*, July 9, 2009.

[22] "Final Count in Costa Rica," *Latin News Daily*, February 22, 2010.

[23] "Chinchilla wins in the first round," *Latin American Regional Report: Caribbean & Central America*, February 2010.

[24] Manuel D. Arias, "En Costa Rica: ni el PRI ni Chávez," *La Nación* (Costa Rica), October 17, 2009; Eduardo Ulibarri, "Nueva década, ¿nueva política?" *La Nación* (Costa Rica), January 10, 2010.

[25] Carlos A. Villalobos, "Confianza en el Gobierno desciende a su peor nivel," *La Nación* (Costa Rica), January 19, 2010; Carlos A. Villalobos, "Chinchilla y Guevara obtendrían empate técnico en 2.a ronda," *La Nación* (Costa Rica), January 17, 2010.

[26] "Costa Rica: Chinchilla win consolidates PLN power," *Oxford Analytica*, February 9, 2010; Tim Padgett, "Costa Rica's Generational and Gender Changes," *Time*, February 10, 2010; Alex Leff, "Costa Ricans Choose Chinchilla and Continuity," *Americas Quarterly*, February 11, 2010; "Chinchilla wins in the first round," *Latin American Regional Report: Caribbean & Central America*, February 2010.

[27] "Costa Ricans elect Latin America's fifth female president," *Latin American Weekly Report*, February 11, 2010.

[28] Nicholas Casey, "Costa Rica Victor Girds for Gridlock," *Wall Street Journal*, February 9, 2010.

[29] "Costa Rica: Government seeks green credentials," *Oxford Analytica*, October 21, 2008.

[30] Ministerio Del Ambiente y Energia, "Sistema Nacional de Áreas Protegidas," available at http://www.sinac.go.cr/planificacionasp.php.

[31] "Costa Rica: Expertos alertan sobre riesgo de incumplir objeticos ambientales," *Agence France Presse*, October 8, 2009.

[32] Alejandra Vargas, "Costa Rica irá a cumbre de Copenhague a dar su ejemplo," *La Nación* (Costa Rica), December 2, 2009.

[33] "Costa Rica taxing firms that dump wastewater into rivers," *EFE News Service*, April 7, 2009.

[34] Alejandra Vargas, "Costa Rica irá a cumbre de Copenhague a dar su ejemplo," *La Nación* (Costa Rica), December 2, 2009.

[35] Esteban A. Mata, "Óscar Arias se opone a exploración petrolera," *La Nación* (Costa Rica), March 24, 2009.

[36] Alejandra Vargas, "Costa Rica irá a cumbre de Copenhague a dar su ejemplo," *La Nación* (Costa Rica), December 2, 2009.

[37] Costa Rica: Government seeks green credentials," *Oxford Analytica*, October 21, 2008.

[38] Ibid.

[39] Alejandra Vargas, "Costa Rica irá a cumbre de Copenhague a dar su ejemplo," *La Nación* (Costa Rica), December 2, 2009.

[40] Alvaro Murillo, "Arias pide cambiar deuda por reforestación," *La Nación* (Costa Rica), September 23, 2009.

[41] "Costa Rica: Nation Seeks Big Emissions Cut," *Latin America Data Base NotiCen*, December 17, 2009.

[42] Ibid; Alvaro Murillo, "Arias pide cambiar deuda por reforestación," *La Nación* (Costa Rica), September 23, 2009.

[43] Alejandra Vargas, "Costa Rica irá a cumbre de Copenhague a dar su ejemplo," *La Nación* (Costa Rica), December 2, 2009.

[44] Ana Cristina Camacho Sandoval, "Zonas costeras y marinas necesitan esquemas de conservación," *La Nación* (Costa Rica), November 18, 2009.

[45] Oscar Núñez Olivas, "Costa Rica, 'paraíso ecológico', arrastra graves problems ambientales," *Agence France Presse*, November 12, 2009.

[46] The most current U.N. data reflects importation rates from 2007. An international agreement that Costa Rica has signed would prevent the country from importing ozone depleting substances as of this year (2010). Jairo Villegas, "País lidera compra per cápita de contaminantes de ozono," *La Nación* (Costa Rica), April 26, 2009.

[47] Oscar Arias, "Region's real enemies: poverty and ignorance," *Miami Herald*, August 19, 2008.

[48] Tim Rogers, "Central American leaders to vie for Obama's ear; Nicaragua and Costa Rica are jockeying for leadership roles at the Summit of the Americas in Trinidad and Tobago," *Miami Herald*, March 25, 2009.

[49] Andres Oppenheimer, "Arias' brilliant response to anti-American leaders," *Miami Herald*, May 3, 2009; Hillary Rodham Clinton, Secretary of State, "Remarks at the Top of the Daily Press Briefing," July 7, 2009. For additional information on the Fifth Summit of the Americas, see CRS Report R40074, *Fifth Summit of the Americas, Port of Spain, Trinidad and Tobago, April 2009: Background, Expectations, and Results*. For more information on the 2009 political crisis in Honduras, see CRS Report R41064, *Honduran Political Crisis, June 2009-January 2010*.

[50] U.S. Department of State, Office of the Spokesman, "Debt for Nature Agreement to Conserve Costa Rica's Forests," October 17, 2007. For more information on the Tropical Forest Conservation Act, see CRS Report RL31286, *Debt-forNature Initiatives and the Tropical Forest Conservation Act: Status and Implementation*, by Pervaze A. Sheikh.

[51] For more information on the Mérida Initiative, see CRS Report R40135, *Mérida Initiative for Mexico and Central America: Funding and Policy Issues*, by Clare Ribando Seelke.

[52] Dulue Mbachu, "Costa Rica, Panama in the Crossfire," *International Relations and Security Network (ISN)*, October 7, 2009.

[53] "Chinchilla wins in the first round," *Latin American Regional Report: Caribbean & Central America*, February 2010.

[54] U.S. Department of State, Office of the Spokesman, "Letter of Agreement Signed with Costa Rica," June 18, 2009.

[55] Oscar Arias, "Region's real enemies: poverty and ignorance," *Miami Herald*, August 19, 2008.

[56] "Costa Rican president says Merida Plan funds 'insufficient,'" *BBC Monitoring*, March 31, 2009.

[57] For more information on Article 98 sanctions, see CRS Report RL33337, *Article 98 Agreements and Sanctions on U.S. Foreign Aid to Latin America*, by Clare Ribando Seelke.

[58] "Row over 'abolished' army," *Latin American Security & Strategic Review*, January 2009.

[59] Argentina, Bolivia, Uruguay, and Venezuela have stopped sending students to WHINSEC.

[60] For more information on the School of the Americas and the Western Hemisphere Institute for Security Cooperation, see CRS Report RL3 0532, *U.S. Army School of the Americas: Background and Congressional Concerns*, by Richard F. Grimmett and Mark P. Sullivan and CRS Report RS20892, *Western Hemisphere Institute for Security Cooperation*, by Richard F. Grimmett.

[61] U.S. Southern Command, "Posture Statement of Admiral James G. Stavridis, United States Navy Commander, United States Southern Command, Before the 111th Congress Senate Armed Services Committee," March 17, 2009.

[62] For more information on the Dominican Republic-Central America-United States Free Trade Agreement, see CRS Report RL3 1870, *The Dominican Republic-Central America-United States Free Trade Agreement (CAFTA-DR)*, by J. F. Hornbeck.

[63] "Latin America Economy: What's at Stake with CAFTA," *Economist Intelligence Unit*, May 14, 2003.

[64] "Scandal Topples Costa Rican Vice President, Clouds Outlook as CAFTA Referendum Nears," *Latin America Data Base NotiCen*, September 27, 2007.

[65] "Costa Rica: Arias is undermined despite 'yes' vote," *Oxford Analytica*, October 9, 2007.

[66] "Costa Rica: Arias sneaks Cafta-DR referendum," *Latin News Weekly Report*, October 11, 2007.

[67] "Country Profile: Costa Rica," *Economist Intelligence Unit*, 2008.

[68] "Costa Rica: Arias concedes defeat on CAFTA-DR deadline," *Latin American Weekly Report*, February 7, 2008.

[69] "Country Report: Costa Rica," *Economist Intelligence Unit*, October 2008.

[70] "Bush firma decreto para que Costa Rica se una al Cafta," *Reuters*, December 23, 2008.

[71] U.S. Department of Commerce data, as presented by *Global Trade Atlas*, February 2010.

In: Central America: Profiles and U.S. Relations
Editor: Brian J. Durham

ISBN: 978-1-61470-122-4
© 2011 Nova Science Publishers, Inc.

Chapter 4

EL SALVADOR PROFILE

U.S. Department of State

Official Name: Republic of El Salvador

GEOGRAPHY

Area: 20,742 sq. km. (8,008 sq. mi.); about the size of Massachusetts.
Cities: *Capital*--San Salvador (pop. 1.6 million). *Other cities*--Santa Ana, San Miguel, Soyapango, and Apopa.
Terrain: Mountains separate country into three distinct regions--southern coastal belt, central valleys and plateaus, and northern mountains.
Climate: Tropical, distinct wet and dry seasons.

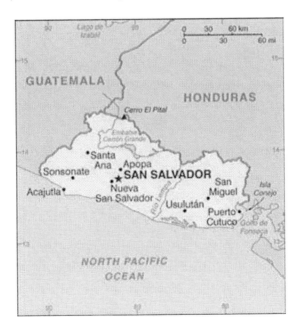

Flag of El Salvador

PEOPLE

Nationality: *Noun and adjective*--Salvadoran(s).
Population (2009 est.): 7.2 million.
Annual population growth rate (2009 est.): 1.7%.
Ethnic groups: Mestizo 90%, indigenous 1%, Caucasian 9%.
Religion (2003 est.): About 57% Roman Catholic, with significant and growing numbers of Protestant groups.
Language: Spanish.
Education: Free through high school. *Attendance* (grades 1-9)--92.4%. *Literacy*--86.1% nationally; 77.6% in rural areas.
Health: *Infant mortality rate* (2006)--22/1,000 (source: UNICEF). *Life expectancy at birth* (2008)--72.1 years.
Work force (about 2.4 million, 2009): *Agriculture*--21%; *retail, hotels, and restaurants*--29%; *industry*--15%; *construction*--5%; *other services*--30% (2009).

GOVERNMENT

Type: Republic.
Constitution: December 20, 1983.
Independence: September 15, 1821.
Branches: *Executive*--president and vice president. *Legislative*--84-member Legislative Assembly. *Judicial*--independent (Supreme Court).
Administrative subdivisions: 14 departments.
Political parties (represented in the legislature): Farabundo Marti National Liberation Front (FMLN), Nationalist Republican Alliance (ARENA), National Conciliation Party (PCN), Christian Democratic Party (PDC), and Democratic Change (CD).
Suffrage: Universal at 18.

ECONOMY

GDP (2010): $21.8 billion; PPP GDP (2010): $43.98 billion.
GDP annual real growth rate (2010): 0.7%-1.0%.
Per capita income (2009): $3,429; PPP per capita income (2010): $7,300.
Agriculture (11% of GDP, 2010): *Products*--coffee, sugar, livestock, corn, poultry, and sorghum. *Arable, cultivated, or pasture land*--68% (2005).

Industry (29.1% of GDP, 2010): *Types*--textiles and apparel, medicines, food and beverage processing, clothing, chemical products, petroleum products, electronics, call centers.

Trade (2010): *Exports*--\$4.5 billion: textiles and apparel, ethyl alcohol, coffee, sugar, medicines, iron and steel products, tuna, light manufacturing, and paper products. *Major markets*--U.S. 48.3%, Central American Common Market (CACM) 35.5%. *Imports*--\$8.5 billion: petroleum, iron products, machines and mechanical devices, cars, medicines, consumer goods, foodstuffs, capital goods, and raw industrial materials. *Major suppliers*--U.S. 36.5%, CACM 19.5%.

PEOPLE

El Salvador's population numbers about 7.2 million. Almost 90% is of mixed Indian and Spanish extraction. About 1% is indigenous; very few Indians have retained their customs and traditions. The country's people are largely Roman Catholic and Protestant. Spanish is the language spoken by virtually all inhabitants. The capital city of San Salvador has about 1.6 million people; an estimated 37.3% of El Salvador's population lives in rural areas.

HISTORY

The Pipil Indians, descendants of the Aztecs, and the Pocomames and Lencas were the original inhabitants of El Salvador.

The first Salvadoran territory visited by Spaniards was Meanguera Island, located in the Gulf of Fonseca, where Spanish Admiral Andres Nino led an expedition to Central America and disembarked on May 31, 1522. In June 1524, the Spanish Captain Pedro de Alvarado started a war to conquer Cuscatlan. His cousin Diego de Alvarado established the village of San Salvador in April 1525. In 1546, Charles I of Spain granted San Salvador the title of city.

During the subsequent years, the country evolved under Spanish rule; however, toward the end of 1810 many people began to express discontent. On November 5, 1811, when Priest Jose Matias Delgado rang the bells of La Merced Church in San Salvador calling for insurrection, the people began to band together for freedom.

In 1821, El Salvador and the other Central American provinces declared their independence from Spain. When these provinces were joined with Mexico in early 1822, El Salvador resisted, insisting on autonomy for the Central American countries. In 1823, the United Provinces of Central America was formed of the five Central American states under Gen. Manuel Jose Arce. When this federation was dissolved in 1838, El Salvador became an independent republic. El Salvador's early history as an independent state--as with others in Central America--was marked by frequent revolutions; not until the period 1900-30 was relative stability achieved. Following a deterioration in the country's democratic institutions in the 1970s a period of civil war followed from 1980-1992. More than 75,000 people are estimated to have died in the conflict. In January 1992, after prolonged negotiations, the opposing sides signed peace accords which ended the war, brought the military under civilian control, and allowed the former guerillas to form a legitimate political party and participate in elections.

GOVERNMENT AND POLITICAL CONDITIONS

El Salvador is a democratic republic governed by a president and an 84-member unicameral Legislative Assembly. The president is elected by universal suffrage by absolute majority vote and serves for a 5-year term. A second round runoff is required in the event that no candidate receives more than 50% of the first round vote. Members of the assembly are elected based on the number of votes that their parties obtain in each department (circumscriptive suffrage) and serve for 3-year terms. The country has an independent judiciary and Supreme Court. Legislative and municipal elections were held in January 2009, and presidential elections were held in March 2009.

Political Landscape

Hard-line conservatives, including some members of the military, created the Nationalist Republican Alliance party (ARENA) in 1981. ARENA almost won the election in 1984 with solid private sector and rural farmer support. By 1989, ARENA had attracted the support of business groups. Multiple factors contributed to ARENA victories in the 1988 legislative and 1989 presidential elections, including allegations of corruption in the ruling Christian Democratic party which had poor relations with the private sector, and historically low prices for the nation's main agricultural exports.

The successes of Alfredo Cristiani's 1989-94 administration in achieving a peace agreement to end the civil war and in improving the nation's economy helped ARENA--led by former San Salvador mayor Armando Calderon Sol--keep both the presidency and a working majority in the Legislative Assembly in the 1994 elections. ARENA's legislative position was weakened in the 1997 elections, but it recovered its strength, helped by divisions in the opposition, in time for another victory in the 1999 presidential race, bringing President Francisco Guillermo Flores Perez to office. Flores concentrated on modernizing the economy and strengthening bilateral relations with the United States. Under his presidency El Salvador committed itself to combating international terrorism, including sending troops to aid in the reconstruction of Iraq. El Salvador also played a key role in negotiations for the Central American Free Trade Agreement (CAFTA-DR).

Taking advantage of both public apprehension of Flores' policies and ARENA infighting, the chief opposition party, the Farabundo Marti National Liberation Front (FMLN), was able to score a significant victory against ARENA in the March 2003 legislative and municipal elections. ARENA, left with only 29 seats in the 84-seat Legislative Assembly, was forced to court the right-wing National Conciliation Party (PCN) in order to form a majority voting bloc. However, in 2003 the PCN entered into a loose partnership with the FMLN, further limiting ARENA's ability to maneuver in the legislature.

Despite these constraints, ARENA made a strong showing in the March 2004 presidential election, which was marked by an unprecedented 67% voter turnout. ARENA candidate Elias

Antonio "Tony" Saca handily defeated the FMLN candidate and party head Shafik Handal, garnering 57.7% of the votes cast. The defeat of the FMLN's presidential candidate rekindled an internal FMLN struggle between hardliners and more moderate members who saw the party's 2004 defeat as a call for reform.

In January 2009 legislative and municipal elections, the incumbent ARENA party garnered 32 assembly deputies and 122 mayoralties, while the opposition FMLN won 35 legislative seats and 75 city halls (plus 21 additional mayoralties in which they participated as part of a coalition). The PCN, PDC, and CD carried 11, 5, and 1 assembly seats, respectively. The new assembly took office in May 2009. In October 2009, twelve ARENA deputies left the party to form a new movement, the Great Alliance for National Unity (GANA), and two other deputies (one each from ARENA and the PCN) left their parties to become independents. As of January 2010, the assembly was composed as follows: FMLN - 35 seats, ARENA - 19 seats, GANA - 12 seats, PCN - 10 seats, PDC - 5 seats, CD - 1 seat, independent deputies - 2 seats. In December 2009, former President Antonio Saca was expelled from ARENA for his suspected involvement in the defection of the GANA deputies.

On March 15, 2009, FMLN candidate Mauricio Funes won El Salvador's presidential elections, defeating ARENA candidate Rodrigo Avila. Final vote totals were 51.3% for the FMLN and 48.7% for ARENA. The elections marked the first time since the 1992 peace agreement that ended the civil war that an FMLN candidate was elected president and the first left-of-center government in El Salvador's history. President Funes was inaugurated on June 1, 2009.

Human Rights and Post-War Reforms

During the 12-year civil war, human rights violations by both the government security forces and left-wing guerillas were rampant. The accords established a Truth Commission under UN auspices to investigate the most serious cases. The commission recommended that those identified as human rights violators be removed from all government and military posts. Thereafter, the Legislative Assembly granted amnesty for political crimes committed during the war. Among those freed as a result were the Salvadoran Armed Forces (ESAF) officers convicted in the November 1989 Jesuit murders and the FMLN ex-combatants held for the 1991 murders of two U.S. servicemen. The peace accords also established the Ad Hoc Commission to evaluate the human rights record of the ESAF officer corps.

In accordance with the peace agreements, the constitution was amended to prohibit the military from playing an internal security role except under extraordinary circumstances. Demobilization of Salvadoran military forces generally proceeded on schedule throughout the process. The Treasury Police, National Guard, and National Police were abolished, and military intelligence functions were transferred to civilian control. By 1993--9 months ahead of schedule--the military had cut personnel from a war-time high of 63,000 to the level of 32,000 required by the peace accords. By 1999, ESAF strength stood at less than 15,000, including uniformed and non-uniformed personnel, consisting of personnel in the army, navy, and air force. A purge of military officers accused of human rights abuses and corruption was completed in 1993 in compliance with the Ad Hoc Commission's recommendations. The military's new doctrine, professionalism, and complete withdrawal from political and economic affairs have made it one of the most respected institutions in El Salvador.

More than 35,000 eligible beneficiaries from among the former guerrillas and soldiers who fought in the war received land under the peace accord-mandated land transfer program, which ended in January 1997. The majority of them also received agricultural credits.

National Civilian Police

The National Civilian Police (PNC), created to replace the discredited public security forces, deployed its first officers in March 1993 and was present throughout the country by the end of 1994. The PNC has about 16,000 officers. The United States, originally through the International Criminal Investigative Training Assistance Program (ICITAP) and subsequently through the Department of State's Bureau for International Narcotics and Law Enforcement Affairs, led international support for the PNC and the National Public Security Academy (ANSP), providing about $32 million in non-lethal equipment and training since 1992.

Judiciary

Following the peace accords, both the Truth Commission and the Joint Group identified weaknesses in the judiciary and recommended solutions, including the replacement of all the magistrates on the Supreme Court. This recommendation was fulfilled in 1994 when an entirely new court was elected, but weaknesses remain. The process of replacing judges in the lower courts, and of strengthening the attorney generals' and public defender's offices, has moved slowly. The government continues to work in all of these areas with the help of international donors, including the United States. Action on peace accord-driven constitutional reforms designed to improve the administration of justice was largely completed in 1996 with legislative approval of several amendments and the revision of the Criminal Procedure Code--with broad political consensus.

Principal Government Officials

President--Carlos Mauricio FUNES Cartagena
Vice President--Salvador SANCHEZ CEREN
Minister of Foreign Relations--Hugo Roger MARTINEZ Bonilla
Ambassador to the United States--Francisco ALTSCHUL Fuentes
Representative to the OAS--Luis MENENDEZ Castro (interim)
Representative to the UN--Carmen Maria GALLARDO de Hernandez

El Salvador maintains an **Embassy** in the United States at 1400 16th Street NW, Washington, DC, 20036 (tel: 202-595-7500). There are consulates in Atlanta, GA; Brentwood, NY; Boston, MA; Chicago, IL; Dallas, TX; Elizabeth, NJ; Houston, TX; Las Vegas, NV; Los Angeles, CA; Miami, FL; New York, NY; Nogales, AZ; Santa Ana, CA; San Francisco, CA; and Woodbridge, VA.

ECONOMY

The Salvadoran economy continues to benefit from a commitment to free markets and careful fiscal management. The economy has been growing at a steady and moderate pace since the signing of peace accords in 1992, and poverty was cut from 66% in 1991 to 37.8% in 2009. Much of the improvement in El Salvador's economy is a result of the privatization of the banking system, telecommunications, public pensions, electrical distribution and some electrical generation; reduction of import duties; elimination of price controls; and improved enforcement of intellectual property rights. Capping those reforms, on January 1, 2001, the U.S. dollar became legal tender in El Salvador. The economy is now fully dollarized.

The Salvadoran Government has maintained fiscal discipline during post-war reconstruction and reconstruction following earthquakes in 2001 and hurricanes in 1998 and 2005. Taxes levied by the government include a value added tax (VAT) of 13%, income tax of 20%, excise taxes on alcohol and cigarettes, and import duties. The VAT accounted for about 49.7% of total tax revenues in 2010. El Salvador's public external debt in December 2009 was about $11.2 billion, 53% of GDP.

Years of civil war, fought largely in the rural areas, had a devastating impact on agricultural production in El Salvador. The agricultural sector experienced significant recovery, buoyed in part by higher world prices for coffee and sugarcane and increased diversification into horticultural crops. Seeking to develop new growth sectors and employment opportunities, El Salvador created new export industries through fiscal incentives for free trade zones. The largest beneficiary has been the textile and apparel (maquila) sector, which directly provides approximately 80,000 jobs. Services, including retail and financial, have also shown strong employment growth, with about 59% of the total labor force now employed in the sector.

Remittances from Salvadorans working in the United States are an important source of income for many families in El Salvador. In 2010, the Central Bank estimated that remittances totaled $3.5 billion. UN Development Program (UNDP) surveys show that an estimated 22.3% of families receive remittances.

Under its export-led growth strategy, El Salvador has pursued economic integration with its Central American neighbors and negotiated trade agreements with the Dominican Republic, Chile, Mexico, Panama, Taiwan, Colombia, and the United States. In 2010, Central America signed an Association Agreement with the European Union that includes the establishment of a free trade area. The Central American countries are negotiating a free trade agreement with Canada. El Salvador is negotiating a partial-scope agreement with Cuba that is expected to be finalized during 2011. El Salvador also expects to begin Pacific Arc forum negotiations to reach a trade agreement aimed at creating a common production platform; forum members are Mexico, Guatemala, El Salvador, Honduras, Nicaragua, Costa Rica, Panama, Colombia, Peru, Chile, and Ecuador. Exports and Imports both grew by 17.8% in 2010. As in previous years, the large trade deficit was offset by family remittances.

The U.S.-Central America-Dominican Republic Free Trade Agreement (CAFTA-DR), implemented between El Salvador and the United States on March 1, 2006, provides El Salvador preferential access to U.S. markets. Textiles and apparel, shoes, and processed foods are among the sectors that benefit. In addition to trade benefits, CAFTA-DR also provides trade capacity building, particularly in the environment and labor areas, and a framework for additional reforms on issues such as intellectual property rights, dispute resolution, and customs that will improve El Salvador's investment climate. For sensitive sectors such as agriculture, the agreement includes generous phase-in periods to allow Salvadoran producers an opportunity to become more competitive.

U.S. support for privatization of the electrical and telecommunications markets markedly expanded opportunities for U.S. investment in the country. More than 300 U.S. companies have established either a permanent commercial presence in El Salvador or work through representative offices in the country. The U.S. Department of Commerce maintains a Country Commercial Guide for U.S. businesses seeking detailed information on business opportunities in El Salvador.

On November 29, 2006, the Government of El Salvador and the Millennium Challenge Corporation (MCC) signed a 5-year, $461 million anti-poverty Compact to stimulate economic growth and reduce poverty in the country's northern region. The grant seeks to improve the lives of approximately 850,000 Salvadorans through investments in education, public services, enterprise development, and transportation infrastructure. The Compact entered into force in September 2007, and it is expected that incomes in the region will increase by 20% over the 5-year term of the Compact, and by 30% within 10 years of the start of the Compact.

Natural Disasters

Located on the Pacific's earthquake-prone Ring of Fire and at latitudes plagued by hurricanes, El Salvador's history is a litany of catastrophe, including the Great Hurricane of 1780 that killed 22,000 in Central America and earthquakes in 1854 and 1917 that devastated El Salvador and destroyed most of the capital city. More recently, an October 1986 earthquake killed 1,400 and seriously damaged the nation's infrastructure. In 1998, Hurricane Mitch killed 10,000 in the region, although El Salvador--lacking a Caribbean coast--suffered less than Honduras and Nicaragua. Major earthquakes in January and February of 2001 took another 1,000 lives and left thousands more homeless and jobless. El Salvador's largest volcano, Santa Ana (also known by its indigenous name Ilamatepec), erupted in October 2005, spewing sulfuric gas, ash, and rock on surrounding communities and coffee plantations, killing two people and permanently displacing 5,000. Also in October 2005, Hurricane Stan unleashed heavy rains that caused flooding throughout El Salvador. In all, the flooding caused 67 deaths and more than 50,000 people were evacuated at some point during the crisis. Damages from the storm were estimated at $355.6 million. In November 2008, rains from Tropical Storm Ida caused flooding and mudslides that killed at least 199 and left extensive property damage in the departments of Cuscatlan, La Paz, San Vicente, and San Salvador. In 2010 property evacuation operations by the authorities prevented a higher number of deaths. In June 2010, Tropical Storm Alex killed 5 people and damaged 349 homes, and in September 2010, Tropical Storm Matthew killed 3 people and damaged 141 homes.

FOREIGN RELATIONS

El Salvador is a member of the United Nations and several of its specialized agencies, the Organization of American States (OAS), the Central American Common Market (CACM), the Central American Parliament, and the Central American Integration System (SICA). It actively participates in the Central American Security Commission (CASC), which seeks to promote regional arms control. From 2002-2003, El Salvador was chair of the OAS anti-terrorism coordinating body, CICTE. El Salvador also is a member of the World Trade Organization and is pursuing regional free trade agreements. An active participant in the Summit of the Americas process, El Salvador has chaired a working group on market access under the Free Trade Area of the Americas initiative. El Salvador has joined its six Central American neighbors in signing the Alliance for Sustainable Development, known as the Conjunta Centroamerica-USA or CONCAUSA to promote sustainable economic development in the region.

El Salvador enjoys normal diplomatic and trade relations with all of its neighboring countries including Honduras, with which it has previously had territorial disputes. While the two nations continue to disagree over the status of their maritime borders in the Gulf of Fonseca, they have agreed to settle their land-border disputes with the International Court of Justice (ICJ). In September 1992, the Court awarded most of the territory in question to Honduras. In January 1998, Honduras and El Salvador signed a border demarcation treaty to implement the terms of the ICJ decree although delays continue due to technical difficulties.

U.S.-SALVADORAN RELATIONS

U.S.-Salvadoran relations remain close and strong. U.S. policy toward El Salvador promotes the strengthening of El Salvador's democratic institutions, rule of law, judicial reform, national reconciliation and reconstruction, and economic opportunity and growth. El Salvador was a committed member of the coalition of nations fighting against terrorism and sent 11 rotations of troops to Iraq to support Operation Iraqi Freedom from 2003 through 2008.

The U.S. and Salvadoran Governments cooperate closely to combat narcotics trafficking and organized crime. El Salvador hosts the International Law Enforcement Academy, which provides training to police, prosecutors, and other officials from across the Latin American region. El Salvador's Air Force installation near Comalapa Airport houses a monitoring facility that surveils narco-trafficking routes in the Eastern Pacific. The Federal Bureau of Investigation (FBI) and El Salvador's National Civilian Police jointly operate the Transnational Anti-Gang unit, which addresses the growing problem of street gangs in both countries. In January 2009, the U.S. and El Salvador signed letters of agreement committing both countries to work jointly under the Merida Initiative to fight crime and drug trafficking.

U.S. ties to El Salvador are dynamic and growing. More than 19,000 American citizens live and work full-time in El Salvador. Most are private business people and their families, but a small number of American citizen retirees have been drawn to El Salvador by favorable tax conditions. The Embassy's consular section provides a full range of citizenship services to this community. The American Chamber of Commerce in El Salvador is located at World Trade Center, Torre 2, local No. 308, 89 Av. Nte. Col. Escalon, phone: 2263-9494.

In: Central America: Profiles and U.S. Relations
Editor: Brian J. Durham

ISBN: 978-1-61470-122-4
© 2011 Nova Science Publishers, Inc.

Chapter 5

EL SALVADOR: POLITICAL, ECONOMIC, AND SOCIAL CONDITIONS AND U.S. RELATIONS

Clare Ribando Seelke

SUMMARY

Throughout the last few decades, the United States has maintained a strong interest in El Salvador, a small Central American country with a population of 7.2 million. During the 1980s, El Salvador was the largest recipient of U.S. aid in Latin America as its government struggled against the Farabundo Marti National Liberation Front (FMLN) insurgency during a 12-year civil war. A peace accord negotiated in 1992 brought the war to an end and formally assimilated the FMLN into the political process as a political party. After the peace accords were signed, U.S. involvement shifted toward helping the government rebuild democracy and implement market- friendly economic reforms.

Mauricio Funes of the FMLN was inaugurated to a five-year presidential term in June 2009. Funes won a close election in March 2009, marking the first FMLN presidential victory and the first transfer in political power between parties since the end of El Salvador's civil war. Funes' victory followed strong showings by the FMLN in the January 2009 municipal and legislative elections, in which the party won a plurality of the seats in the National Assembly and the largest share of the municipal vote.

President Funes still has relatively high approval ratings (69% in November 2010), but faces a number of political, economic, and social challenges. The National Assembly is fragmented, which means that Funes has to form coalitions with other parties in order to advance his legislative agenda. The global financial crisis and U.S. recession negatively impacted El Salvador's economy, increasing the country's already widespread poverty. A three-year $790 million agreement signed with the International Monetary Fund (IMF) in March 2010 is helping support economic recovery, but will constrain the Funes' government's future fiscal policies. In addition to these political and economic challenges, El Salvador's violent crime rates remain among the highest in the world and still need to be addressed.

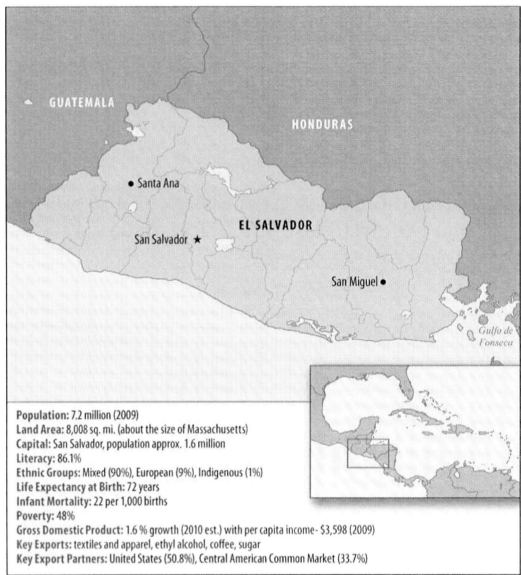

Source: Map prepared by CRS. Data gathered from: U.S. Department of State, "Background Note: El Salvador," July 2010; World Bank, World Development Indicators; Economist Intelligence Unit.; U.N. Economic Commission for Latin America and the Caribbean.

Figure 1. Map and Data on El Salvador.

Maintaining close ties with the United States has been a primary foreign policy goal of successive Salvadoran governments. Although some members of Congress expressed reservations about working with an FMLN administration, relations between El Salvador and the United States have remained friendly. After a March 8, 2010, meeting with President Funes at the White House, President Obama said that he was "very favorably impressed by the steps that [Funes is taking] to try to break down political divisions within the country ... focusing on prosperity at every level of Salvadorian society." Both leaders pledged to continue working together to expand trade through the Dominican Republic-Central America-

United States Free Trade Agreement (CAFTA-DR), foster development, and combat organized crime. U.S. bilateral assistance, which totaled an estimated $57 million in FY20 10, as well as assistance provided through the Central American Regional Security Initiative (CARSI), is supporting those bilateral goals.

POLITICAL, ECONOMIC AND SOCIAL CONDITIONS

FMLN Victory

On June 1, 2009, Mauricio Funes of the leftist Farabundo Martí National Liberation Front (FMLN), a party that was formerly an anti-government revolutionary movement, was inaugurated to a five-year term as President of El Salvador. Funes, a former television journalist and the first FMLN presidential candidate without a guerilla past, defeated Rodrigo Ávila of the conservative Nationalist Republican Alliance (ARENA) 51 %-49% in a March 2009 election. Born in San Salvador in 1959, Funes earned a liberal arts degree from the Central American University (UCA) José Simeón Cañas. He then spent more than 20 years working as a print, radio, and television journalist, becoming one of the most popular and well-respected figures in his field. In 2007, he was chosen to serve as the FMLN's 2009 presidential candidate, reportedly because party leaders thought that he would bring a modern face to the party.

Despite some concerns about potential fraud and a few cases of inter-party violence in the weeks preceding the vote, the election was conducted relatively peacefully after an extremely polarizing campaign.[1] During the campaign, ARENA sought to tie Funes to the more hard-line members of the FMLN and asserted that an FMLN victory would lead to a deterioration in relations with the United States and the installation of an authoritarian political system. Funes attempted to project a moderate image, campaigning on the slogan, "hope is born, change is coming," but also promising to maintain close ties with the United States, implement CAFTA-DR, and keep the U.S. dollar as El Salvador's currency.[2]

Funes' presidential victory is a first for the FMLN, which fought a 12-year civil war against the U.S.-backed Salvadoran government before officially transforming into a political party following the signing of a peace accord in 1992. Some 70,000 Salvadorans (1.4% of the population) were killed during the conflict.[3] The presidential victory followed a strong showing by the FMLN in the January 2009 municipal and legislative elections, in which it won 49.5% of the municipal vote and a plurality in the National Assembly. Funes' election has been described as a watershed moment in the history of El Salvador. However, a recent analysis of Salvadoran voting behavior since 1992 concluded that Funes' victory occurred at least partially as a result of a gradual shift leftward among Salvadoran voters that was already evident by early 2008.[4]

President Funes and the Major Challenges Facing his Administration

Since the election, President Funes has pursued moderate policies, which has caused periodic friction between him and more radical members of his party, including Vice

President Salvador Sánchez Cerén. President Funes has stated that he seeks to emulate President Lula da Silva of Brazil, a leader who has instituted social welfare programs while advancing market-oriented economic policies. According to observers, Funes' cabinet includes competent leaders from a variety of ideological backgrounds. President Funes has also created a permanent Economic and Social Council, composed of leaders from business, academia, churches, unions, government, and popular organizations, to advise his government. Funes has generally been able to secure legislative support for his initiatives from the FMLN; the Grand Alliance for National Unity (GANA) party, a dissident faction that split from ARENA in October 2009; and the center-right National Conciliation Party (PCN). While the Funes Administration has restored diplomatic relations with Cuba, it has also sought to build ties with the United States by, in part, not aligning itself with the government of Hugo Chávez in Venezuela and the Bolivarian Alliance for the Americas (ALBA).[5]

President Funes continues to enjoy strong approval ratings (69% in November 2010[6]), but analysts remain divided over how well his Administration has performed thus far. Some observers have credited Funes' pragmatic approach to governance with helping his administration secure much-needed support from the International Monetary Fund (IMF). Others have expressed concerns, however, that he may be straying too far away from his FMLN base, particularly since forming a legislative alliance with dissident members of ARENA and forming his own political movement called the "Citizens' Movement for Change."[7] Some analysts maintain that the Funes government has struggled to respond to the country's significant public security challenges without resorting to repressive policies.[8] However, according to a November 2010 survey conducted by the University of Central America's Public Opinion Institute (IUDOP), 60% of Salvadorans polled felt that police performance had improved under President Funes. Most analysts concur that the Funes government needs to find a way to jumpstart the country's economy, which 52% of Salvadorans polled by IUDOP said had worsened in the past year.

Rebuilding a Faltering Economy

The Funes government is struggling to boost El Salvador's economy, which contracted by 3.4% in 2009, largely as a result of the U.S. recession. Since the United States is El Salvador's most important trading and investment partner, the U.S. economic slowdown caused remittances, investment, tourism revenues, and demand for Salvadoran exports to decline in 2009. According to El Salvador's Central Bank, remittances, which contribute some 16% of the country's GDP, fell by 8.5% in 2009 as compared to the year before.[9] In November 2009, Funes' efforts to repair the Salvadoran economy were dealt a significant blow when Tropical Storm Ida and related flooding caused 190 deaths and wrought millions of dollars in damages to agriculture and infrastructure in the country. By the second quarter of 2010, however, an uptick in remittances, domestic demand, and exports—particularly sales of non-traditional products—had helped the Salvadoran economy begin to expand. Although the economy now appears to be on an upward trajectory, annual Gross Domestic Product (GDP) growth is expected to reach just over 1.0% for 2010, and significant challenges remain, including how to spur private investment.[10]

The Funes government has taken both short and medium-term steps to respond to the country's economic challenges. Upon taking office, President Funes called for austerity, emphasizing the need to reduce excess spending, better target subsidies, and combat tax evasion and corruption. He also announced an "Anti-Crisis" plan focused on boosting social spending, constructing new housing, and improving public utilities and road infrastructure. President Funes and the IMF agreed to a $790 million stand-by agreement in March 2010 premised on the idea that as the Salvadoran economy recovers, the government will strive to improve tax administration, restrict spending, and reallocate energy subsidies.[11] A medium-term challenge for the Funes government will be determining how to boost the economy with targeted social spending and infrastructure projects without exceeding the fiscal deficit targets recommended by the IMF. In addition to trying to raise tax revenues, President Funes has secured loans totaling approximately $600 million from the World Bank and $450 million from the Inter-American Development Bank to fund anti-poverty efforts, fiscal reform programs, and the creation of an export guarantee fund.

Should the Salvadoran economy continue to falter, broader debates may emerge within the Funes government about the proper economic course for the country to follow, including whether or not to maintain a dollarized economy.[12] El Salvador achieved notable stability and economic growth in the 1990s following the Salvadoran government's embrace of a "neo-liberal" economic model, cutting government spending, privatizing state-owned enterprises, and, in 2001, adopting the dollar as its national currency. As expected, dollarization led to lower interest rates, low inflation, and easier access to capital markets, but it also took away the government's ability to use monetary and exchange rate adjustments to cushion the economy from external shocks (such as the global financial crisis and U.S. recession). After posting strong growth rates in the 1 990s, El Salvador registered only 2% growth from 2000-2004 and 3.6% growth from 2005-2008. Even before the economy contracted in 2009, El Salvador's growth rates had not been high enough to improve living standards among the Salvadoran people, approximately 48% of whom continued to live in poverty in 2009 (roughly the same percentage as in 2001).[13] Emigration has reduced rural unemployment and infused some households with extra income in the form of remittances, but has also caused significant social disruptions.[14]

Confronting Crime and Violence

The Funes Administration is also confronting the related problems of crime and violence that have plagued El Salvador since its civil war. Pervasive poverty and inequality, unemployment and underemployment, drug trafficking, corruption, and illicit firearms have all contributed to the current situation. In 2009, El Salvador recorded approximately 4,365 murders, which is 34% higher than in 2008, a year in which the country had a murder rate of 52 per 100,000 inhabitants, one of the highest in the world.[15] As many as 30,000 Salvadoran youth belong to *maras* (street gangs), which Salvadoran National Police (PNC) officials maintain are responsible for just under half of all homicides and a majority of extortion occurring in the country.[16] In early September 2010, the MS- 13 and 18th Street gangs[17] jointly organized a three-day strike in response to new anti-gang legislation that paralyzed the country's transport system. Drug trafficking organizations and organized criminal groups, both Salvadoran and international, have also increased their illicit activities in the country, including money laundering.[18] In September 2010, the PNC seized two plastic barrels containing a combination of Euros and U.S. dollars worth $15 million.[19]

President Funes had hoped to move away from the *mano dura* (firm hand)[20] policies towards gangs and crime enacted by previous ARENA administrations, but escalating violence, including two gang attacks on buses that killed 17 people in June 2010, has forced him to adopt a number of tough measures.[21] In November 2009, President Funes issued an emergency decree deploying military troops to assist police forces in fighting crime on the streets until enough police can be recruited, trained, and equipped to handle the task alone, a process which may take several years. Several thousand troops are now involved in securing border crossings, carrying out joint patrols with police in high-crime areas, and, since July 2010, in securing the country's prisons.[22] In September 2010, El Salvador's Congress enacted a law outlawing the MS-13, 18th Street, and other criminal gangs and the financing of their activities. Human rights organizations have opposed the law, predicting that it will result in a return to repressive police tactics against gangs. Salvadoran government officials have discounted those predictions, maintaining that the law is focused on helping police build stronger anti-gang investigations that will stand up in court.[23]

These highly publicized crime control efforts have been accompanied by other, less visible, changes in the areas of prevention, prison reform and rehabilitation, and institutional/legal reform. For 2011, the Funes government increased funding for prevention programs to roughly 14% of the Ministry of Security' budget (from a historic average of just over 1%).[24] In order to deal with the dire situation in the country's prisons, three new prisons are under construction, corrupt prison staff have been purged, and a draft law to provide more rehabilitation programs in the prison system is being developed. Many argue that more needs to be done in this area, however, given that the prisons currently house close to 25,000 prisoners, a significant percentage of whom have yet to be sentenced, in facilities designed to hold roughly 8,000 inmates.[25] With respect to institutional reform and anti-corruption efforts, the Inspector General of the PNC has dismissed at least 20 police officers found guilty of corruption or ties with criminal groups and suspended hundreds more pending ongoing investigations.[26] In order to provide additional tools for law enforcement to use in criminal investigations and prosecutions, President Funes shepherded a wiretapping law through the National Assembly. He is reportedly considering whether or not to propose a security tax to fund government efforts to enhance public security as was done by President Álvaro Uribe in Colombia.[27] Perhaps partially as a result of these efforts, statistics indicate that El Salvador's murder rate from January 2010 to October 2010 was 8 percent lower than the same period in 2009.[28]

RELATIONS WITH THE UNITED STATES

Throughout the last few decades, the United States has maintained a strong interest in the political and economic situation in El Salvador. During the 1980s, El Salvador was the largest recipient of U.S. military aid in Latin America as its government struggled against the FMLN insurgency. After the 1992 peace accords were signed, U.S. involvement and assistance shifted toward helping successive ARENA governments rebuild democracy and implement market-friendly economic reforms. The Administration of Tony Saca (2004-2009) cooperated in counternarcotics operations, supported the U.S. coalition forces in Iraq, and implemented the Dominican Republic- Central America-United States Free Trade Agreement (CAFTA-DR).

Although some analysts predicted that a Funes victory could complicate U.S.-Salvadoran relations, most others predicted that bilateral relations would remain friendly regardless of who won the March 2009 elections. During his inauguration, which was attended by Secretary of State Hillary Clinton, Funes asserted his desire to "broaden, strengthen, and renew" El Salvador's relations with the United States.[29] While some FMLN officials have made anti-American remarks, Funes has repeatedly referred to the United States as a "strategic partner." Funes has also pledged to maintain El Salvador's dollarized economy, to continue the implementation of CAFTA-DR, and to allow the continued use of Comalapa International Airport as a Forward Operating Location (FOL) for U.S. anti-drug forces in the hemisphere.

President Obama has spoken with President Funes several times since his election, congratulating Funes on his victory and meeting him in person at the Fifth Summit of the Americas. El Salvador's Foreign Minister Hugo Martinez met with Secretary of State Hillary Clinton and Assistant Secretary Arturo Valenzuela in December 2009 to discuss U.S. relations with El Salvador, particularly those concerning migration. These high-level contacts culminated in President Funes' first visit to the White House, which took place on March 8, 2010. After that meeting, President Obama thanked President Funes for his help in resolving the situation in Honduras and expressed "how interested the United States is in continuing to be an equal partner with El Salvador and other countries in the region."[30]

Evidence of the strong ties between El Salvador and the United States also emerged in the aftermath of Hurricane Ida, when the Obama Administration gave $840,000 in emergency aid and the House passed H.Con.Res. 213 (Mack), expressing solidarity with the people of El Salvador who were victimized by the storm. This initial assistance was followed by the inclusion of an additional $25 million for reconstruction efforts in El Salvador in the FY20 10 supplemental appropriations measure (P.L. 111-212).

Table 1. U.S. Assistance to the El Salvador: FY2009-FY2011 U.S. $ Millions

Account	FY2009	FY2010 (est.)	FY2011 req.
INCLE	0.0	0.0	0.0
ESF	27.0[a]	25.0[b]	0.0
FMF	3.5	1.0	4.8
IMET	1.6	1.8	1.8
GHCS	6.0	5.5	3.1
DA	21.2	23.9	26.5
TOTAL	59.3	57.1	36.2

Sources: U.S. Department of State, Congressional Budget Justification for Foreign Operations: FY20 11.

Notes: GHCS= Global Health and Child Survival (includes total funds provided by the U.S. Agency for International Development and the State Department); DA=Development Assistance; ESF=Economic Support Fund; FMF=Foreign Military Financing; IMET=International Military Education and Training; INCLE=International Narcotics Control and Law Enforcement; NADR=Non-proliferation, Anti-terrorism and Related Programs.

a. This $27 million is from a pot of $255.6 million included in the FY2009 Supplemental Appropriations Act (P.L. 111-32) to assist developing countries affected by the global financial crisis.

b. This supplemental assistance was provided for reconstruction efforts in P.L. 111-212.

U.S. Foreign Aid

Recent bilateral funding to El Salvador amounted to roughly $59.3 million in FY2009 and $57.1 million in FY2010, including $25 million in supplemental assistance for reconstruction efforts associated with Tropical Storm Ida. The Obama Administration requested $36.2 million in bilateral assistance for El Salvador for FY2011. In the absence of FY20 11 appropriations legislation, Congress has passed a series of continuing resolutions (P.L. 111-242 as amended) to fund government programs, with the latest CR set to expire on March 4, 2011. The CRs continue funding most foreign aid programs at the FY2010-enacted level, with some exceptions.

In addition to funding reconstruction efforts, U.S. bilateral assistance to El Salvador seeks to help enhance citizen security, promote trade and investment, reduce poverty, improve healthcare and education, and strengthen government institutions.

El Salvador receives some foreign assistance beyond the bilateral funds appropriated annually through the foreign operations budget. There are approximately 175 U.S. Peace Corps volunteers serving in El Salvador who are engaged in projects related to health and sanitation, environmental issues, and municipal development. USAID's Office of Foreign Disaster Assistance (OFDA) provides assistance in response to natural disasters, including, most recently, $100,000 provided in May 2010 in response to Tropical Storm Agatha. In November 2006, El Salvador signed a five- year, $461 million compact with the Millennium Challenge Corporation (MCC), which is discussed below.

El Salvador also benefits from regional trade capacity building assistance and regional anti-gang assistance funded through global funds appropriated to the State Department's Bureau of International Narcotics and Law Enforcement. El Salvador also receives assistance under the Central America Regional Security Initiative (CARSI, formerly known as Mérida-Central America), a package of counternarcotics and anticrime assistance for the region. CARSI programs in El Salvador focus on bolstering government capacity to inspect and interdict unauthorized drugs, goods, arms, and people; implement anti-gang programs; and carry out police and judicial reform. From FY2008-FY20 10, Congress appropriated $248 for Central America, a portion of which was intended for El Salvador. For FY20 11, the Obama Administration requested $100 million for CARSI.

Millennium Challenge Corporation (MCC) Compact

In late November 2006, El Salvador signed a five-year, $461 million compact with the Millennium Challenge Corporation (MCC) to develop its northern border region, where more than 53% of the population lives in poverty. The compact includes (1) $88 million for technical assistance and financial services to farmers and rural businesses; (2) $100 million to strengthen education and training and improve public services in poor communities; and (3) $233 million to rehabilitate the Northern Transnational Highway and some secondary roads. The MCC compact has been designed to complement the CAFTA-DR and regional integration efforts. Although many have praised its potential, some have questioned why the compact was not designed to encourage communities to channel remittance flows into collective projects that could generate employment and improve local infrastructure.[31] By the end of September 2010, some $112.5 million in MCC assistance had been disbursed for programs in El Salvador.[32]

Counter-Narcotics Issues

Although El Salvador is not a major producer of illicit drugs, it does serve as a transit country for narcotics, mainly cocaine and heroin, cultivated in the Andes and destined for the United States via land and sea. In 2009, Salvadoran officials seized 3.8 kilograms of cocaine/crack cocaine (a majority seized at sea by the Salvadoran Navy), 323 kilograms of marijuana, and 5 kilograms of heroin.[33] Both the Anti-Narcotics Division (DAN) of the PNC and the Salvadoran Navy coordinated closely with their U.S. counterparts. U.S. counternarcotics assistance focuses on improving the interdiction capabilities of Salvadoran law enforcement agencies; increasing transparency, efficiency, and respect for human rights within the criminal justice system; and aiding Salvadoran efforts to fight transnational gangs. Insufficient funding and equipment for the PNC continued to hinder bilateral efforts, as well as a lack of progress on investigating and prosecuting money laundering crimes.[34] In 2010, the Salvadoran National Assembly passed an asset forfeiture law, as well as a law allowing the Attorney General's office to perform wiretapping. On December 8, 2010, the U.S. and Salvadoran governments announced the creation of a new Wiretapping Center in El Salvador to help officials in the Attorney General's office intercept and analyze telecommunications.[35]

Comalapa International Airport in El Salvador serves as one of two Forward Operating Locations (FOLs) for U.S. anti-drug forces in the hemisphere. The FOL extends the reach of detection and monitoring aircraft into the Eastern Pacific drug smuggling corridors, through which more than half of the narcotics destined for the United States transit.[36] Although the U.S. lease on the airport was set to expire in 2010, El Salvador signed an agreement in April 2009 that will allow the United States to continue using Comalapa as an FOL for an additional five years.[37] El Salvador is also the home of the U.S.-backed International Law Enforcement Academy (ILEA), which provides police management and specialized training to officials from all of the countries of the region.

Migration Issues

Beyond financial linkages, the United States is home to some 2.5 million Salvadoran migrants, approximately one-third of El Salvador's population. The movement of large numbers of poor Salvadorans to the United States has eased pressure on El Salvador's social service system and labor market while providing the country with substantial remittances. Remittances sent from Salvadoran workers totaled some $3.5 billion in 2009, some $8.5% lower than in 2008.[38] Through November 2010, remittances sent from the United States to El Salvador were reportedly 2.4% higher than last year, although still much lower than in 2008.[39]

Following a series of earthquakes in El Salvador in 2001 and a determination that the country was temporarily incapable of handling the return of its nationals, the U.S. government granted Temporary Protected Status (TPS) to an estimated 220,000 eligible Salvadoran migrants. TPS has been extended several times, and is currently scheduled to expire in March 2012.

Nonetheless, many Salvadoran migrants continue to be deported from the United States, including 20,830 in FY2010, 41.4% of which were deported on criminal grounds.[40] The United States is working with the Salvadoran government in a joint effort to improve the deportation process. In December 2009, a bi-national working group consisting of migration authorities from both countries was formed in Washington, DC. Two of the group's goals are to expedite the deportation process in order to avoid immigrants spending unnecessary time in U.S. detention centers and to address more general concerns about the current deportation process.[41]

U.S. Trade and CAFTA-DR

The United States is El Salvador's main trading partner, purchasing 48% of its exports and supplying close to 34% of its imports. More than 300 U.S. companies currently operate in El Salvador, many of which are based in the country's 13 free trade zones. Since the 1980s, El Salvador has benefitted from preferential trade agreements, such as the Caribbean Basin Initiative and later the Caribbean Basin Trade Partnership Act (CBTPA) of 2000, which have provided some of its exports, especially apparel and related items, duty-fee entry into the U.S. market. As a result, the composition of Salvadoran exports to the United States has shifted from agricultural products, such as coffee and spices, to apparel and textiles. Since the expiration of global textile quotas on December 31, 2004, Salvadoran apparel producers have had trouble competing with goods from cheaper Asian producers.

On December 17, 2004, despite strong opposition from the FMLN, El Salvador became the first country in Central America to ratify the Dominican Republic-Central America-United States Free Trade Agreement (CAFTA-DR). El Salvador was also the first country to pass the agreement's required legislative reforms, implementing CAFTA-DR on March 1, 2006. Some Salvadoran officials have attributed increases in employment, exports, and investment to the agreement's implementation. Although the country's apparel exports to the United States declined during the first year CAFTA-DR was in effect, El Salvador saw a 21% rise in non-apparel exports to the United States, with significant increases in ethanol, food stuffs, and metal products. Salvadoran exports to the United States increased by 10% in 2007 and 9% in 2008 as a result of a slight recovery in textile and apparel exports and an increase in non-traditional exports. U.S. exports to El Salvador have also increased, rising by 16% in 2006, 7.5% in 2007, and 6.5% in 2008. These positive trends were reversed in 2009, however, as a result of the U.S. recession. Salvadoran exports to the United States fell by 3.9% and U.S. exports to El Salvador fell close to 18%.[42] Exports to the United States have recovered in 2010, however, with sales from January to September roughly 21% higher than during the same period in 2009.

End Notes

[1] Some 5,000 national and international electoral observers supervised the proceedings while 20,000 members of the Salvadoran military and police provided security. "El Salvador: 20,000 Policías y Soldados en Comicios," *Associated Press*, March 4, 2009; "El Salvador prepares to vote," *Latin News Daily*, March 13, 2009.

[2] Maureen Meyer, "Election Season in El Salvador," *Washington Office on Latin America*, January 15, 2009.

[3] Priscilla B. Hayner, *Unspeakable Truths: Facing the Challenge of Truth Commissions*, (New York, NY: Routledge, 2002).

[4] Dinorah Azpuru, "The Salience of Ideology: Fifteen Years of Presidential Elections in El Salvador," *Latin American Politics and Society*, Summer 2010.

[5] President Chávez launched a Bolivarian Alternative for the Americas (ALBA) in 2004 as an alternative to the Free Trade Area of the Americas. ALBA advocates a socially oriented trade block that includes mechanisms for poverty reduction, and cooperation in a range of areas including health, education, culture, investment, and finance. Currently, eight countries in the region have joined ALBA. Venezuela and Cuba were the first countries to launch ALBA in 2004, while Bolivia joined in 2006, and Nicaragua in 2007. In 2008, the Caribbean nation of Dominica joined in January, while Honduras joined in August, but subsequently withdrew in January 2010 under the de facto government of Roberto Micheletti. In June 2009, Ecuador, St. Vincent and the Grenadines, and Antigua and Barbuda joined ALBA.

[6] "Mantiene Funes Popularidad Pese a Deterioro Económico," *Agencia Mexicana de Noticias*, December 7, 2010.

[7] "Is El Salvador's First Left-Leaning President Changing the Country's Internal Political Realities for the Better? Are U.S. Policy Makers About to Make a Major Mistake?" *Council on Hemispheric Affairs (COHA)*, February 17, 2010; "Confessions of a Leftist Party: The FMLN's Dilemma in the Face of Funes' Centrist Policies," *COHA*, June 28, 2010.

[8] "Expectations for Change and Challenges of Governance: The First Year of President Mauricio Funes," *Center for Democracy in the Americas*, June 2010.

[9] "Salvador's Central Bank Says Migrants Sent 8.5 Percent Less Money Home in 2009," *AP*, January 12, 2010.

[10] "Country Report: El Salvador," *Economist Intelligence Unit (EIU)*, December 2010.

[11] International Monetary Fund (IMF), "Press Release 10/95: IMF Executive Board Approves US$790 Million Standby Arrangement for El Salvador," March 17, 2010; IMF, *El Salvador: 2010 Article IV Consultation and First Review Under the Stand-By Arrangement*, IMF Country Report No. 10/307, October 2010.

[12] "Talk of Scrapping Dollar Spices up Budget Debate," *Latin American Weekly Report*, November 25, 2010.

[13] U.N. Economic and Social Commission for Latin America and the Caribbean (ECLAC), *Social Panorama of Latin America, 2010*, December 2010.

[14] Sarah Gammage, "Exporting People and Recruiting Remittances: A Development Strategy for El Salvador?," *Latin American Perspectives*, November 2006.

[15] "El Salvador: President Mauricio Funes to Fight Crime with Guns, Phone Taps, and More Police," *Noticen: Central American & Caribbean Affairs*, March 11, 2010. U.N. Development Program (UNDP), "Informe Sobre Desarrollo Humano Para América Central 2009-2010: Abrir Espacios a la Seguridad Ciudadana y el Desarrollo Humano," October 2009.

[16] CRS Interview with Salvadoran National Police officials, December 2010.

[17] The major gangs operating in Central America with ties to the United States are the "18th Street" gang (also known as M-18), and their main rival, the Mara Salvatrucha (MS-13). The 18th Street gang was formed by Mexican youth in the Rampart section of Los Angeles in the 1960s who were not accepted into existing Hispanic gangs. It was the first Hispanic gang to accept members from all races and to recruit members from other states. MS-13 was created during the 1980s by Salvadorans in Los Angeles who had fled the country's civil conflict. Both gangs later expanded their operations to Central America. CRS Report RL34112, *Gangs in Central America*, by Clare Ribando Seelke.

[18] Stephen S. Dudley, Drug Trafficking Organizations in Central America: Transportistas, Mexican Cartels, and Maras, Woodrow Wilson International Center for Scholars, Working Paper Series on U.S.-Mexico Security Cooperation, May 2010; "Salvadoran Leader Speaks of Criminal Gangs' Links to Drug Cartels," *Los Angeles Times*, September 11, 2010.

[19] CRS Interview with Salvadoran National Police officials, December 2010.

[20] El Salvador's Congress passed strict *mano dura* ("firm hand") anti-gang reforms in 2003 and 2004 that outlawed gang membership, enhanced police power to search and arrest suspected gang members, and stiffened penalties for convicted gang members. Changes in legislation were accompanied by the use of joint military and police patrols to round up gang suspects. While these reforms initially provided a way for Salvadoran leaders to show that they were cracking down on gangs, recent studies have cast serious doubts on their effectiveness. Gang roundups exacerbated prison overcrowding. Most youth arrested under mano dura provisions have been subsequently released for lack of evidence. In addition, many gang members are now hiding or removing their tattoos, changing their dress, and avoiding the use of hand signals, making them harder to identify and arrest.

[21] "Funes Loses Patience with Gangs," *Latin American Weekly Report*, June 24, 2010.

[22] "El Salvador: Investment Depends on Fighting Crime," *Oxford Analytica*, September 3, 2010.

[23] Alex Renderos, "El Salvador Moves Against Criminal Gangs," *Los Angeles Times*, September 4, 2010. CRS interview with officials from El Salvador's National Civilian Police, December, 2010.

[24] Ibid.

[25] Benjamin Witte-Lebhar, "Deadly Blaze Underscores Crisis in El Salvador's Prison System," *Noticen: Central American & Caribbean Affairs*, December 2, 2010.

[26] Rep. Jim McGovern, "Many Challenges Facing El Salvador: President Funes Deserves U.S. Support," House Proceedings, *Congressional Record*, vol. 156, part 132 (September 28, 2010).

[27] Christian Völkel, "Government Proposes Security Tax in El Salvador," *IHS Global Insight Daily Analysis*, November 11, 2010.

[28] Homicide statistics are from the Department of Forensic Statistics at the Institute of Legal Medicine in El Salvador.

[29] Mauricio Funes, "Discurso Toma de Posesión," *Gobierno de la Republica de El Salvador*, June 1, 2009.

[30] The White House, Office of the Press Secretary, "Remarks by President Obama and President Funes of El Salvador after Meeting," March 8, 2010.

[31] The MCC compact also includes $45 million to cover program administration and evaluation. See http://www.mcc.gov/documents/factsheet-112906-elsalvador.pdf; Marcela Sánchez, "Putting Remittances to Work," *Washington Post*, December 9, 2006.

[32] Millennium Challenge Corporation, "Compact Implementation Status Report: El Salvador Compact Progress," July – September 2010.

[33] U.S. Department of State, *International Narcotics Control Strategy Report*, March 1, 2010.

[34] Ibid.

[35] "U.S. and El Salvador Sign Agreement for New Wiretapping Center," *Targeted News Service*, December 8, 2010.

[36] U.S. Southern Command, "Fact Sheet: Forward Operating Locations," February 5, 2009.

[37] "Amplián Permanencia de Centro Antidrogas de EU en El Salvador," *Agencia Mexicana de Noticias*, April 2, 2009.

[38] "Salvador's Central Bank Says Migrants Sent 8.5 Percent Less Money Home in 2009," *AP*, January 12, 2010.

[39] "Central American Officials Show Mixed Feelings on Remittances," *Business News Americas*, December 21, 2010.

[40] Information provided to CRS by the Department of Homeland Security, Immigration and Customs Enforcement, Office of Detention and Removal.

[41] Grupo de Trabajo Binacional El Salvador - Estados Unidos Verifica Proceso de Deportacion," Ministerio de Relaciones Exteriores de El Salvador, Janaury 12, 2010.

[42] U.S. Department of Commerce statistics, as presented by *World Trade Atlas*, 2010.

In: Central America: Profiles and U.S. Relations
Editor: Brian J. Durham

ISBN: 978-1-61470-122-4
© 2011 Nova Science Publishers, Inc.

Chapter 6

GUATEMALA PROFILE

U.S. Department of State

Official Name: Republic of Guatemala

GEOGRAPHY

Area: 108,890 sq. km. (42,042 sq. mi.); about the size of Tennessee.
Cities: *Capital*--Guatemala City (metro area pop. 2.5 million). *Other major cities*--Quetzaltenango, Escuintla.
Terrain: Mountainous, with fertile coastal plain.
Climate: Temperate in highlands; tropical on coasts.

Guatemala Flag

PEOPLE

Nationality: *Noun and adjective*--Guatemalan(s).
Population (2009 est.): 14.36 million.
Annual population growth rate (2009 est.): 2.4%.
Ethnic groups: Mestizo (mixed Spanish-Indian), indigenous.
Religions: Roman Catholic, Protestant, traditional Mayan.
Languages: Spanish, 24 indigenous languages (principally Kiche, Kaqchikel, Q'eqchi, and Mam).
Education: *Years compulsory*--6. *Attendance*--41%. *Literacy*--70.6%.
Health: *Infant mortality rate* (2008/2009)--30/1,000. *Life expectancy* (2005)--69 yrs.
Work force salaried breakdown: *Services*--42%; *industry and commerce*--37%; *agriculture*--14%; *construction, mining, utilities, transportation, and communications*--7%. Fifty percent of the population engages in some form of agriculture, often at the subsistence level outside the monetized economy.

GOVERNMENT

Type: Constitutional democratic republic.
Constitution: May 1985; amended November 1993.
Independence: September 15, 1821.
Branches: *Executive*--president (4-year term; 1 term limit). *Legislative*--unicameral 158-member Congress (4-year term). *Judicial*--13-member Supreme Court of Justice (5-year term).
Subdivisions: 22 departments (appointed governors); 331 municipalities with elected mayors and city councils.
Major political parties: National Union for Hope (UNE), Grand National Alliance (GANA), Patriot Party (PP), Guatemalan Republican Front (FRG), National Advancement Party (PAN), Unionists (PU), Encounter for Guatemala (EG).
Suffrage: Universal for adults 18 and over who are not serving on active duty with the armed forces or police. A variety of procedural obstacles have historically reduced participation by poor, rural, and indigenous people, but implementation in 2007 of voting reform legislation nearly doubled the number of polling places, resulting in higher participation in rural areas, including among indigenous people.

ECONOMY

Real GDP (2009 est.): $23.7 billion.
Real GDP growth (2009 est.): 0.6%.
Per capita GNI, PPP (2008): $4,690.
Natural resources: Oil, timber, nickel, gold.
Agriculture (13.4% of GDP): *Products*--coffee, sugar, bananas, cardamom, vegetables, flowers and plants, timber, rice, rubber.
Manufacturing (18.3% of GDP): *Types*--prepared food, clothing and textiles, construction materials, tires, pharmaceuticals.
Trade (2009): *Exports*--$7.2 billion: coffee, bananas, sugar, crude oil, chemical products, clothing and textiles, vegetables. *Major markets*--U.S. 40.7%, Central American Common Market (CACM) 27.5%, Mexico 5.9%. *Imports*--$11.5 billion: machinery and equipment, fuels, mineral products, chemical products, vehicles and transport materials, plastic materials and products. *Major suppliers*--U.S. 36.5%, CACM 11.4%, Mexico 10.3%, China 5.3%.

PEOPLE

More than half of Guatemalans are descendants of indigenous Mayan peoples. Westernized Mayans and mestizos (mixed European and indigenous ancestry) are known as Ladinos. Most of Guatemala's population is rural, though urbanization is accelerating. The predominant religion is Roman Catholicism, into which many indigenous Guatemalans have incorporated traditional forms of worship. Protestantism and traditional Mayan religions are practiced by an estimated 40% and 1% of the population, respectively. Though the official language is Spanish, it is not universally understood among the indigenous population. The peace accords signed in December 1996 provide for the translation of some official documents and voting materials into several indigenous languages.

HISTORY

The Mayan civilization flourished throughout much of Guatemala and the surrounding region long before the Spanish arrived, but it was already in decline when the Mayans were defeated by Pedro de Alvarado in 1523-24. The first colonial capital, Ciudad Vieja, was ruined by floods and an earthquake in 1542. Survivors founded Antigua, the second capital, in 1543. Antigua was destroyed by two earthquakes in 1773. The remnants of its Spanish colonial architecture have been preserved as a national monument. The third capital, Guatemala City, was founded in 1776.

Guatemala gained independence from Spain on September 15, 1821; it briefly became part of the Mexican Empire, and then for a period belonged to a federation called the United Provinces of Central America. From the mid-19th century until the mid-1980s, the country passed through a series of dictatorships, insurgencies (particularly beginning in the 1960s), coups, and stretches of military rule with only occasional periods of representative government.

1944 to 1986

In 1944, Gen. Jorge Ubico's dictatorship was overthrown by the "October Revolutionaries," a group of dissident military officers, students, and liberal professionals. A civilian President, Juan Jose Arevalo, was elected in 1945 and held the presidency until 1951. Social reforms initiated by Arevalo were continued by his successor, Col. Jacobo Arbenz. Arbenz permitted the communist Guatemalan Labor Party to gain legal status in 1952. The army refused to defend the Arbenz government when a U.S.-backed group led by Col. Carlos Castillo Armas invaded the country from Honduras in 1954 and quickly took over the government. Gen. Miguel Ydigoras Fuentes took power in 1958 following the murder of Colonel Castillo Armas.

In response to the increasingly autocratic rule of Ydigoras Fuentes, a group of junior military officers revolted in 1960. When they failed, several went into hiding and established close ties with Cuba. This group became the nucleus of the forces that were in armed insurrection against the government for the next 36 years. Four principal left-wing guerrilla groups--the Guerrilla Army of the Poor (EGP), the Revolutionary Organization of Armed People (ORPA), the Rebel Armed Forces (FAR), and the Guatemalan Labor Party (PGT)-- conducted economic sabotage and targeted government installations and members of government security forces in armed attacks. These organizations combined to form the Guatemalan National Revolutionary Unity (URNG) in 1982.

Shortly after President Julio Cesar Mendez Montenegro took office in 1966, the army launched a major counterinsurgency campaign that largely broke up the guerrilla movement in the countryside. The guerrillas then concentrated their attacks in Guatemala City, where they assassinated many leading figures, including U.S. Ambassador John Gordon Mein in 1968. Between 1966 and 1982, there was a series of military or military-dominated governments.

On March 23, 1982, army troops commanded by junior officers staged a coup to prevent the assumption of power by Gen. Angel Anibal Guevara, the hand-picked candidate of outgoing President and Gen. Romeo Lucas Garcia. They denounced Guevara's electoral victory as fraudulent. The coup leaders asked retired Gen. Efrain Rios Montt to negotiate the departure of Lucas and Guevara.

Rios Montt was at this time a lay pastor in the evangelical protestant "Church of the Word." He formed a three-member military junta that annulled the 1965 constitution, dissolved Congress, suspended political parties, and canceled the electoral law. After a few months, Rios Montt dismissed his junta colleagues and assumed the de facto title of "President of the Republic."

Guerrilla forces and their leftist allies denounced Rios Montt. Rios Montt sought to defeat the guerrillas with military actions and economic reforms; in his words, "rifles and beans." The government began to form local civilian defense patrols (PACs). Participation was in theory voluntary, but in reality, many Guatemalans, especially in the heavily indigenous northwest, had no choice but to join either the PACs or the guerrillas. Rios Montt's conscript army and PACs recaptured essentially all guerrilla territory--guerrilla activity lessened and was largely limited to hit-and-run operations. However, Rios Montt won this partial victory at an enormous cost in civilian deaths, in what was probably the most violent period of the 36-year internal conflict, resulting in about 200,000 deaths of mostly unarmed indigenous civilians.

On August 8, 1983, Rios Montt was deposed by his own Minister of Defense, Gen. Oscar Humberto Mejia Victores, who succeeded him as de facto President of Guatemala. Rios Montt survived to found a political party (the Guatemalan Republic Front) and to be elected President of Congress in 1995 and 2000. Awareness in the United States of the conflict in Guatemala, and its ethnic dimension, increased with the 1983 publication of the book *I, Rigoberta Menchu, An Indian Woman in Guatemala.*

General Mejia allowed a managed return to democracy in Guatemala, starting with a July 1, 1984 election for a Constituent Assembly to draft a democratic constitution. On May 30, 1985, after 9 months of debate, the Constituent Assembly finished drafting a new constitution, which took effect immediately. Vinicio Cerezo, a civilian politician and the presidential candidate of the Christian Democracy Party, won the first election held under the new constitution with almost 70% of the vote, and took office on January 14, 1986.

1986 to 2007

Upon its inauguration in January 1986, President Cerezo's civilian government announced that its top priorities would be to end the political violence and establish the rule of law. Reforms included new laws of habeas corpus and amparo (court-ordered protection), the creation of a legislative human rights committee, and the establishment in 1987 of the Office of Human Rights Ombudsman. Cerezo survived coup attempts in 1988 and 1989, and the final 2 years of Cerezo's government were also marked by a failing economy, strikes, protest marches, and allegations of widespread corruption.

Presidential and congressional elections were held on November 11, 1990. After a runoff ballot, Jorge Serrano was inaugurated on January 14, 1991, thus completing the first transition from one democratically elected civilian government to another.

The Serrano administration's record was mixed. It had some success in consolidating civilian control over the army, replacing a number of senior officers and persuading the military to participate in peace talks with the URNG. Serrano took the politically unpopular step of recognizing the sovereignty of Belize. The Serrano government reversed the economic slide it inherited, reducing inflation and boosting real growth.

On May 25, 1993, Serrano illegally dissolved Congress and the Supreme Court and tried to restrict civil freedoms, allegedly to fight corruption. The "autogolpe" (or self-initiated coup) failed due to unified, strong protests by most elements of Guatemalan society, international pressure, and the army's enforcement of the decisions of the Court of Constitutionality, which ruled against the attempted takeover. Serrano fled the country.

On June 5, 1993, the Congress, pursuant to the 1985 constitution, elected the Human Rights Ombudsman, Ramiro De Leon Carpio, to complete Serrano's presidential term. De Leon, not a member of any political party and lacking a political base but with strong popular support, launched an ambitious anticorruption campaign to "purify" Congress and the Supreme Court, demanding the resignations of all members of the two bodies.

Despite considerable congressional resistance, presidential and popular pressure led to a November 1993 agreement brokered by the Catholic Church between the administration and Congress. This package of constitutional reforms was approved by popular referendum on January 30, 1994. In August 1994, a new Congress was elected to complete the unexpired term.

Under De Leon, the peace process, now brokered by the United Nations, took on new life. The government and the URNG signed agreements on human rights (March 1994), resettlement of displaced persons (June 1994), historical clarification (June 1994), and indigenous rights (March 1995). They also made significant progress on a socioeconomic and agrarian agreement. National elections for president, the Congress, and municipal offices were held in November 1995. With almost 20 parties competing in the first round, the presidential election came down to a January 7, 1996 runoff in which National Advancement Party (PAN) candidate Alvaro Arzu defeated Alfonso Portillo of the Guatemalan Republican Front (FRG) by just over 2% of the vote. Under the Arzu administration, peace negotiations were concluded, and the government signed peace accords ending the 36-year internal conflict in December 1996. The human rights situation also improved during Arzu's tenure, and steps were taken to reduce the influence of the military in national affairs.

In a December 1999 presidential runoff, Alfonso Portillo (FRG) won 68% of the vote to 32% for Oscar Berger (PAN). Portillo's impressive electoral triumph, with two-thirds of the vote in the second round, gave him a claim to a mandate from the people to carry out his reform program. In February 2004, Portillo fled to Mexico to escape corruption charges. In October 2008, Mexican authorities extradited former president Portillo (2000-2004) to Guatemala to face corruption charges. In March 2010, a Guatemalan court ruled to approve Portillo's extradition to the United States to face money-laundering charges after domestic charges are resolved.

Oscar Berger of the Grand National Alliance (GANA) party won the November 9, 2003 presidential election, receiving 54.1% of the vote. His opponent, Alvarado Colom Caballeros of the National Unity for Hope (UNE) party, received 45.9% of the vote.

Álvaro Colom of the National Unity for Hope (UNE) party won the November 4, 2007 presidential election against retired General Otto Perez Molina with 52.8% of the vote versus 47.2%.

GOVERNMENT

Guatemala's 1985 constitution provides for a separation of powers among the executive, legislative, and judicial branches of government. The 1993 constitutional reforms included an increase in the number of Supreme Court justices from 9 to 13. The reforms reduced the terms of office for president, vice president, and congressional representatives from 5 years to 4 years, and for Supreme Court justices from 6 years to 5 years; they increased the terms of mayors and city councils from 2-1/2 years to 4 years.

The president and vice president are directly elected through universal suffrage and limited to one term. A vice president can run for president after 4 years out of office. The Supreme Court consists of 13 justices who are elected by the Congress from a list of 26 qualifying candidates submitted by the bar association, law school deans, a university rector, and appellate judges. The Supreme Court and local courts handle civil and criminal cases. There also is a separate Constitutional Court.

Members of Congress are elected through a modified proportional representation system via the D'Hondt method; 127 members are chosen from lists in 23 electoral districts, and 31 members are chosen from a national list. Guatemala City and 331 other municipalities are governed by similarly elected mayors or councils. Guatemala has 22 administrative subdivisions (departments) administered by governors appointed by the president.

Principal Government Officials

President--Álvaro COLOM Caballeros
Vice President--Rafael ESPADA
Minister of Foreign Affairs--Haroldo RODAS
Minister of Government--Carlos MENOCAL Chavez
Minister of Defense--Abraham VALENZUELA González
Ambassador to the U.S.--Francisco VILLAGRAN de León
Ambassador to the UN--Gert ROSENTHAL
Ambassador to the OAS--Jorge SKINNER-KLEE

The Guatemalan embassy is located at 2220 R Street, NW, Washington, DC 20008 (tel. 202-745-4952; email: INFO@Guatemala). Consulates are in Washington, New York, Miami, Chicago, Houston, San Francisco, Denver, and Los Angeles, and honorary consuls in Montgomery, San Diego, Ft. Lauderdale, Atlanta, Leavenworth, Lafayette, New Orleans, Minneapolis, Philadelphia, Pittsburgh, San Juan, Providence, Memphis, San Antonio, and Seattle. See the State Department Web page: http://www.state

POLITICAL CONDITIONS

Congressional, municipal, and first-round presidential elections took place on September 9, 2007. The final round of presidential elections took place on November 4, 2007. Inauguration for the new president and the new Congress took place on January 14, 2008. The next presidential elections are scheduled for September 2011.

Common and violent crime, aggravated by a legacy of violence and vigilante justice, presents a serious challenge. Impunity remained a major problem, primarily because democratic institutions, including those responsible for the administration of justice, have developed only a limited capacity to cope with this legacy. Guatemala's judiciary is independent; however, it suffers from inefficiency, corruption, and intimidation.

In early December 2006, the government and the UN agreed to the creation of the joint International Commission Against Impunity in Guatemala (CICIG). On August 1, 2007, the Guatemalan Congress approved the agreement, and on January 11, 2008, Guatemala and the United Nations inaugurated the work of CICIG. An earlier Guatemala-UN agreement was ruled unconstitutional in 2004 before it was ratified by the Guatemalan Congress. In July 2009, the Guatemalan Congress approved an extension of CICIG's mandate to September 4, 2011. The UN Verification Mission in Guatemala (MINUGUA) ceased its 10-year project of monitoring peace accord implementation and human rights problems in November 2004 with UN Secretary General Kofi Annan declaring Guatemala had made "enormous progress in managing the country's problems through dialogue and institutions".

ECONOMY

After the signing of the final peace accord in December 1996, Guatemala was well-positioned for rapid economic growth over the next several years, until a financial crisis in 1998 disrupted the course of improvement. The subsequent collapse of coffee prices left what was once the country's leading export sector in depression and had a severe impact on rural income. On a more positive note, Guatemala's macroeconomic management is sound, preserving stability and mitigating the slowdown in growth brought on by the global economic crisis in late 2008. While Guatemala's foreign debt levels are modest, recent deficit spending and low tax collection have limited the space for further accumulation of debt. President Colom has continued programs initiated by prior governments to promote foreign investment, enhance competitiveness, and expand investment in the export and tourist sectors. These programs and the implementation of the U.S.-Central America-Dominican Republic Free Trade Agreement (CAFTA-DR) led to increases in foreign direct investment (FDI) inflows from $592 million in 2006 to $753 million in 2008. According to official projections, FDI inflows declined 25.8% in 2009 to $559 million as a result of the global economic crisis.

Guatemala's economy is dominated by the private sector, which generates about 90% of GDP. Agriculture contributes 13.4% of GDP and accounts for 26% of exports. Most manufacturing is light assembly and food processing, geared to the domestic, U.S., and Central American markets. Over the past several years, tourism and exports of textiles, apparel, and nontraditional agricultural products such as winter vegetables, fruit, and cut flowers have boomed, while more traditional exports such as sugar, bananas, and coffee continue to represent a large share of the export market.

The United States is the country's largest trading partner, providing 36.5% of Guatemala's imports and receiving 40.7% of its exports. The government's involvement is small, with its business activities limited to public utilities--some of which have been privatized--ports and airports, and several development-oriented financial institutions.

Guatemala ratified the U.S.-Central America Free Trade Agreement (CAFTA-DR) on March 10, 2005, and the agreement entered into force between Guatemala and the U.S. on July 1, 2006. CAFTA-DR eliminates customs tariffs on as many categories of goods as possible; opens services sectors; and creates clear and readily enforceable rules in areas such as investment, government procurement, intellectual property protection, customs procedures, electronic commerce, the use of sanitary and phyto-sanitary measures to protect public health, and resolution of business disputes. It also provides for protection of internationally recognized labor rights and environmental standards.

At only 10.4% of GDP in 2009, Guatemala's tax collection is low compared to the Latin American average of 14.5%. In addition to raising overall tax revenues, continuing priorities include increasing transparency and accountability in public finances, broadening the tax base, strengthening the enforcement of tax laws, and completing implementation of financial sector reforms.

The United States, along with other donor countries--especially France, Italy, Spain, Germany, and Japan--and the international financial institutions, have increased development project financing since the signing of the peace accords. However, donor support remains contingent upon Guatemalan Government reforms and counterpart financing.

According to the World Bank, Guatemala has one of the most unequal income distributions in the hemisphere. The wealthiest 20% of the population consumes 51% of Guatemala's GDP. As a result, about 51% of the population lives on less than $2 a day and 15% on less than $1 a day. Guatemala's social development indicators, such as infant mortality, chronic child malnutrition, and illiteracy, are among the worst in the hemisphere. The United States has provided disaster assistance and food aid in response to natural disasters including Hurricane Stan, which caused extensive mudslides in Guatemala in October 2005, and in response to El Niño-related drought in 2009 and 2010.

NATIONAL SECURITY

Guatemala is a signatory to the Rio Pact and is a member of the Conference of Central American Armed Forces (CFAC). Guatemala has deployed its troops to UN peacekeeping operations in Haiti and the Congo and has observers in several other locations. The president is commander in chief. The Minister of Defense is responsible for policy. Day-to-day operations are the responsibility of the military chief of staff and the national defense staff.

An agreement signed in September 1996, which is one of the substantive peace accords, mandated that the mission of the armed forces change to focus exclusively on external threats. However, Presidents Colom, Berger, Portillo, and Arzu used a constitutional clause to order the army to temporarily support the police in response to a nationwide wave of violent crime.

The 1996 accord calls for a one-third reduction in the army's authorized strength and budget--achieved under President Berger--and for a constitutional amendment to permit the appointment of a civilian Minister of Defense. A constitutional amendment to this end was defeated as part of a May 1999 plebiscite, but discussions on how to achieve this objective continue between the executive and legislative branches.

As of March 2010, the army numbered around 16,100 troops, having gone well beyond its accord-mandated target of reducing its strength from 50,000 to 33,000 troops. President Colom has increased the cap on troop levels to 20,000. Not only was this reduction the most profound transformation of any Central American military in the last 50 years, it also indicates the effective control the civilian government has over the military. President Berger tasked the Ministry of Defense with increasing the professional skills of all soldiers, but military budgets remained limited and troop levels fell as far as 15,500. As part of the army downsizing, the operational structure of 19 military zones was eliminated. Currently, there are 6 brigades with contiguous areas of responsibility throughout the country. The air force operates three main air bases; the navy has two primary port bases. Additionally, recent steps have been taken to redefine the military's mission--the military doctrine has been rewritten, and there has been an increase in cooperation with civil society to help bring about this reform.

FOREIGN RELATIONS

Guatemala's major diplomatic interests are regional security, regional development, and economic integration. Guatemala participates in several regional groups, particularly those related to trade and the environment.

The Council of Central American Ministers of Trade meets on a regular basis to work on regional approaches to trade issues. The council signed a Trade and Investment Framework Agreement (TIFA) with the U.S. in 1998, and was part of the negotiations that led to the creation of CAFTA-DR. Guatemala joined Honduras and El Salvador in signing a free trade agreement with Mexico in 2000, which went into effect the following year. Guatemala also originated the idea for, and is the seat of, the Central American Parliament (PARLACEN).

The U.S. and Central American countries signed the CONCAUSA (Conjunto Centroamerica-USA) agreement at the Summit of the Americas in December 1994. CONCAUSA is a cooperative plan of action to promote clean, efficient energy use; conserve the region's biodiversity; strengthen legal and institutional frameworks and compliance mechanisms; and improve and harmonize environmental protection standards.

Guatemala has a long-standing claim to a large portion of Belize; the territorial dispute caused problems with the United Kingdom and later with Belize following its 1981 independence from the U.K. In December 1989, Guatemala sponsored Belize for permanent observer status in the Organization of American States (OAS). In September 1991, Guatemala recognized Belize's independence and established diplomatic ties, while acknowledging that the boundaries remained in dispute. In anticipation of an effort to bring the border dispute to an end in early 1996, the Guatemalan Congress ratified two long-pending international agreements governing frontier issues and maritime rights. In 2001, Guatemala and Belize agreed to a facilitation process led by the OAS to determine the land and maritime borders separating the two countries. National elections in Guatemala put a temporary halt to progress, but discussions resumed in November 2005. After being named Foreign Minister in 2008, Haroldo Rodas made clear his intention to reinvigorate discussions with Belize, and the two countries signed an agreement to submit the dispute to the International Court of Justice at The Hague for resolution. The agreement is pending ratification by simultaneous plebiscites in both countries.

U.S.-GUATEMALAN RELATIONS

Relations between the United States and Guatemala traditionally have been close, although at times strained by human rights and civil/military issues. U.S. policy objectives in Guatemala include:

- Supporting the institutionalization of democracy and implementation of the peace accords;
- Encouraging respect for human rights and the rule of law, and the efficient functioning of the International Commission Against Impunity in Guatemala (CICIG);
- Supporting broad-based economic growth and sustainable development and maintaining mutually beneficial trade and commercial relations, including ensuring that benefits of CAFTA-DR reach all sectors of the Guatemalan populace;
- Cooperating to combat money laundering, corruption, narcotics trafficking, alien-smuggling, and other transnational crime, including through programs funded under the Central American Regional Security Initiative; and

- Supporting Central American integration through support for resolution of border/territorial disputes.

The United States, as a member of "the Friends of Guatemala," along with Colombia, Mexico, Spain, Norway, and Venezuela, played an important role in the UN-moderated peace accords, providing public and behind-the-scenes support. The U.S. strongly supports the six substantive and three procedural accords, which, along with the signing of the December 29, 1996 final accord, form the blueprint for profound political, economic, and social change. To that end, the U.S. Government has committed over $500 million to support peace implementation since 1997.

Violent criminal activity continues to be a problem in Guatemala, including murder, rape, and armed assaults against persons of all nationalities. In recent years the number of violent crimes reported by U.S. citizens has steadily increased, though the number of Americans traveling to Guatemala has also increased.

Most U.S. assistance to Guatemala is provided through the U.S. Agency for International Development's (USAID) offices for Guatemala. USAID/Guatemala's current program builds on the gains of the peace process that followed the signing of the peace accords in December 1996, as well as on the achievements of its 1997-2004 peace program. The current program works to advance U.S. foreign policy objectives by focusing on Guatemala's potential as Central America's largest economy and trading partner of the United States, but also recognizes the country's lagging social indicators and high rate of poverty. The three areas of focus for USAID/Guatemala's program are modeled after the Millennium Challenge Account areas--ruling justly, economic freedom, and investing in people, and are as follows:

More responsive, transparent governance, through:

- Strengthened justice; and
- Greater transparency and accountability of governments.

Open, diversified and expanding economies, through:

- Laws, policies, and regulations that promote trade and investment;
- More competitive, market-oriented private enterprises; and
- Broader access to financial markets and services.

Healthier, better educated people, through:

- Increased and improved quality of social sector (health and education) investments; and
- Increased use of quality maternal-child and reproductive health services, particularly in rural areas.

In: Central America: Profiles and U.S. Relations
Editor: Brian J. Durham

ISBN: 978-1-61470-122-4
© 2011 Nova Science Publishers, Inc.

Chapter 7

HONDURAS PROFILE

U.S. Department of State

Official Name: Republic of Honduras

GEOGRAPHY

Area: 112,090 sq. km. (43,278 sq. mi.); slightly larger than Virginia.
Cities: *Capital*--Tegucigalpa (1,150,000); San Pedro Sula (800,000-900,000).
Terrain: Mountainous.
Climate: Tropical to subtropical, depending on elevation.

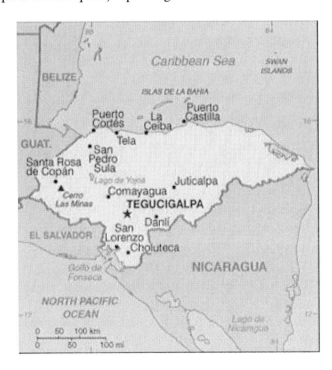

Flag of Honduras

PEOPLE

Nationality: *Noun and adjective*--Honduran(s).
Population (2010 est.): 8.0 million.
Population growth rate (2010 est.): 1.94%.
Ethnic groups: 90% mestizo (mixed Amer-Indian and European); others of European, Arab, African, or Asian ancestry; and indigenous Indians.
Religions: Roman Catholic; Protestant minority.
Language: Spanish.
Education (2003): *Years compulsory*--6. *Attendance*--94% overall, 61% at junior high level. *Literacy*--83.3%.
Health: *Infant mortality rate*--26/1,000. *Life expectancy*--70.5 yrs.
Work force: *Services*--42.2%; *natural resources/agriculture*--35.9%; *manufacturing*--16.3%; *construction/housing*--5.6%.

GOVERNMENT

Type: Democratic constitutional republic.
Independence: September 15, 1821.
Constitution: 1982; with amendments.
Branches: *Executive*--president, directly elected to 4-year term. *Legislative*--unicameral National Congress, elected for 4-year term. *Judicial*--Supreme Court of Justice (appointed for a 7-year term by Congress and confirmed by the president); several lower courts.
Political parties: National Party, Liberal Party, Innovation and National Unity Party, Christian Democratic Party, and the Democratic Unification Party.
Suffrage: Universal and compulsory at age 18.
Administrative subdivisions: 18 departments.

Economy (2009 est.)
GDP: $14.8 billion.
Growth rate (2009): -2.1%.
Per capita GDP: $1,829 (official exchange rate); $3,130 (PPP, IMF).
Natural resources: Arable land, forests, minerals, and fisheries.
Agriculture (14.2% of GDP): *Products*--coffee, bananas, shrimp and lobster, sugar, fruits, basic grains, and livestock.
Manufacturing (27.9% of GDP): *Types*--textiles and apparel, cement, wood products, cigars, and foodstuffs.

Services (57.9% of GDP).

Trade: *Exports (goods)*--$5.2 billion: apparel, auto parts, coffee, shrimp, bananas, palm oil, gold, zinc/lead concentrates, soap/detergents, melons, lobster, pineapple, lumber, sugar, and tobacco/tobacco products. *Major market*--U.S. (59.5%). *Imports (goods)*--$7.79 billion: fabrics, yarn, machinery, chemicals, petroleum, vehicles, processed foods, metals, agricultural products, plastic articles, and paper articles. *Major source*--U.S. (50.1%).

PEOPLE

About 90% of the population is mestizo. There also are small minorities of European, African, Asian, Arab, and indigenous Indian descent. A majority of Hondurans are Roman Catholic, but Protestant churches are growing in number. While Spanish is the predominant language, some English is spoken along the northern coast and is prevalent on the Caribbean Bay Islands. Several indigenous Indian languages and Garífuna (a mixture of Afro-indigenous languages) are also spoken. The restored Mayan ruins near the Guatemalan border in Copan reflect the great Mayan culture that flourished there for hundreds of years until the early 9th century. Columbus landed at mainland Honduras (Trujillo) in 1502, and named the area "Honduras" (meaning "depths") for the deep water off the coast. Spaniard Hernan Cortes arrived in 1524.

HISTORY

Honduras was originally inhabited by indigenous tribes, the most powerful of which were the Mayans. The western-central part of Honduras was inhabited by the Lencas. These autonomous groups had their conflicts but maintained their commercial relationships with each other and with other populations as distant as Panama and Mexico.

On July 30, 1502, Christopher Columbus first saw Honduran soil and he claimed the territory in the name of his sovereigns, Ferdinand of Aragon and Isabella of Castile.

In 1523, the first expeditionary forces arrived under the command of Gil Gonzales de Avila, who hoped to rule the new territory. In 1524, Cristobal de Olid arrived with the same intent on behalf of Hernan Cortes. Olid founded the colony Triunfo de la Cruz and tried to establish an independent government. When Cortes learned of this, he decided to reestablish his own authority by sending a new expedition, headed by Francisco de las Casas. Olid, who managed to capture his rivals, was betrayed by his men and assassinated. Cortes then traveled to Honduras to firmly establish his government in the city of Trujillo before returning to Mexico in 1526. Honduras formed part of the colonial era Captaincy General of Guatemala. The cities of Comayagua and Tegucigalpa developed as early mining centers.

By October 1537, the Lenca chief, Lempira, a warrior of great renown, had managed to unify more than two hundred native tribes in order to offer an organized resistance against penetration by the Spanish conquerors. After a long battle, Governor Montejo gained the Valley of Comayagua, established Comayagua city in another location, and vanquished the indigenous peoples in Tenampua, Guaxeregui, and Ojuera.

Independence

Honduras gained independence from Spain in 1821. The country was then briefly annexed to the Mexican Empire. In 1823, Honduras joined the newly formed United Provinces of Central America federation, which collapsed in 1838. Gen. Francisco Morazan-- a Honduran national hero--led unsuccessful efforts to maintain the federation. Honduras' agriculture-based economy was dominated in the 1900s by U.S. companies that established vast banana plantations along the north coast. Foreign capital, plantation life, and conservative politics held sway in Honduras from the late 19th century until the mid-20th century.

Military Rule

Authoritarian Gen. Tiburcio Carias Andino controlled Honduras during the Great Depression, until 1948. In 1955--after two authoritarian administrations and a strike by banana workers--young military reformists staged a coup that installed a provisional junta and paved the way for constituent assembly elections in 1957. This assembly appointed Ramon Villeda Morales as President and transformed itself into a national legislature with a 6-year term. In 1963, conservative military officers preempted constitutional elections and deposed Villeda in a bloody coup. The armed forces, led by Gen. Lopez Arellano, governed until 1970. Popular discontent continued to rise after a 1969 border war with El Salvador, known as "the Soccer War." A civilian President--Ramon Cruz of the National Party--took power briefly in 1970 but proved unable to manage the government. In 1972, Gen. Lopez staged another coup. Lopez adopted more progressive policies, including land reform, but his regime was brought down in the mid-1970s by corruption scandals. The regimes of Gen. Melgar Castro (1975-78) and Gen. Paz Garcia (1978-82) largely built the current physical infrastructure and telecommunications system of Honduras. The country also enjoyed its most rapid economic growth during this period, due to greater international demand for its products and the availability of foreign commercial lending.

Seven Consecutive Democratic Elections

Following the overthrow of Anastasio Somoza in Nicaragua in 1979 and general instability in El Salvador at the time, Hondurans elected a constituent assembly in 1980 and voted in general elections in 1981. A new constitution was approved in 1982, and the Liberal Party government of President Roberto Suazo Cordoba took office. Suazo relied on U.S. support during a severe economic recession, including ambitious social and economic development projects sponsored by the U.S. Agency for International Development (USAID). Honduras became host to the largest Peace Corps mission in the world, and nongovernmental and international voluntary agencies proliferated.

As the 1985 election approached, the Liberal Party interpreted election law as permitting multiple presidential candidates from one party. The Liberal Party claimed victory when its presidential candidates, who received 42% of the vote, collectively outpolled the National Party candidate, Rafael Leonardo Callejas. Jose Azcona Hoyo, the candidate receiving the most votes among the Liberals, assumed the presidency in 1986. With the endorsement of the Honduran military, the Azcona administration ushered in the first peaceful transfer of power between civilian presidents in more than 30 years.

Nationalist Rafael Callejas won the following presidential election, taking office in 1990. The nation's fiscal deficit ballooned during Callejas' last year in office. Growing public dissatisfaction with the rising cost of living and with widespread government corruption led voters in 1993 to elect Liberal Party candidate Carlos Roberto Reina with 56% of the vote. President Reina, elected on a platform calling for a "moral revolution," actively prosecuted corruption and pursued those responsible for human rights abuses in the 1980s. He created a modern attorney general's office and an investigative police force, increased civilian control over the armed forces, transferred the police from military to civilian authority, and restored national fiscal health.

Liberal Carlos Roberto Flores Facusse took office in 1998. Flores inaugurated programs of reform and modernization of the Honduran government and economy, with emphasis on helping Honduras' poorest citizens while maintaining the country's fiscal health and improving international competitiveness. In October 1998, Hurricane Mitch devastated Honduras, leaving more than 5,000 people dead and 1.5 million displaced. Damages totaled nearly $3 billion.

Ricardo Maduro Joest of the National Party won the 2001 presidential elections, and was inaugurated in 2002. Maduro's first act as President was to deploy a joint police-military force to the streets to permit wider neighborhood patrols in the ongoing fight against the country's massive crime and gang problem. Maduro was a strong supporter of U.S. counterterrorism efforts and joined the U.S.-led coalition in Iraq with an 11-month contribution of 370 troops. Under President Maduro's guidance, Honduras also negotiated and ratified the U.S.-Central America Free Trade Agreement (CAFTA), received debt relief, became the first Latin American country to sign a Millennium Challenge Account compact with the U.S., and actively promoted greater Central American integration. While the Maduro administration implemented a number of successful economic and security policies, reliable polling data revealed widespread popular rejection of Honduran institutions, underscoring the lack of public faith in the political class, the media, and the business community.

Jose Manuel "Mel" Zelaya Rosales of the Liberal Party won the November 27, 2005, presidential elections with less than a 4% margin of victory, the smallest margin ever in Honduran electoral history. Zelaya's campaign theme was "citizen power," and he vowed to increase transparency and combat narcotrafficking, while maintaining macroeconomic stability. The Liberal Party won 62 of the 128 congressional seats, just short of an absolute majority. Zelaya's presidency was marked by a series of controversies as his policies and rhetoric moved closer in line with that of Venezuelan President Hugo Chavez. Zelaya signed on to Chavez' Bolivarian Alternative for the Americas (ALBA) in August 2008, and the treaty was ratified by the National Congress in October 2008. In the final year of Zelaya's term, he began advocating that a referendum be added to the November 2009 elections regarding reform of the constitution. Zelaya proposed that an informal poll be held on June 28 to gauge public support for his proposal. However, Honduran courts ruled that Zelaya's plans were unconstitutional and directed that government agencies desist from providing support to carry out the poll. Zelaya ignored the rulings.

Coup d'état

Army soldiers entered Zelaya's residence in the early hours of June 28, 2009, the day of the poll, forcibly seized Zelaya and expelled him to Costa Rica. The National Congress met in an emergency session that same day, declared Zelaya was no longer president, and swore in President of Congress Roberto Micheletti as the new President of the Republic. Micheletti replaced all the cabinet members who did not accept Zelaya's ouster. As reflected in resolutions by the Organization of American States (OAS) and the United Nations General Assembly, the events of June 28 constituted a coup d'état against a democratically elected government.

Zelaya's forced removal was universally condemned by the international community, and the OAS issued an immediate and unanimous call for Zelaya's unconditional return to office. With support from the United States, the OAS designated Nobel Peace Prize laureate and then-Costa Rican President Oscar Arias as mediator to reach a peaceful, diplomatic resolution of the crisis. Through the Arias-led negotiations, the San Jose Accord, a 12-point plan for restoration of constitutional order, was drafted. The plan called for restoration of Zelaya as president, but with a consensus-based "unity government;" establishment of a truth commission and a verification commission under the auspices of the OAS; amnesty for political crimes committed by all sides related to the coup; and early elections to establish a successor as rapidly as possible. In early October 2009, negotiations were moved to Tegucigalpa and renamed the Guaymuras process. On October 30, 2009, President Zelaya and Roberto Micheletti signed the Tegucigalpa-San Jose Accord. However, President Zelaya broke off his participation in the process of implementing the Tegucigalpa-San Jose Accord after Micheletti announced on November 6, 2009, that he would form a new cabinet without Zelaya.

On November 29, 2009, Hondurans elected Porfirio "Pepe" Lobo as President in a previously scheduled free and fair election that attracted broad voter participation. Lobo received the largest number of votes for a presidential candidate in Honduran history. President Lobo was sworn in on January 27, 2010. After assuming office, Lobo formed a government of national unity and convened a truth commission, as set forth in the Tegucigalpa-San Jose Accord. However, as of August 2010, several countries in Latin America had not recognized the Lobo government, and Honduras' participation remained suspended from the OAS.

GOVERNMENT

The 1982 constitution provides for a strong executive, a unicameral National Congress, and a judiciary appointed by the National Congress. The president is directly elected to a 4-year term by popular vote. The Congress also serves a 4-year term; congressional seats are assigned to the parties' candidates in proportion to the number of votes each party receives in the various departments. The judiciary includes a Supreme Court of Justice (one president and 14 magistrates chosen by Congress for a 7-year term), courts of appeal, and several courts of original jurisdiction--such as labor, tax, and criminal courts. For administrative purposes,

Honduras is divided into 18 departments, with 298 mayors and municipal councils selected for 4-year terms.

POLITICAL CONDITIONS

Reinforced by the media and several political watchdog organizations, concerted efforts to protect human rights and civil liberties continued up to the June 28, 2009, coup. In the immediate aftermath of Zelaya's expulsion from Honduras, the de facto Micheletti regime used troops to shut down dissenting media outlets and imposed curfews to prevent anti-coup protestors from forming large groups to voice their opposition. The de facto regime issued a decree on September 27, 2009, suspending most civil liberties and invoking a state of emergency. The de facto regime also issued an executive order giving the executive the right to close any media service it deemed a threat to national security or public order, without a court order. On October 19, 2009, the de facto regime published a decree abrogating its earlier suspension of civil liberties. The human rights situation significantly deteriorated during the de facto regime's control with widespread reports of beatings by security forces and other abuses. In addition, the regime's movement of security forces into the large cities, in order to maintain its rule, resulted in a significant increase in crime and drug trafficking as traditional security force activities were curtailed. Since his inauguration, President Lobo has taken important steps indicating his government's commitment to human rights, including the appointment of a special advisor for human rights issues. However, since March 2010, the killings of 8 journalists have raised concerns.

Organized labor is relatively strong in Honduras, representing approximately 8% of the overall work force and 13% of the apparel workforce.

Political Parties

The two major parties are the slightly left-of-center Liberal Party and the slightly-right-of-center National Party. The three much smaller registered parties--the Christian Democratic Party, the Innovation and National Unity Party, and the Democratic Unification Party--hold a few seats each in the Congress, but have never come close to winning the presidency.

Principal Government Officials

President--Porfirio LOBO Sosa
First designate-Vice President--Maria Antonieta Guillen de BOGRAN
Minister of Foreign Relations--Mario Miguel CANAHUATI
President of Congress--Juan Orlando HERNÁNDEZ
Ambassador to the United States--Jorge Ramon Hernández-Alcerro
Ambassador to the United Nations--Mary Elizabeth FLORES Flake

Honduras maintains an embassy in the United States at 3007 Tilden Street NW, Washington, DC 20008 (tel. 202-966-7702). For more information concerning entry and exit requirements, travelers may contact the Consular office at 1014 M Street NW, Washington, DC 20001; telephone (202) 682-5948; e-mail: consulado.washington@hondurasemb.org. Honduras also has consulates in Atlanta, Chicago, Houston, Miami, Los Angeles, New Orleans, New York, Phoenix, and San Francisco and an Honorary Consul in San Juan, Puerto Rico. For tourist information or suggestions, please contact the Honduras Institute of Tourism at 1-800-410-9608 (in the United States) or at 1-800-222-TOUR (8687) (within Honduras only) or visit the web site at http://www.hondurastips.honduras.com/.

ECONOMY

Honduras, with an estimated per capita gross domestic product (GDP) of $1,829 in 2009, is one of the poorest countries in the western hemisphere, with about 65% of the population living in poverty. In 2009, Honduras' GDP fell by 2.1%. Reasons for this contraction included the worldwide economic downturn and the political crisis surrounding the forced removal of President Zelaya from power. Previously, the economy grew by more than 6% per year from 2004 to 2007, and by 4% in 2008. The Honduran Central Bank projects that GDP growth for 2010 will be between 2.2% and 3%.

Historically dependent on exports of agricultural goods, the Honduran economy has diversified in recent decades and now has a strong export-processing (*maquila*) industry, primarily focused on assembling textile and apparel goods for re-export to the United States, as well as automobile wiring harnesses and similar products. Despite the recent economic diversification, there continues to be a large subsistence farming population with few economic opportunities. Honduras also has extensive forest, marine, and mineral resources, although widespread slash-and-burn agricultural methods and illegal logging continue to destroy Honduran forests.

Because of a strong commercial relationship with the United States, Honduras was hit hard by the international economic downturn, especially in the maquila industry, where orders were estimated to decline about 40%, and where about 30,000 workers lost their jobs in 2008 and 2009 out of a pre-crisis workforce of 145,000. The maquila sector began to see an upswing toward the end of 2009 as the U.S. economy stabilized, and it has begun re-expanding its employment base. About one-third of the Honduran workforce was considered either unemployed or underemployed in 2009.

Roughly 1 million Hondurans have migrated to the United States. Remittance inflows from Hondurans living abroad, mostly in the United States, are the largest source of foreign income and a major contributor to domestic demand. Remittances totaled $2.8 billion in 2009, down 11.8% from 2008 levels; that is equivalent to about one-fifth of Honduras' GDP.

NATIONAL SECURITY

With the cessation of the 1980s civil wars in El Salvador and Nicaragua, the Honduran armed forces refocused their orientation toward combating transnational threats such as narcoterrorism and organized crime. Honduras supports efforts at regional integration and deployed troops to Iraq in support of Operation Iraqi Freedom. In 1999, the constitution was amended to abolish the position of military commander in chief of the armed forces, thus codifying civilian authority over the military.

FOREIGN RELATIONS

Honduras is a member of the United Nations, the World Trade Organization (WTO), the Organization of American States (OAS--membership suspended July 2009 as a result of the June 28, 2009, coup), the Central American Parliament (PARLACEN), the Central American Integration System (SICA), the Conference of Central American Armed Forces (CFAC), and the Central American Security Commission (CASC). Honduras is also a signatory to the Rio Pact, and a member of the Central American Defense Council (CONDECA). During 1995-96, Honduras--a founding member of the United Nations--served as a nonpermanent member of the UN Security Council for the first time. Honduras is a party to all UN and OAS counterterrorism conventions and protocols.

Honduras is a strong proponent of Central American cooperation and integration, and before the June 2009 coup was working toward the implementation of a regional customs union and Central American passport, which would ease border controls and tariffs among Honduras, Guatemala, Nicaragua, and El Salvador.

In 1969, El Salvador and Honduras fought the brief "Soccer War" over disputed border areas. The two countries formally signed a peace treaty in 1980, which put the border dispute before the International Court of Justice (ICJ). In 1992, the IJC awarded most of the disputed territory to Honduras, and in January 1998, Honduras and El Salvador signed a border demarcation treaty to implement the terms of the ICJ decree, although delays continue due to technical difficulties. However, Honduras and El Salvador maintain normal diplomatic and trade relations. Honduras also has unresolved maritime border disputes with El Salvador, Jamaica, and Cuba.

U.S.-HONDURAN RELATIONS

Overview

Honduras has traditionally been an ally of the United States and generally supports U.S. initiatives in international fora. There was close cooperation with Honduras in the areas of counternarcotics and counterterrorism before June 2009, but because the de facto regime was not recognized as the legitimate government, these activities were suspended. The U.S. recognized the November 2009 presidential election and is cooperating with the Lobo administration to combat poverty, to improve education and health standards for all Hondurans, to strengthen the rule of law and respect for human rights, and to increase Honduras' ability to fight transnational crime and provide a safe environment for all of its citizens. Honduras was among the first countries to sign an International Criminal Court (ICC) Article 98 Agreement with the U.S., and the Honduran port of Puerto Cortes is part of the U.S. Container Security Initiative (CSI). Honduras was also the first Central American country to sign a letter of agreement (LOA) to implement the Merida Initiative, now known as the Central American Regional Security Initiative (CARSI).

During the 1980s, Honduras supported U.S. policy opposing a revolutionary Marxist government in Nicaragua and an active leftist insurgency in El Salvador. The Honduran Government also played a key role in negotiations that culminated in the 1990 Nicaraguan elections. Honduras continues to participate in the UN observer mission in the Western Sahara, contributed 370 troops for stabilization in Iraq, and remains interested in participating in other UN peacekeeping missions.

In 2004, the United States signed the U.S.-Central America Free Trade Agreement (CAFTA) with Honduras, El Salvador, Nicaragua, Guatemala, Costa Rica, and the Dominican Republic. The legislatures of all signatories except Costa Rica ratified CAFTA in 2005, and the agreement entered into force in the first half of 2006. CAFTA eliminates tariffs and other barriers to trade in goods, services, agricultural products, and investments. Additionally, CAFTA is expected to solidify democracy, encourage greater regional integration, and provide safeguards for environmental protection and labor rights. The United States is Honduras' chief trading partner and the largest investor in Honduras.

The United States maintains a small presence at a Honduran military base; until suspension as a result of the June 2009 coup, the two countries conducted joint peacekeeping, counternarcotics, humanitarian, disaster relief, and civic action exercises. U.S. troops conduct and provide logistics support for a variety of bilateral and multilateral exercises--medical, engineering, peacekeeping, counternarcotics, and disaster relief--for the benefit of the Honduran people and their Central American neighbors. U.S. forces--regular, reserve, and National Guard--benefit greatly from these exercises. These activities resumed once constitutional government was restored.

U.S. Policy Toward Honduras

U.S. policy toward Honduras is aimed at consolidating democracy, protecting human rights, and promoting the rule of law, and U.S. policy regarding the June 2009 coup pursued those aims. U.S. Government programs are aimed at promoting a healthy and more open economy capable of sustainable growth, improving the climate for business and investment while protecting U.S. citizen and corporate rights, and promoting the well-being of the Honduran people. The United States also works with Honduras to meet transnational challenges--including the fight against terrorism, narcotics trafficking, money laundering, illegal migration, and trafficking in persons--and encourages and supports Honduran efforts to protect the environment. The goals of strengthening democracy and promoting viable economic growth are especially important given the geographical proximity of Honduras to the United States. An estimated 1 million Hondurans reside in the United States, 600,000 of whom are believed to be undocumented; consequently, immigration issues are an important item on our bilateral agenda.

U.S.-Honduras ties are further strengthened by numerous private sector contacts, with an average of between 80,000 and 110,000 U.S. citizens visiting Honduras annually and about 15,000 Americans residing there. More than 200 American companies operate in Honduras.

Economic and Development Assistance

In order to help strengthen Honduras' democratic institutions and improve living conditions, the United States has provided substantial economic assistance. The United States has historically been the largest bilateral donor to Honduras. The planned USAID budget for Honduras is $49.5 million for fiscal year 2010. Over the years, U.S. foreign assistance has helped advance such objectives as fostering democratic institutions, improving education and the health status of the population, increasing private sector employment and income, helping Honduras manage its arrears with international financial institutions, providing humanitarian aid, increasing agricultural production, and providing loans to microbusinesses.

1998's Hurricane Mitch left hundreds of thousands homeless, devastated the road network and other public infrastructure, and crippled key sectors of the economy. Estimates show that Hurricane Mitch caused $8.5 billion in damages to homes, hospitals, schools, roads, farms, and businesses throughout Central America, including more than $3 billion in Honduras alone. In response, the United States provided more than $461 million in immediate disaster relief and humanitarian aid over the years 1998-2001. This supplemental assistance was designed to help repair water and sanitation systems; replace housing, schools, and roads; provide agricultural inputs; provide local government crisis management training; grant debt relief; and encourage environmental management expertise. Additional resources were utilized to maintain anti-crime and drug assistance programs.

In June 2005, Honduras became the first country in the hemisphere to sign a Millennium Challenge Account (MCA) compact with the U.S. Government. Under the compact, the U.S. Millennium Challenge Corporation was to invest $215 million over 5 years to help Honduras improve its road infrastructure, diversify its agriculture, and transport its products to market. Honduras failed the corruption indicator required for continued funding into 2008. MCC planned to closely follow Honduras' progress on reducing corruption under an approved "remediation plan."

The Peace Corps has been active in Honduras since 1962, and currently the program is one of the largest in the world. In 2009, there were approximately 180 Peace Corps Volunteers working in the poorest parts of Honduras. Volunteers work in six project areas including: HIV/AIDS Prevention and Child Survival, Youth Development, Protected Areas Management, Business, Water and Sanitation, and Municipal Development.

The U.S. Government strongly supports the professionalization of the civilian police force as an important element in strengthening the rule of law in Honduras. The American Embassy in Tegucigalpa provides specialized training to police officers.

Security Assistance

The role of the Honduran armed forces has changed significantly in recent years as many institutions formerly controlled by the military are now under civilian authority. The annual defense and police budgets are approximately $75 million with very modest increases in the past few years. Prior to the June 28, 2009, political crisis, Honduras received modest U.S. security assistance funds and training. During the coup regime, there was no official U.S.-Honduran military interaction.

Historically, in the absence of a large security assistance program, defense cooperation has taken the form of increased participation by the Honduran armed forces in military-to-military contact programs and bilateral and multilateral combined exercises oriented toward peacekeeping, disaster relief, humanitarian/civic assistance, and counternarcotics. The U.S. Joint Task Force Bravo (JTF-Bravo), stationed at the Honduran Soto Cano Air Base, plays a vital role in supporting combined exercises in Honduras and in neighboring Central American countries. JTF-Bravo plays a critical role in helping the United States respond to natural disasters in Central America by serving as a platform for rescue missions, repairing critical infrastructure, and in meeting high priority health and sanitation needs. JTF-Bravo forces have helped deliver millions of dollars worth of privately donated goods to those in need. JTF-Bravo also provides logistical support to interagency partners in the region that combat illegal trafficking activities.

U.S. Business Opportunities

The U.S. is the chief trading partner for Honduras, supplying 50% of Honduran imports and purchasing 60% of Honduran exports in 2009. Bilateral trade between the two nations totaled $6.7 billion in 2009. U.S. Exports to Honduras in 2009 totaled $3.4 billion, a 30% decline from 2008. U.S. imports from Honduras are up 7.8% since the implementation of CAFTA, while U.S. exports to Honduras have grown by 48.9% in that period.

CAFTA eliminates most tariffs and other barriers for U.S. goods destined for the Central American market, provides protection for U.S. investments and intellectual property, and creates more transparent rules and procedures for conducting business. CAFTA also aims to eliminate intra-Central American tariffs and facilitate increased regional trade, benefiting U.S. companies manufacturing in Honduras. With CAFTA implemented, about 80% of U.S. goods now enter the region duty-free, with tariffs on the remaining 20% to be phased out by 2016.

Leading U.S. exports in 2009 included: textile yarn and fabric, petroleum and petroleum products, cereals and cereal preparations, low value shipments, and apparel. Nearly all textile and apparel goods that meet CAFTA's rules of origin became duty-free and quota-free immediately, thus promoting new opportunities for U.S. fiber, yarn, fabric, and apparel manufacturers. Honduras is the seventh-largest exporter of apparel and textile products by volume to the U.S. market behind countries such as Mexico and China; Honduras is first among Central American and Caribbean countries.

The stock of U.S. investments in Honduras at the end of 2008, on a historical cost basis, was $700 million, according to the U.S. Department of Commerce. Foreign direct investment (FDI) in Honduras declined significantly in 2009, totaling $484.5 million, down 46.2% from 2008. The majority of FDI in 2009 was directed to the telecommunications, food, and consumer trade sectors. The United States continued to be the largest investor in Honduras in 2009, accounting for $343.4 million, or 70.7%, of the total inflow. Obstacles to foreign investment include public insecurity, weak judicial protection of investor rights, and corruption.

In: Central America: Profiles and U.S. Relations
Editor: Brian J. Durham

ISBN: 978-1-61470-122-4
© 2011 Nova Science Publishers, Inc.

Chapter 8

HONDURAN-U.S. RELATIONS

Peter J. Meyer

SUMMARY

On January 27, 2010, Porfirio "Pepe" Lobo Sosa was inaugurated President of Honduras, assuming power after seven months of domestic political crisis and international isolation that had resulted from the June 28, 2009, ouster of President Manuel Zelaya. While the strength of Lobo's National Party in the legislature has enabled the government to secure passage of much of its policy agenda, the Lobo Administration has made only limited progress in addressing the challenges inherited as a result of the political crisis. Several efforts to foster political reconciliation, including the creation of a truth commission and the passage of a measure to enable constitutional reform, have done little to lesson domestic polarization. Moreover, human rights abuses have continued, and the country has failed to secure recognition from some sectors of the international community.

In addition to the political problems inherited as a result of the 2009 ouster, Lobo has had to contend with a weak economy. Honduras suffered an economic contraction of 2.1% in 2009 as the global financial crisis, together with the domestic political crisis, led to significant declines in tourism, remittances, and export earnings. Lobo has pushed a number of reforms through Congress designed to restore macroeconomic stability, strengthen public finances, and encourage sustained economic growth. Although these reforms have generated considerable opposition from some sectors of Honduran society, they have the support of the international financial institutions, which are now providing Honduras with access to much needed development financing. The economy picked up in 2010, with estimated growth of 2.8%, and is expected to grow by 3.7% in 2011. Nonetheless, significant development challenges remain. Approximately 60% of Honduras' 8 million citizens live under the poverty line and the country continues to perform poorly on a number of social indicators.

Although relations were strained during the political crisis, the United States has traditionally had a close relationship with Honduras. Broad U.S. policy goals include a strengthened democracy with an effective justice system that protects human rights and promotes the rule of law, and the promotion of sustainable economic growth with a more open economy and improved living conditions. In addition to providing Honduras with substantial amounts of foreign assistance ($51 million in FY20 10) and maintaining significant military and economic ties, the United States cooperates with Honduras on transnational issues such as migration, crime, narcotics trafficking, trafficking in persons, and port security.

The 111th Congress expressed considerable interest in Honduras as a result of the 2009 political crisis and its aftermath. Several resolutions were introduced and multiple hearings were held. Issues such as ongoing human rights abuses, reintegration of Honduras into the international community, and U.S. policy toward Honduras may continue to be of interest to the 112th Congress.

This report examines current political and economic conditions in Honduras as well as issues in Honduran-U.S. relations.

RECENT DEVELOPMENTS

On January 13, 2011, the Honduran National Congress approved a measure that would grant referendums, plebiscites, and citizen initiatives the power to address "issues of fundamental importance to national life," potentially including constitutional changes. The measure needs to be passed again during the new session of Congress that began on January 25, 2011, in order to take effect. (For more information, see "Constitutional Reform")

On January 13, 2011, the Honduran press reported that the country had a homicide rate of 77 per 100,000 residents in 2010, four times the Latin American average and one of the highest rates in the world.

On December 28, 2010, a radio reporter was killed in Honduras, becoming the 10th journalist to be killed in Honduras in 2010. (For more information, see "Press Freedom and the Killing of Journalists").

On November 14, 2010, the Honduran National Congress approved a legislative decree to freeze the price of basic foodstuffs for 90 days in response to sharp increases in prices stemming from local shortages.

On November 10, 2010, the Inter-American Development Bank (IDB) approved a $45.8 million loan for Honduras to promote the stability and strengthening of the Honduran financial system and expand access to financial services.

On November 9, 2010, the World Bank approved a $74.7 million loan to Honduras to address its short-term fiscal situation and initiate reforms intended to improve the country's long-term fiscal balance.

On October 14, 2010, the Honduran National Statistics Institute (INE) published the results of its latest household census, which found that 60% of Hondurans live below the poverty line.

On October 1, 2010, the International Monetary Fund (IMF) approved $202 million in financial support to Honduras to restore macroeconomic stability and advance economic reforms consistent with the country's poverty reduction and growth objectives.

On September 22, 2010, Secretary of State Clinton signed a Memorandum of Understanding with President Lobo outlining the Building Remittance Investment for Development Growth and Entrepreneurship (BRIDGE) Initiative, which will develop relationships with in-county financial institutions to maximize the development impact of remittance flows from the United States. (For more information, see "Remittances").

On September 17, 2010, Honduras completed its five-year, $205 million economic growth compact with the Millennium Challenge Corporation (MCC).

POLITICAL SITUATION

Background

A Central American nation of 8 million people, Honduras enjoyed 27 years of uninterrupted democratic, constitutional governance prior to the forced removal of President Manuel Zelaya from office in June 2009. The Liberal (PL) and National (PN) parties have been Honduras' two dominant political parties since the military relinquished political control in 1982. Both have traditionally been based around patron-client networks and there appear to be few ideological differences between them. Both parties have generally been considered to be ideologically center- right; however, the PL is heterogeneous and includes some center-left factions.[1]

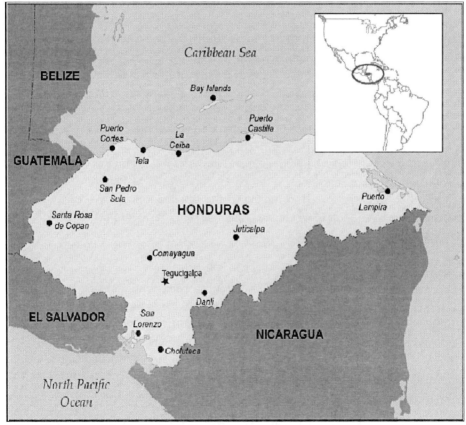

Source: Map Resources. Adapted by CRS Graphics.

Figure 1. Map of Honduras.

Manuel Zelaya of the PL was elected president in November 2005, narrowly defeating the PN's Porfirio Lobo. As a wealthy landowner who founded a somewhat left-leaning faction within the PL, Zelaya was regarded as a moderate when he was inaugurated to a four-year term in January 2006.[2] As his term progressed, however, Zelaya advanced a number of populist policies, including a 60% increase in the minimum wage in December 2008.[3] Zelaya also forged closer relations with Venezuelan President Hugo Chávez, joining initiatives such as PetroCaribe, which provides oil at preferential discounted rates, and the Bolivarian Alternative for the Americas (ALBA), a socially oriented trade block.[4] Although Zelaya's populist policies allowed him to maintain considerable support among certain sectors of Honduran society, they alienated many within the traditional economic and political elite. Likewise, his Administration's inability to achieve concrete results on a number of issues of importance—such as poverty and violent crime—significantly weakened his public standing.[5]

Political Crisis[6]

Detention and Expulsion of Zelaya

On June 28, 2009, the Honduran military detained President Zelaya and flew him to forced exile in Costa Rica. The ouster followed several months of political polarization between Honduran governmental institutions resulting from Zelaya's intention to hold a non-binding referendum and eventually amend the constitution. After the military deposed the President, the Honduran Supreme Court[7] asserted that an arrest warrant had been issued for Zelaya as a result of his noncompliance with judicial decisions that had declared the non-binding referendum unconstitutional. However, the military's actions halted the judicial process before a trial could be held.[8] The Honduran National Congress then adopted a resolution to replace Zelaya with the PL President of Congress, Roberto Micheletti.[9]

The United States and the rest of the international community universally condemned Zelaya's ouster and called for his return. They leveled a series of diplomatic and economic sanctions against the Micheletti government and pushed for a negotiated agreement to end the crisis. Although Zelaya clandestinely returned to Honduras in September 2009, he was never restored to office and was forced to remain in the Brazilian embassy—where he had taken refuge—until January 27, 2010, when newly inaugurated President Porfirio Lobo granted him safe passage to the Dominican Republic.[10]

Micheletti Government

Micheletti insisted that he took office through a "constitutional succession" throughout the seven months between Zelaya's forced removal and the inauguration of President Lobo.[11] While in power, Micheletti and the Honduran National Congress passed a 2009 budget and annulled more than a dozen decrees and reforms approved under Zelaya, including Honduras' accession to ALBA.[12] Prior to adjourning in mid-January 2010, the Honduran National Congress named Micheletti a "deputy-for-life," and offered life-long security to Micheletti and some 50 other Honduran officials involved in his government or the ouster of Zelaya.[13] Although Micheletti received substantial support from some sectors of Honduran society, an October 2009 poll found that just 36% of Hondurans approved of Micheletti's job in office and 59% believed he rarely or never did what was in the interest of the Honduran people. The same poll found that 42% of Hondurans recognized Zelaya as president, while 36% recognized Micheletti.[14]

During his government, Micheletti maintained tight control of Honduran society, severely restricting the political opposition. On the day of Zelaya's ouster, security forces patrolled the streets; a curfew was put in place and a number of local and international television and radio stations were shut down or intimidated.[15] Over the next several months, the Micheletti government periodically implemented curfews—often with little or no prior notification—and issued decrees restricting civil liberties.[16] The Inter-American Commission on Human Rights (IACHR), an autonomous body of the Organization of American States (OAS), asserts that during the Micheletti government, serious violations of human rights occurred, including "deaths, an arbitrary declaration of a state of emergency, suppression of public demonstrations through disproportionate use of force, criminalization of public protest, arbitrary detentions of thousands of persons, cruel, inhuman and degrading treatment and grossly inadequate conditions of detention, militarization of Honduran territory, a surge in incidents of racial discrimination, violations of women's rights, serious and arbitrary restrictions on the right to freedom of expression, and grave violations of political rights."[17]

November 2009 Elections

Results

On November 29, 2009, Honduras held general elections to fill nearly 3,000 posts nationwide, including the presidency and all 128 seats in the unicameral National Congress.[18] Former President of Congress and 2005 National Party (PN) presidential nominee Porfirio Lobo easily defeated his closest rival, former Vice President Elvin Santos of the Liberal Party (PL), 5 6.6% to 38.1%. Three minor party candidates won a combined 5.3% of the presidential vote. [19] Lobo's PN also won an absolute majority in the unicameral National Congress, with 71 of the 128 seats (see **Figure 2** for the change in the legislative balance of power). The election was a major defeat for the PL, which has traditionally had the broadest base of support in Honduras. On top of its poor presidential showing, it won just 45 seats in Congress, down from 62 in 2005.[20] According to some analysts, many Hondurans held the PL responsible for the country's political crisis as a result of Zelaya and Micheletti both belonging to the party. Likewise, traditional PL supporters were divided over the ouster, leading many from the Zelaya-allied faction to stay home on election day.[21]

Legitimacy

There has been considerable debate—both in Honduras and the international community— concerning the legitimacy of the November 2009 elections. Supporters of the elections note that the electoral process was initiated, and the members of the autonomous Supreme Electoral Tribunal (TSE) were chosen, prior to Zelaya's ouster. They also note that the candidates were selected in internationally observed primary elections in November 2008,[22] and that election day was largely[23] free of political violence.[24] Nonetheless, some Hondurans and international observers have argued that the Micheletti government's suppression of opposition media and demonstrators prevented a fair electoral campaign from taking place. This led to election boycotts and a number of left-leaning candidates for a variety of offices withdrawing from the elections, including an independent presidential candidate and some incumbent Members of Congress.[25] It also led organizations that traditionally observe elections in the hemisphere, such as the OAS, the EU, and the Carter Center, to cancel their electoral observation missions.[26] Critics of the elections also assert that the electoral turnout, which was just under 50% (five points lower than 2005), demonstrated a rejection of the elections by the Honduran people. Supporters of the elections counter this assertion by arguing that Lobo won more absolute votes in 2009 than Zelaya did in 2005, and that the electoral rolls are artificially inflated—distorting the turnout rate—as a result of Honduras not purging the rolls of those who have died or migrated abroad.[27] Although a growing number of Hondurans and members of the international community have recognized Lobo as the legitimate President of Honduras, some have refused to do so.[28]

Challenges for the Lobo Administration

One year after his inauguration to a four-year term, President Lobo continues to face daunting challenges stemming from Honduras' seven-month political crisis. Several efforts to foster political reconciliation, including the creation of a truth commission and the passage of a measure to enable constitutional reform, have done little to lesson domestic polarization. There has also been little improvement in the country's poor human rights situation. Murders of journalists, political activists, and human rights defenders have continued and law enforcement officials have proven unwilling or unable to bring those responsible to justice. Moreover, efforts to reintegrate Honduras into the international system have been unsuccessful in winning formal recognition from a number of Latin American nations.

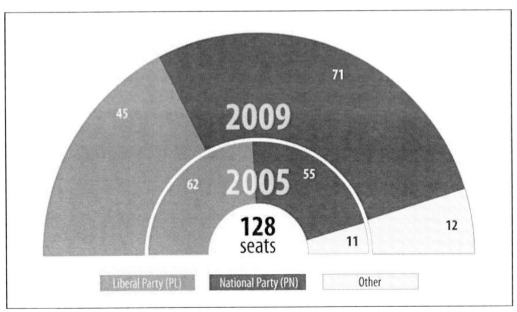

Source: CRS Graphics.

Figure 2. Party Affiliation in the Unicameral Honduran National Congress (2005 and 2009 Election Results).

Additional challenges for the Lobo Administration include fostering economic development and improving citizen security. As one of the poorest counties in the hemisphere, Honduras has long struggled to improve economic growth and reduce social disparities. The poor security situation—with high rates of violent crime, increasing flows of narcotics, and low levels of confidence in public institutions—is another long-running problem that previous governments have struggled to tackle. While the strength of Lobo's National Party in the legislature has enabled the government to secure passage of several policies designed to address these issues, there have been few improvements thus far (see "Economic and Social Conditions" and "Crime, Violence, and Drug Trafficking" below).

Political Reconciliation

President Lobo has taken a number of steps to ease the political polarization in Honduras, but still faces significant challenges. Upon taking office in late January 2010, Lobo arranged safe passage out of the country for former President Zelaya and immediately signed a bill providing political amnesty to Zelaya and those who removed him from office. The amnesty covers political and common crimes committed prior to and after the removal of President Zelaya, but does not include acts of corruption or violations of human rights.[29] President Lobo also appointed a national unity cabinet with representatives of each of the five official political parties—including the small left-wing Democratic Unification Party (UD)—and pledged to engage in dialogue with all sectors of Honduran society. Since then, Lobo has established a truth commission to investigate the events surrounding the 2009 ouster, pushed for a measure to grant greater power to citizen initiatives, and sought to clear the way for Zelaya to return to Honduras. Zelaya has insisted that he will not return to Honduras until the corruption charge against him, which he maintains is politically-motivated, is dropped.[30]

Truth Commission

In April 2010, President Lobo established a Truth and Reconciliation Commission (CVR) to investigate the events before and after the ouster of President Zelaya and to make recommendations so that these events will not be repeated.[31] The CVR officially began its work on May 4, 2010 and is expected to present a report in March 2011.[32] Led by former Guatemalan Vice President Eduardo Stein, the CVR has two additional international representatives, Canadian diplomat Michael Kergin and former Peruvian judicial official María Amadilia Zavala Valladares. The two Honduran representatives on the commission are Julieta Castellas, the rector of the National Autonomous University of Honduras (UNAH), and Jorge Omar Casco, the former rector of UNAH.

Reflecting the ongoing political polarization in Honduras, the CVR has been criticized by both the right and the left. Critics on the right fear that the commission could be used as a means to promote the constitutional reforms that former President Zelaya proposed in the lead up to the country's political crisis. In June 2010, President Lobo even suggested that some extremist elements on the right were plotting to overthrow him as a result of his reconciliation efforts.[33] Human rights groups criticized President Lobo for establishing the CVR on his own without consultation with civil society groups. Likewise, the National Popular Resistance Front[34] (FNRP, *Frente Nacional de Resistencia Popular*)—an umbrella group of those who were opposed to Zelaya's removal—views the CVR as an attempt to "whitewash" the ouster. As a result, Zelaya called on officials from his government not to cooperate with the CVR and the FNRP established an alternative truth commission composed of human rights advocates such as Nobel Peace Prize Laureates Rigoberta Menchu of Guatemala and Adolfo Pérez Esquivel of Argentina.[35]

Constitutional Reform

Much like the truth commission, Lobo's attempt to initiate political reforms has largely failed to reduce polarization. As noted above, President Zelaya was pushing for reforms to the constitution at the time of his ouster. Supporters of Zelaya's effort maintained that reforms were necessary because the country had changed significantly since the constitution was completed in 1982 by a constituent assembly elected under the military government. Those who opposed the effort accused Zelaya of wanting to perpetuate himself in power. Since Zelaya's removal, the FNRP has continued to push for a new constituent assembly to draft a new constitution and provide greater rights to traditionally excluded sectors of the Honduran population. It claims to have gathered over 1.3 million signatures in support of its initiative, which—if verified—would surpass the number of votes received by Lobo in November 2009.[36]

President Lobo, who never ruled out the idea of abstract constitutional changes as a candidate, called for a national dialogue to discuss potential political reforms in October 2010. After consulting with each of the political parties and various sectors of Honduran society, Lobo proposed a measure that would grant greater power to citizen initiatives. It would amend the constitutional provisions governing referendums and plebiscites to allow such citizen initiatives to address "issues of fundamental importance to national life," potentially including constitutional changes. Lobo's proposal was approved on January 13, 2011, but needs to be passed again during the new session of Congress that began on January 25, 2011, in order to take effect. Although some members of the FNRP that are linked to the Zelaya faction of the Liberal Party have been willing to engage in dialogue with Lobo about the proposed reforms, the more hard-line sectors of the FNRP have refused to do so and maintain that anything less than a national constituent assembly to draft a new constitution is insufficient.[37]

Human Rights

Another key challenge for the Lobo government is curtailing the increase in human rights violations that has occurred since the forced removal of President Zelaya. In March 2010, the U.S. State Department released its 2009 human rights report on Honduras. The report details numerous human rights violations that occurred in the aftermath of the ouster, including "unlawful killings by members of the police and government agents," "arbitrary and summary killings committed by vigilantes and former members of the security forces," and "arbitrary detention and disproportionate use of force by security forces."[38]

Similar human rights abuses appear to have continued since President Lobo's January 2010 inauguration. Following a May 2010 visit to Honduras, the Inter-American Commission on Human Rights (IACHR) expressed deep concern over murders of, and threats against, journalists, political activists, and human rights defenders, as well as the absence of effective investigations into these crimes. The IACHR also expressed concerns that the dismissal of judges opposed to Zelaya's ouster was politicizing the justice system, and that Lobo's appointment of several high- ranking military officers accused of participating in Zelaya's removal to positions in the government was remilitarizing society.[39] Although the Lobo Administration has taken some steps to improve the human rights situation—such as providing the Human Rights Unit in the Attorney General's Office an independent budget for the first time and creating a new Ministry of Justice and Human Rights—Honduran and international human rights organizations assert that the Honduran government has made little progress, especially with regard to bringing human rights violators to justice.[40] According to a December 2010 Human Rights Watch report, at least 18 journalists, political activists, and human rights defenders were killed in Honduras in 2010.[41]

Press Freedom and the Killing of Journalists

International human rights observers have been particularly concerned about declining press freedom in Honduras as media outlets and journalists have been the subjects of attacks. In the aftermath of Zelaya's forced removal in June 2009, human rights organizations strongly criticized the new Micheletti government for its attacks on press freedom, including government intimidation of journalists and media outlets and the temporary shutdown and interruptions of radio and television broadcasts. Press rights groups maintain that media workers were often targeted and foreign journalists were expelled. The IACHR issued a report in December 2009 asserting that there were serious violations of freedom of expression under Micheletti. The report maintained that the media became extremely polarized during the year, with those journalists and media supportive of the new Micheletti government subject to attacks by those who opposed Zelaya's ouster, and those perceived as encouraging support for resistance to the government subject to severe restrictions by state actions and attacks by private citizens.

Threats to press freedom have continued under the Lobo Administration. As noted above, the IACHR reported in May 2010 that it received information about threats and attacks directed against journalists to intimidate and impede their journalistic work.[42] In 2010, at least ten journalists were murdered in Honduras, making the country among the most dangerous in the world for the media.[43] According to a July 2010 report by the independent, nonprofit Committee to Protect Journalists, there is no evidence to "confirm a political conspiracy or coordinated effort behind the killings." Nonetheless, the report asserts that "the murders occurred in a politically charged atmosphere of violence and lawlessness" and "the government's ongoing failure to successfully investigate crimes against journalists and other social critics—whether by intention, impotence, or incompetence—has created a climate of pervasive impunity."[44]

Press rights groups have repeatedly urged President Lobo to combat the crime wave against journalists. The IACHR and the Office of the Special Rapporteur for Freedom of Expression have repeatedly called on the Honduran government to take all necessary measures to prevent thse murders, protect at-risk journalists, and make progress in investigating the crimes.[45] The Inter American Press Association recommended that the Lobo Administration request international technical assistance, establish special prosecutors' offices, and adopt a number of legal, judicial, and penal reforms.[46] Honduran officials have asserted that there is nothing to indicate that journalists are being attacked because of their work, and that the murdered journalists were most likely the victims of the widespread, random crime that has plagued Honduras in recent years.[47] Nevertheless, the Honduran government has requested assistance from the United States, Spain, and Colombia in investigating alleged human rights violations, including the killing of journalists.[48]

International Recognition

Although President Lobo has made considerable strides in his first year toward reintegrating Honduras into the international community, he has had difficulty gaining recognition from a number of countries in the region. Following the ouster of President Zelaya, many nations expressed concern about the state of democracy in Latin America and the possibility that the events of June 28, 2009 could serve as an example for other countries. Not a single nation recognized the Micheletti government, and since Zelaya was not returned to office prior to the November 2009 election, a number of countries refused to recognize the result.[49] While some countries have granted formal recognition to President Lobo since his inauguration, many South American nations—such as Argentina, Brazil, Ecuador, and Venezuela—have refused to do so.

At this juncture, Honduras is participating in the United Nations and the international financial institutions, but remains suspended from participation in the OAS.[50] Secretary of State Clinton has called on Latin American nations to welcome Honduras back into the inter-American community, but countries such as Brazil want to see more changes in Honduras before extending recognition. Brazilian officials and OAS Secretary General José Miguel Insulza have suggested that allowing former President Zelaya to return home would pave the way for the OAS member- states to readmit Honduras.[51] According to the Inter-American Democratic Charter, the votes of two-thirds of the OAS member-states are required to lift a suspension.

ECONOMIC AND SOCIAL CONDITIONS

Background

The Honduran economy has experienced significant changes since the 1990s. Traditional agricultural exports of coffee and bananas are still important, but nontraditional sectors, such as shrimp farming and the *maquiladora*, or export-processing industry, have grown significantly. In 1998, Honduras was devastated by Hurricane Mitch, which killed more than 5,000 people and caused billions of dollars in damage. The gross domestic product declined by 1.4% in 1999, and the country felt the effects of the storm for several years, with roads and bridges washed out, the agricultural sector hard hit, and scores of orphaned children, many of whom joined criminal gangs. Spurred on by substantial U.S. foreign assistance, however, the economy rebounded. Between 2000 and 2008, the country experienced average growth of over 5%.[52] Honduras is now classified by the World Bank as a lower middle income developing economy, with a per capita income of $1,800 (2009).[53]

Over the past decade, Honduras has benefited from several debt-reduction programs. In 2005, Honduras signed a three-year poverty reduction and growth facility agreement with the International Monetary Fund (IMF), making the country eligible for about $1 billion in debt relief under the IMF and World Bank's Heavily Indebted Poor Countries (HIPC) Initiative.[54] The agreement imposed fiscal and monetary targets on the government, and required Honduras to maintain firm macroeconomic discipline and develop a comprehensive poverty reduction strategy. In 2006, the Inter-American Development Bank (IDB) implemented a debt forgiveness program for its poorest members. Honduras benefitted from a reduction of $1.4

billion in foreign debt, freeing government resources to finance poverty alleviation.[55] Largely as a result of these programs, Honduras' net public debt declined from nearly 46% of gross domestic product (GDP) in 2005 to about 19.1% in 2007.[56] Honduran debt has been climbing again in recent years, however, as increased domestic spending and decreased government revenue have contributed to growing fiscal deficits.

Despite experiencing relatively strong growth and benefitting from debt reduction programs, Honduras continues to face significant development challenges. The country remains one of the most impoverished nations in Latin America. According to the most recent household census conducted by the Honduran National Statistics Institute, 60% of Honduras' 8 million citizens live under the poverty line—defined as being unable to acquire the basic basket of household goods.[57] Likewise, Honduras has an infant mortality rate of 27 per 1,000; chronic malnutrition for one out of four children under five years of age; and a significant HIV/AIDS crisis, with an adult infection rate of 1.5% of the population. The Garifuna community (descendants of freed black slaves and indigenous Caribs from St. Vincent) concentrated in northern coastal areas has been especially hard hit by the HIV/AIDS epidemic. The World Bank maintains that development indicators have improved over the past decade because of increased public spending on health and education, but further progress is uncertain. It notes that the country remains vulnerable to external shocks, including declines in prices for agricultural exports and natural disasters such as hurricanes and droughts.[58]

Crises and Recovery

The global financial crisis and domestic political crisis took a significant toll on the Honduran economy. Honduras was already experiencing significant declines in remittances, tourism, and export earnings as a result of the financial crisis at the time of President Zelaya's forced removal from office.[59] The ouster exacerbated these economic problems, as the international community, which had been expected to finance 20% of the country's budget, imposed a series of economic sanctions on Honduras.[60] International financial institutions withheld access to some $485 million in loans and other transfers, the European Union and United States terminated $126 million in aid, and Venezuela—which provided 50% of Honduras' petroleum imports in 2008—stopped supplying the country with subsidized oil.[61] Domestic opponents of the ouster placed additional pressure on the economy, engaging in strikes, transportation blockades, and other measures designed to paralyze economic activity.[62] Some economists estimated that the political crisis cost Honduras 180,000 jobs and $20 million daily in lost trade, aid, tourism, and investment.[63] Overall, the Honduran economy contracted by 2.1% in 2009.[64]

Since his inauguration, President Lobo has pushed for reforms designed to restore macroeconomic stability, strengthen public finances, and encourage sustained economic growth. The Honduran National Congress has approved several of Lobo's proposals, including an energy reform intended to better target subsidies to the poor, and a comprehensive tax reform expected to generate additional revenue equivalent to 2.5% of GDP. The National Congress also approved a measure de-indexing teachers' wages from changes in the minimum wage in an effort to slow the growth of expenditure on public sector salaries, which absorb 73% of all government revenue. [65] These efforts have been criticized by business groups opposed to tax increases and public sector workers pushing for wage increases. However, they have been supported by the international financial institutions, providing the Lobo Administration with access to much needed development financing. In October and November 2010, the International Monetary Fund (IMF), the Inter-American Development Bank (IDB), and the World Bank approved a combined $322.5 million in financial support for Honduras to support the Lobo Administration's efforts to improve the country's long-term fiscal balance and implement the reforms necessary to achieve the country's poverty reduction and growth objectives.[66] The Honduran economy grew by 2.8% in 2010 and is expected to grow by 3.7% in 2011.[67]

ISSUES IN U.S.-HONDURAN RELATIONS

The United States has had close relations with Honduras over many years. The bilateral relationship became especially close in the 1980s when Honduras returned to democratic rule and became the lynchpin for U.S. policy in Central America. At that time, the country became a staging area for U.S.-supported excursions into Nicaragua by anti-Sandinista forces known as the Contras. Economic linkages intensified in the 1 980s after Honduras became a beneficiary of the Caribbean Basin Initiative providing duty-free importation of Honduran goods into the United States, and more recently with the entrance into force of the Dominican Republic-Central America-United States Free Trade Agreement (CAFTA-DR) in 2006.

Relations between the United States and Honduras were strained in 2009 because of the country's political crisis. Following Zelaya's ouster, the United States cut off almost all contact with the Honduran government. It suspended some foreign assistance, minimized cooperation with the Honduran military, and revoked the visas of members and supporters of the Micheletti government, which assumed power following Zelaya's removal.[68] Micheletti reacted angrily to U.S. policy toward his government, declaring, "it isn't possible for anyone, no matter how powerful they are, to come over here and tell us what we have to do."[69]

Relations have improved considerably since the inauguration of President Lobo, whose efforts to foster national reconciliation and solidify democratic processes in Honduras led the United States to restore foreign assistance and resume cooperation on other issues. According to the March 2010 congressional testimony of then Principal Deputy Assistant Secretary of State, Craig Kelly, U.S. policy towards Honduras is now focused on helping Honduras deal with its numerous daunting challenges, including: (1) improving the human-rights climate, especially regarding allegations of serious human rights abuses and reports that persons have been targeted for their political views; (2) combating high levels of corruption, crime, and drug-trafficking; (3) promoting and implementing social and economic reforms to reduce poverty and inequality levels that are among the highest in the hemisphere; and (4) helping Honduras contend with a severe economic crisis that could further destabilize the country.[70] In pursuit of its policy goals, the United States provides Honduras with substantial amounts of foreign assistance, maintains significant military and economic ties, and engages on transnational issues such as illegal migration, crime, narcotics trafficking, trafficking in persons, and port security.

U.S. Foreign Assistance

The United States has provided considerable foreign assistance to Honduras over the past three decades. In the 1980s, the United States provided about $1.6 billion in economic and military aid as the country struggled amid the region's civil conflicts. In the 1990s, U.S. assistance to Honduras began to wane as regional conflicts subsided and competing foreign assistance needs grew in other parts of the world. Hurricane Mitch changed that trend as the United States provided almost $300 million in assistance to help the country recover from the 1998 storm. As a result of the influx of aid, total U.S. assistance to Honduras for the 1 990s amounted to around $1 billion. With Hurricane Mitch funds expended by the end of 2001, U.S. foreign aid levels to Honduras again began to decline.

Recent foreign aid funding to Honduras amounted to $40.5 million in FY2008, $40.2 million in FY2009, and $50.2 million in FY20 10.[71] The continuing resolution (P.L. 111-242, as amended) scheduled to expire on March 4, 2011, continues funding most foreign aid programs at the FY20 10 enacted level. For FY20 12, the Obama Administration has requested nearly $68 million in foreign aid for Honduras, including $55 million in Development Assistance (DA), $11 million in Global Health and Child Survival assistance (GHCS), and $1 million in Foreign Military Financing (FMF). (See **Table 1** below). U.S. assistance supports a variety of projects designed to enhance security, strengthen democracy, improve education and health systems, conserve the environment, and build trade capacity. Most assistance to the country is managed by the U.S. Agency for International Development (USAID) and the State Department.

Honduras receives some foreign assistance beyond the bilateral funds appropriated annually through the foreign operations budget. The Peace Corps, which has been active in the country since 1963, provides nearly 180 volunteers to work on projects related to HIV/AIDS prevention and child survival, protected area management, water and sanitation, and business, municipal and youth development. The Millennium Challenge Corporation (MCC) provided Honduras with $205 million[72] for a five-year economic growth compact that was completed in September 2010. The compact had two components: a rural development project to provide farmers with skills to grow and market new crops, and a transportation project to improve roads and highways to link farmers and other businesses to ports and major production centers in Honduras.[73] USAID's Office of Foreign Disaster Assistance (OFDA) provides assistance in response to natural disasters. USAID/OFDA provided Honduras with $150,000 to respond to flooding and other damage during the 2010 hurricane season.[74] Honduras also receives assistance under the Central America Regional Security Initiative (CARSI, formerly known as Mérida-Central America), a package of counternarcotics and anticrime assistance for the region.[75] From FY2008-FY2010, Congress appropriated $248 for Central America, a portion of which was intended for Honduras. For FY20 12, the Obama Administration has requested $100 million for CARSI.

Military Cooperation

The United States maintains a troop presence of about 600 military personnel known as Joint Task Force (JTF) Bravo at Soto Cano Air Base. JTF Bravo was first established in 1983 with about 1,200 troops who were involved in military training exercises and in supporting

U.S. counterinsurgency and intelligence operations in the region. In the aftermath of Hurricane Mitch in 1998, U.S. troops provided extensive assistance in the relief and reconstruction effort. Today, U.S. troops in Honduras support such activities as disaster relief, medical and humanitarian assistance, counternarcotics operations, and search and rescue operations that benefit Honduras and other Central American countries. Regional exercises and deployments involving active duty and reserve components also provide training opportunities for thousands of U.S. troops.

The June 28, 2009 ouster of President Manuel Zelaya led some to reassess the state of U.S.- Honduran military cooperation. As a result of the Honduran military's role in Zelaya's removal, the United States suspended joint military activities as well as some military assistance to the country.[76] The events in Honduras also led some analysts to question the effectiveness of U.S. foreign military training programs.[77] They argued that such programs have not obtained their desired outcomes given that General Romeo Vasquez Velasquez— who had received U.S. training—led the effort to remove President Zelaya, and the Honduran military reportedly cut off contact with the United States prior to the ouster.[78] Nevertheless, U.S.-Honduran military cooperation resumed following the election of President Lobo, with the United States restoring aid and resuming its training of Honduran officers.[79]

Table 1. U.S. Bilateral Assistance to Honduras, FY2007-FY2011 (U.S. $ in Thousands)

Account	FY2008	FY2009	FY2010	FY2011 (req.)[a]	FY2012 (req.)[b]
Global Health and Child Survival (GHCS) (USAID)	12,035	11,750	11,000	11,000	10,000
Global Health and Child Survival (GHCS) (State)	1,000	1,000	1,000	1,000	1,000
Development Assistance (DA)	15,149	21,382	37,491	53,934	55,266
Economic Support Funds (ESF)	—	—	—	—	—
Foreign Military Financing (FMF)	496	—	—	1,300	1,000
International Military Education and Training (IMET)	936	329	700	700	700
International Narcotics & Law Enforcement (INCLE)	744	—	—	—	—
Nonproliferation, Antiterrorism & Demining (NADR)	—	—	—	—	NA
Food Aid	10,150	5,771	—	—	NA
Total	40,510	40,232	50,191	67,934	67,966

Sources: U.S. Department of State, *Executive Budget Summary: Function 150 & Other International Programs, Fiscal Year 2012*, February 14, 2011; U.S. Department of State, Office of the Director of Foreign Assistance.

Notes: Global Health and Child Survival (USAID) was formerly called "Child Survival and Health," but was relabeled with the FY20 10 budget request. Likewise, Global Health and Child Survival (State) was formerly called "Global HIV/AIDS Initiative," but was re-labeled with the FY20 10 budget request.

a. Since Congress has yet to pass FY2011 appropriations legislation, government programs are currently funded by a series of continuing resolutions (P.L. 111-242 as amended), with the latest extension set to expire on March 4, 2011. The continuing resolution, as amended, continues funding most foreign aid programs at the FY20 10 enacted level.

b. Country-level figures for the NADR and P.L. 480 accounts are not yet available for the FY2012 request.

Economic Linkages

U.S. trade and investment linkages with Honduras have increased greatly since the early 1980s. In 1984, Honduras became one of the first beneficiaries of the Caribbean Basin Initiative (CBI), the unilateral U.S. preferential trade arrangement providing duty-free importation for many goods from the region. In the late 1980s, Honduras benefitted from production-sharing arrangements with U.S. apparel companies for duty-free entry into the United States of certain apparel products assembled in Honduras. As a result, *maquiladoras* or export-assembly companies flourished, most concentrated in the north coast region. The passage of the Caribbean Basin Trade Partnership Act in 2000 (CBTPA), which provided Caribbean Basin nations with NAFTA-like preferential tariff treatment, further boosted Honduran *maquiladoras*. Trade relations expanded again following the implementation of the Dominican Republic-Central America-United States Free Trade Agreement (CAFTA-DR), which entered into force with Honduras in April 2006.[80]

Total trade between the United States and Honduras has increased 15% since the implementation of CAFTA-DR, with U.S. exports to Honduras growing by 25% and U.S. imports from Honduras growing by 6%. Total U.S.-Honduran trade in 2010 totaled $8.5 billion. U.S. exports to Honduras amounted to about $4.6 billion, an increase of nearly 37% after a steep decline in 2009. Knit and woven apparel inputs accounted for a substantial portion, as did machinery and petroleum. U.S. imports from Honduras amounted to about $3.9 billion, with knit and woven apparel (assembled products from the *maquiladora* sector) accounting for the greatest share. Other major imports from Honduras include electrical wiring, bananas, seafood, coffee, and gold. In 2010, the United States remained Honduras' top trading partner and Honduras moved up one spot to become the United States 49th largest trading partner.[81]

U.S. foreign direct investment in Honduras amounted to $844 million in 2009, up from $787 million in 2006.[82] More than 150 U.S. companies operate in Honduras. The most significant U.S. investments are in the *maquila* or export assembly sector, fruit production, tourism, energy generation, shrimp farming, animal feed production, telecommunications, fuel distribution, cigar manufacturing, insurance, brewing, food processing, and furniture manufacturing.[83] U.S. businesses operating in Honduras were negatively affected by the country's political crisis in 2009, with the tourism and manufacturing sectors especially hard hit as international travelers stayed away and government-imposed curfews prevented workers from getting to their places of employment.[84]

Despite the increases in trade and investment that have occurred since the implementation of CAFTA-DR, some Honduran and U.S. officials have expressed concerns about the agreement. Honduran officials are concerned about the loss of agricultural jobs in the corn, rice, beef, poultry, and pork sectors since the country opened its market to U.S. agricultural products. Some fear that the loss of agricultural employment could lead to social unrest if not addressed properly through long-term investment.[85] Although CAFTA-DR has provisions to enforce domestic labor codes and improve labor rights, a number of U.S. officials maintain that the provisions are inadequate given the history of non-compliance with labor laws in many Central American nations. The U.S. State Department's most recent Country Reports on Human Rights Practices for Honduras found credible evidence that employees engaged in union organizing were blacklisted within the *maquiladoras* and that union leaders were occasionally targeted with threats and violence.[86]

Migration Issues

Temporary Protected Status

In the aftermath of Hurricane Mitch in 1998, the United States provided temporary protected status (TPS) to eligible Hondurans who may otherwise have been deported from the United States. Originally slated to expire in July 2000, TPS status has now been extended nine times. The most recent TPS extension came on May 5, 2010, when the Secretary of Homeland Security announced that the United States would continue to provide TPS for an additional 18 months, expiring on January 5, 2012 (prior to this extension, TPS would have expired July 5, 2010). According to a *Federal Register* notice on the most recent extension, the Secretary of Homeland Security maintained that the extension was warranted because there continues to be a substantial, but temporary, disruption of living conditions in Honduras resulting from Hurricane Mitch, and the country remains temporarily unable to adequately handle the return of its nationals.[87] Homeland Security estimates that TPS covers an estimated 66,000 Hondurans residing in the United States.[88]

Remittances

Remittances from migrant workers abroad—87% of whom live in the United States—are the largest single source of foreign exchange for Honduras. Between 2002 and 2008, remittances to Honduras more than tripled to $2.7 billion, the equivalent of 20% of GDP. Although remittances declined by over 8% in 2009, they appear to have partially recovered in 2010. The recent decline in remittances is at least partially due to the global financial crisis and U.S. recession, which have left many Honduran immigrants in the United States unemployed. Most remittances from Hondurans abroad are sent to immediate family members, such as parents and children, to supplement their wages.[89]

In September 2010, Secretary of State Clinton signed a Memorandum of Understanding with President Lobo regarding the Building Remittance Investment for Development Growth and Entrepreneurship (BRIDGE) Initiative. Under the Initiative, the United States will work with Honduras to develop and support partnerships with Honduran financial institutions in hopes of maximizing the development impact of remittance flows. The identified financial institutions will be able to leverage the remittances they receive to obtain lower-cost, longer-term financing in international capital markets to fund investments in infrastructure, public works, and commercial development.[90]

Deportations[91]

Deportations to Honduras have increased significantly over the past decade. Approximately 25,600 Hondurans were deported from the United States in FY20 10, making Honduras one of the top recipients of deportees on a per capita basis.[92] Increasing deportations from the United States have been accompanied by similar increases in deportations from Mexico, a transit country for Central American migrants bound for the United States. Honduran policymakers are concerned about their country's ability to absorb the large volume of deportees, as it is often difficult for those returning to the country to find gainful employment. Individuals who do not speak Spanish, who are tattooed, who have criminal records, and/or who lack familial support face additional difficulties re-integrating into Honduran society. In addition to these social problems, leaders are concerned that remittances may start to fall if the current high rates of deportations continue.[93] In 2007, the Honduran Congress approved a motion calling for the United States to halt deportations of undocumented Honduran migrants who live and work in the United States.[94]

Some analysts contend that increasing U.S. deportations of individuals with criminal records has exacerbated the gang problem in Honduras and other Central American countries. By the mid- 1990s, the civil conflicts in Central America had ended and the United States began deporting unauthorized immigrants, many with criminal convictions, back to the region. Between 2000 and 2004, an estimated 20,000 criminals were sent back to Central America, many of whom had spent time in prisons in the United States for drug and/or gang-related offenses. Some observers contend that gang-deportees have "exported" a Los Angeles gang culture to Central America, and that they have recruited new members from among the local populations.[95] Although a recent United Nations study found little conclusive evidence to support their claims, the media and many Central American officials have attributed a large proportion of the rise in violent crime in the region to gangs, particularly gang-deportees from the United States.[96] U.S. Immigration and Customs Enforcement (ICE) does not provide receiving countries with the complete criminal records or gang affiliations of deportees, however, it may provide them with some information regarding deportees' criminal histories and gang affiliations when specifying why the deportees were removed from the United States. Likewise, receiving countries may contact the Federal Bureau of Investigation (FBI) to request criminal history checks on particular criminal deportees once they have arrived. Over 40% of the Hondurans deported from the United States in FY20 10 were removed on criminal grounds.[97]

Crime, Violence, and Drug Trafficking[98]

Honduras, along with neighboring El Salvador and Guatemala, has become fertile ground for gangs and drug trafficking organizations. Fueled by poverty, unemployment, leftover weapons from the conflicts of the 1 980s, and the U.S. deportation of criminals to the region, gangs such as Mara Salvatrucha (MS- 13) and the 18th Street Gang (M- 18) have firmly established themselves in the region. Although estimates of the number of gang members in Central America vary widely, the U.S. Southern Command maintains that there are some 70,000, concentrated largely in Honduras, El Salvador, and Guatemala.[99] At the same time, Mexican Drug Trafficking Organizations (DTOs) have taken control of Central American trafficking corridors to transport cocaine and other narcotics from the Andean region of South America to the United States. The State Department, in its 2010 International Narcotics Strategy Control Report (INCSR), estimated that 200 metric tons of cocaine transited Honduras in 2009, largely through remote and poorly controlled areas, such as the country's north coast.

This confluence of gangs and DTOs has led to increasing rates of crime and violence. According to Vanderbilt University's 2010 Americas Barometer, 14% of Honduran citizens reported that they had been the victim of a crime within the past year.[100] The surge in violent crime has been particularly worrisome. In December 2009, Honduras' top counternarcotics official was ambushed and killed in the capital by gunmen on motorcycles. In September 2010, 18 men working in a shoe factory in San Pedro Sula were apparently massacred by members of a Mexican DTO. And in January 2011, eight people were killed and three were injured when gunmen opened fire on a public bus.[101] Honduras' murder rate was already among the highest in the world in 2008 at 57.9 per 100,000 inhabitants. Nevertheless, it increased to 66.8 per 100,000 in 2009 and reportedly reached 77 per 100,000 in 2010.[102] Many have assumed that gangs are responsible for the increasing number of homicides; however, some recent studies have shown that the highest murder rates are not in large cities—where gangs are primarily located—but in more remote areas along strategic drug trafficking corridors. Although there have been some indications that DTOs are using gangs as hired assassins in Honduras, connections between the DTOs and gangs remain largely anecdotal and unsubstantiated.[103]

Recent Honduran presidents have implemented varying anti-crime strategies; however, none of them have achieved much success. During his term, President Ricardo Maduro (2002-2006) increased the number of police officers and signed legislation that made *maras* (street gangs) illegal and gang membership punishable with 12 years in prison. Although the crackdown won popular support and initially reduced crime, its success was short-lived. Following his election, President Zelaya (2006-2009) replaced the previous administration's zero-tolerance policy with dialogue and other outreach techniques designed to persuade gang members to reintegrate into society.[104] Failure to achieve concrete results, however, led the Zelaya Administration to shift its emphasis toward more traditional anti-gang law enforcement operations. Zelaya increased the number of police and military troops in the streets and conducted raids against suspected criminals. Nonetheless, as reflected in the statistics cited above, crime and violence in Honduras continued unabated.[105]

President Lobo has pledged to crack down on crime and violence, and although he has backed away from his 2005 proposal to reinstate the death penalty in Honduras, he still favors a hard-line approach.[106] Since taking office, Lobo has initiated a new security strategy that has deployed additional police into the poorest neighborhoods of Tegucigalpa and other large cities. In early June 2010, the Honduran National Congress approved a measure authorizing the use of military soldiers to support the police in fighting crime. Military patrols have been deployed in large cities to reinforce police as well as to the remote Atlantic coast region to combat drug trafficking.[107] In November 2010, the Honduran National Congress approved a new anti-terrorism law that reportedly includes measure to strengthen control over land, sea, and air borders, and will allow authorities to better control cash flows into the country.[108]

Although cooperation was temporarily disrupted by the 2009 political crisis, communication and coordination between U.S. law enforcement and intelligence entities and Honduras military and police elements have improved in recent years according to the 2010 INCSR. Through the Central America Regional Security Initiative (CARSI)[109] and other efforts, the United States has supported a variety of anticorruption, anti-gang, police training, and maritime operations programs intended to improve Honduras' counternarcotics capabilities. The United States has also supported efforts to strengthen Honduran judicial institutions, provide positive opportunities for youth at risk of joining gangs, and develop a national crime prevention policy.[110] Moreover, the United States funded construction of a Honduran naval base in Barra de Caratasca in the isolated Mosquitia region of northeastern Honduras to assist in interdiction operations. Overall in 2009, Honduras seized 6.6 metric tons of cocaine, 2,795 stones of crack cocaine, 923 kilograms of marijuana, and nearly 2.8 million pseudoephedrine pills. Despite these efforts, U.S. officials maintain that Honduran citizen security and counternarcotics efforts continue to face a number of challenges, including limited resources, a weak enforcement presence in sparsely populated areas, corruption within the government and law enforcement, and weak criminal investigations and prosecutions.[111]

Human Trafficking

According to the State Department's 2010 Trafficking in Persons (TIP) Report, Honduras is primarily a source and transit country for women and children trafficked for the purpose of commercial sexual exploitation. Many victims are trafficked from rural areas to tourist and urban locales such as Tegucigalpa, San Pedro Sula, and the Bay Islands. Destination countries for trafficked Honduran women and children include the United States, Mexico, Guatemala, El Salvador, and Belize. There are also foreign victims of commercial sexual exploitation in Honduras, most having been trafficked from neighboring countries, including economic migrants en route to the United States.

The State Department maintains that Honduras does not fully comply with the minimum standards for the elimination of trafficking, however, it notes that the government is making significant efforts to do so. As a result, Honduras is considered a so-called "Tier 2" country. The 2010 report recognized the Honduran government's law enforcement actions against sex trafficking offenders and its partnership with international organizations to provide training to government officials and members of civil society. However, the report also maintained that government services for trafficking victims remained virtually non-existent, that laws failed to prohibit trafficking for forced labor, and that the number of trafficking-related convictions had decreased. In the report, the State Department recommended that Honduras amend its anti- trafficking laws to prohibit forced labor; increase efforts to investigate and prosecute all trafficking offenses; convict and sentence traffickers; improve victims' access to shelter, aid, and essential services; develop formal procedures for identifying victims; and initiate efforts to raise awareness of human trafficking.[112]

Port Security

Honduras and the United States have cooperated extensively on port security. For the United States, port security emerged as an important element of homeland security in the aftermath of the September 11, 2001, terrorist attacks. Honduras views such cooperation as important in order to ensure the speedy export of its products to the United States, which in turn could increase U.S. investment in the country. In March 2006, U.S. officials announced the inclusion of the largest port in Honduras, Puerto Cortés, in the U.S. Container Security Initiative (CSI). CSI is operated by the U.S. Customs and Border Protection (CBP) of the Department of Homeland Security, and uses a security regime to ensure that all containers that pose a potential risk for terrorism are identified and inspected at foreign ports before they are placed on vessels destined for the United States. Honduras also participates in the Department of Energy's Megaports Initiative, which supplies ports with equipment capable of detecting nuclear or radioactive materials, and the Secure Freight Initiative (SFI), which deploys equipment capable of scanning containers for radiation and information risk factors before they are allowed to depart for the United States. Puerto Cortés was one of six ports around the world chosen to be part of the first phase of the SFI.[113]

ACKNOWLEDGMENTS

Mark P. Sullivan, Specialist in Latin American Affairs, contributed to this report.

End Notes

[1] *Honduras: A Country Study*, ed. Tim L. Merrill, 3rd ed. (Washington, DC: Library of Congress, Federal Research Division, 1995).

[2] "People Profile: Manuel 'Mel' Zelaya," *Latin News Daily*, November 15, 2005; "Manuel Zelaya to head Honduras and redefine his Party," *Latin America Data Base NotiCen*, December 15, 2005.

[3] The minimum wage decree—which did not affect the maquila sector's monthly minimum wage that fluctuates between 6,000 and 7,000 Lempiras ($318-$370)—increased the rural monthly minimum wage to 4,055 Lempiras ($215) and the urban monthly minimum wage to 5,500 Lempiras ($291). Calculations are based on an exchange rate of $1 U.S. dollar to 18.9 Honduran lempiras. "Elevan a L.5,500 el salario mínimo en Honduras," *El Heraldo* (Honduras), December 24, 2008.

[4] It should be noted that the National Congress ratified Honduras' entrance into both PetroCaribe and ALBA. "Honduras: Congress signs up to Petrocaribe" *Latin American Caribbean & Central America Report*, March 2008; "Honduras: Congress approves Alba, with caveats," *Latin American Caribbean & Central America Report*, October 2008.

[5] Mica Rosenberg, "Protests erupt, gunshots heard after Honduras coup," *Reuters*, June 28, 2009.

[6] For a more detailed examination of the Honduran political crisis, see CRS Report R41064, *Honduran Political Crisis, June 2009-January 2010*.

[7] The U.S. Department of State's 2009 Country Reports on Human Rights Practices states that "although the constitution and the law provide for an independent judiciary," the Honduran judicial system has been "subject to patronage, corruption, and political influence."

[8] Poder Judicial de Honduras, "Expediente Judicial Relación Documentada Caso Zelaya Rosales," available at http://www.poderjudicial.gob.hn/.

[9] "El decreto de la separación de Zelaya," *El Heraldo* (Honduras), June 28, 2009.

[10] "Zelaya deja Honduras tras 4 meses en la Embajada de Brasil," *EFE News Service*, January 27, 2010.

[11] Roberto Micheletti, "Moving Forward in Honduras," *Washington Post*, September 22, 2009.

[12] "Honduras: Micheletti prepares to leave on high note," *Latin News Weekly Report*, January 21, 2010.

[13] "Congreso de Honduras designa a Micheletti 'diputado vitalicio,'" *Agence France Presse*, January 13, 2010; "Más de 50 funcionarios gozarán de seguridad vitalicia," *El Tiempo* (Honduras), January 15, 2010.

[14] "Hondureños ven solución en presidente alternativo y elecciones, según sondeo," *EFE News Service*, October 27, 2009; "Honduras: 42% reconoce a Zelaya como presidente, 36% a Micheletti (encuesta)," *Agence France Presse*, October 28, 2009.

[15] "Honduras: Decretan toque de queda por 48 horas," *La Prensa* (Honduras), June 28, 2009; "Honduras: Media Blackout, Protests Reported," *Stratfor*, June 29, 2009.

[16] "Honduras suspende derechos constitucionales durante toque queda," *Reuters*, July 1, 2009; Amnesty International, "Honduras: human rights crisis threatens as repression increases," August 2009.

[17] Inter-American Commission on Human Rights, *Honduras: Human Rights and the Coup D'état*, Organization of American States, OEA/Ser.L/V/II. Doc. 55, December 30, 2009.

[18] "Elecciones, incierto antídoto contra la crisis socio política," *El Tiempo* (Honduras), August 31, 2009.

[19] "TSE confirma el triunfo de 'Pepe' en las elecciones," *El Heraldo* (Honduras), December 21, 2009.

[20] "Final results in Honduras," *Latin News Daily*, December 22, 2009.

[21] Noé Leiva, "El Partido Liberal de Zelaya, el gran perdedor de los comicios hondureños," *Agence France Presse*, November 30, 2009; "Partido Liberal sacrificó el poder para salvar democracia," *La Tribuna* (Honduras), December 3, 2009.

[22] Former Vice President Elvin Santos, although originally ruled constitutionally ineligible to run by the TSE, became the PL presidential nominee following a series of events that included congressional passage of a special decree and a 52%-32% primary victory by his stand-in-candidate, Mauricio Villeda, over then President of Congress, Roberto Micheletti. "Honduras' Vice President Regains the Right to Run; Elvin Santos is Partido Liberal Presidential Candidate," *Latin America Data Base NotiCen*, March 5, 2009.

[23] A demonstration in San Pedro Sula by those opposed to the government of Roberto Micheletti was forcefully dispersed on election day. "Police fire tear gas on Honduras poll protesters," *Agence France Presse*, November 29, 2009.

[24] José Saúl Escobar Andrade, Enrique Ortez Sequeira, and David Andrés Matamoros Batso, "Honduran Elections," Remarks at the Inter-American Dialogue, Washington, DC, October 22, 2009; International Republican

Institute, "Hondurans Turn Out to Polls in Credible Elections: IRI's Preliminary Statement on Honduras' 2009 National Elections," November 30, 2009.

[25] "Seguidores de Zelaya no particparán en elecciones aunque haya restitución," *EFE News Service*, November 8, 2009; "Renuncian importantes dirigentes del liberalismo," *El Tiempo* (Honduras), November 22, 2009; "Zelayistas dicen que hay incongruencias en la UD," *El Tiempo* (Honduras), November 23, 2009.

[26] Gustavo Palencia, "Honduras busca convencer observadores para cuestionada elección," *Reuters*, November 12, 2009; "La CE dice que no hay tiempo para una misión electoral y envía dos expertos," *EFE News Service*, November 11, 2009.

[27] "Honduras: Tug of War Between Opposition and De Facto Regime Regarding Flow of Voters," *Latin America Data Base NotiCen*, December 3, 2009; "Final results in Honduras," *Latin News Daily*, December 22, 2009.

[28] Frente Nacional de Resistencia Contra el Golpe de Estado, "Comunicado No. 41," November 30, 2009; "El Mercosur anuncia 'pleno desconocimiento' de nuevo gobierno de Honduras," *EFE News Service*, December 8, 2009.

[29] "Lobo secures exit from Honduras for Zelaya," *Latin News Daily*, January 21, 2010; "Congreso aprueba amnistía para delitos políticos comunes conexos," *El Tiempo* (Honduras), January 27, 2010.

[30] "Zelaya promises to return with a bang," *Latin News Weekly Report*, January 6, 2011.

[31] Honduras, Presidencia de la República, Decreto Ejecutivo Número PCM-01 1-20 10.

[32] Thelma Mejía, "Honduras: Lobo reprueba primer año," *Inter Press Service*, January 28, 2011.

[33] Germán Reyes, "Lobo pide no temer a Comisión de Verdad y avala consulta para constituyente," *Agencia EFE*, May 4, 2010; "Presidente hondureño insinúa que se está gestando otro golpe de Estado," *Agence France Presse*, June 8, 2010.

[34] The FNRP initially was formed after Zelaya's ouster as the National Resistance Front Against the Coup d'état. Nominally coordinated by Zelaya from exile, the FNRP is led by an executive committee representative of the movement's composite parts, which include labor unions, worker and campesino organizations, human rights advocates, the Zelaya-allied faction of the Liberal Party, and other civil society groups.

[35] "Zelaya Calls on Former Officials Not to Collaborate with Truth Commission," *ACAN-EFE*, June 8, 2010; "Honduran resistance sets up alternative commission," *Latin News Weekly Report*, July 1, 2010.

[36] "Hondureños reclaman en las calles una Constituyente en del Día del Trabajdor," *Agence France Presse*, May 1, 2010; Frente Nacional De Resistencia Popular, "Comunicado No.74: Avanzamos seguros hacia la Constituyente," September 17, 2010.

[37] "Honduras: Lobo succeeds where Zelaya failed," *Latin American Weekly Report*, January 20, 2011; "Oposición rechaza cambios en Honduras," *La Nación* (Costa Rica), January 24, 2011; "Honduras: Constitutional change tests opposition unity," *Oxford Analytica*, February 14, 2011.

[38] See the full text of the report at http://www.state

[39] IACHR "IACHR Publishes Observations on Follow-up Visit to Honduras," Press Release No. 59/10, June 7, 2010.

[40] Thelma Mejía, "Latin America: Honduras has much to Explain in Human Rights Exam," *Inter Press Service*, November 3, 2010.

[41] Human Rights Watch, *After the Coup: Ongoing Violence, Intimidation, and Impunity in Honduras*, New York, December 2010.

[42] IACHR, "Honduras: Human Rights and the Coup d'État," December 30, 2009, and "IACHR Concerned About Human Rights Violations in Honduras," Press Release, No. 54/10, May 19, 2010.

[43] "Honduras: HRN Radio Reporter Killed," *EFE News Service*, December 28, 2010.

[44] Committee to Protect Journalists, "Journalist murders spotlight Honduran government failures," July 27, 2010.

[45] Inter-American Commission on Human Rights, "Office of the Special Rapporteur Expresses Concern Over New Attacks Against Journalists and Media in Honduras," September 20, 2010.

[46] Inter American Press Association, "IAPA makes recommendations to President Porfirio Lobo to Combat Violence Against Journalists," Press Release, April 27, 2010.

[47] Committee to Protect Journalists, "Journalist murders spotlight Honduran government failures," July 27, 2010.

[48] "Honduras pide ayuda a Colombia, España, y EEUU en investigación sobre DDHH," *Agence France Presse*, January 27, 2011.

[49] "El Mercosur anuncia 'pleno desconocimiento' de nuevo gobierno de Honduras," *EFE News Service*, December 8, 2009.

[50] The OAS member states unanimously voted to suspend Honduras for an unconstitutional interruption of the democratic order in accordance with Article 21 of the Inter-American Democratic Charter on July 4, 2009. According to Article 22 of the Charter, lifting the suspension requires the votes of two thirds of the member states.

[51] "OAS presents report on Honduras," *Latin News Daily*, July 30, 2010; "Chile and Mexico make-up with Honduras," *Latin News Daily*, August 2, 2010.

[52] "Honduras: Country Data," *Economist Intelligence Unit*, February 2011.

[53] World Bank, "World Development Indicators," February 2010, available at http://data.worldbank.org/data-catalog/world-development-indicators.

[54] For more information on the HIPC Initiative, see CRS Report RL33073, *Debt Relief for Heavily Indebted Poor Countries: Issues for Congress*, by Martin A. Weiss.

[55] "Honduras: Country Report," *Economist Intelligence Unit*, April 2007; Nestor Ikeda, "Inter-American Development Bank Forgives Debt of 5 Nations," *Associated Press*, March 17, 2007.

[56] "Honduras: Country Report," *Economist Intelligence Unit*, November 2010.

[57] "Honduras: Poverty drives Lobo's calls for constitutional change," *Latin American Economy & Business*, October 2010.

[58] U.N. Economic Commission for Latin America and the Caribbean, "Social Panorama of Latin America," 2009; World Bank, "Honduras Country Brief," April 22, 2010; World Food Programme, "Country Programme – Honduras," 2008. Also see CRS Report RL32713, *Afro-Latinos in Latin America and Considerations for U.S. Policy*, by Clare Ribando Seelke and June S. Beittel.

[59] "Honduras: Struggling," *Latin American Economy & Business*, October 2009; "Honduras economy: Political crisis takes its toll," *Economist Intelligence Unit*, October 27, 2009.

[60] Keny López de Carballo, "Honduras no puede prescindir de créditos," *La Prensa Grafica* (El Salvador), July 9, 2009.

[61] Robin Emmott, "Aid freeze in post-coup Honduras hurting poor," *Reuters*, November 12, 2009; "Honduras can't touch IMF resources—IMF" *Reuters*, September 9, 2009; "Unión Europea suspende ayuda financiera a Honduras," *Reuters*, July 20, 2009; "Senior State Department Officials Hold Background News Teleconference on Honduras," *CQ Newsmaker Transcripts*, September 3, 2009; "Venezuela halts oil deliveries to Honduras," *EFE News Service*, July 8, 2009; "Negociación solo es para que Zelaya enfrente la justicia," *El Heraldo* (Honduras), July 7, 2009.

[62] "Manifestantes aseguran que hoy paralizan el país," *El Tiempo* (Honduras), July 23, 2009.

[63] Blake Schmidt, "Midence Says Honduras Economy to Shrink After Crisis," *Bloomberg*, August 7, 2009; Laura Figueroa, "Honduras' business leaders hope elections restore investors' faith," *Miami Herald*, December 25, 2009.

[64] "Honduras: Country Report," *Economist Intelligence Unit*, January 2011.

[65] "Honduras: Country Report," *Economist Intelligence Unit*, December 2010; International Monetary Fund, *Honduras: Letter of Intent, Memorandum of Economic and Financial Policies, and Technical Memorandum of Understanding*, September 10, 2010.

[66] "Tracking Trends: Honduras IMF Loan," *Latin News Weekly Report*, October 14, 2010; "BID y BM conceden préstamos por más de USD 120 millones a Honduras," *Agence France Presse*, November 10, 2010.

[67] "Honduras: Country Report," *Economist Intelligence Unit*, January 2011.

[68] "Senior Administration Officials Hold State Department Background Briefing via Teleconference on Honduras," *CQ Newsmaker Transcripts*, June 28, 2009; U.S. Department of State, Office of the Spokesman, "Termination of Assistance and Other Measures Affecting the De Facto Regime in Honduras," September 3, 2009; U.S. Department of State, Office of the Spokesman, "Revocation of Diplomatic Visas," July 28, 2009.

[69] Carlos Salinas, "Honduran de facto leader vows to cling to power over US objections," *El País* (Spain), August 5, 2009.

[70] Testimony of Craig Kelly, Principal Deputy Assistant Secretary of State for Western Hemisphere Affairs, U.S. Department of State, before the House Subcommittee on the Western Hemisphere, March 18, 2010.

[71] In September 2009, the United States terminated about $21.7 million in foreign assistance appropriated for Honduras as a result of the country's political crisis. Some $10.3 million was intended for security assistance and $1 1.4 million was intended for economic and social development programs administered directly by the government of Honduras. The United States would have been legally required to terminate these funds if it had declared Zelaya's ouster a "military coup," although it never did so. Following the inauguration of President Lobo, the United States restored most of the assistance that had been terminated.

[72] The compact was originally for $215 million, but the final $10 million was terminated as a result of the 2009 political crisis.

[73] Millennium Challenge Corporation, "Honduras Overview," available at http://www.mcc.gov/countries/honduras/index.php.

[74] USAID, *Latin America and the Caribbean—Hurricane Season and Floods*, Fact Sheet #6, FY201 1, November 9, 2010.

[75] For more information, see CRS Report R40135, *Mérida Initiative for Mexico and Central America: Funding and Policy Issues*, by Clare Ribando Seelke.

[76] "U.S. suspends joint military activities with Honduras," *EFE News Service*, July 1, 2009; U.S. Department of State, Office of the Spokesman, "U.S. Assistance to Honduras," July 7, 2009.

[77] Adam Isacson, "When your aid recipients stop taking your calls," *Center for International Policy*, June 28, 2008, available at http://www.cipcol.org/.

[78] "U.S. suspends joint military activities with Honduras," *EFE News Service*, July 1, 2009; "Senior Administration Officials Hold State Department Background Briefing via Teleconference on Honduras," *CQ Newsmaker Transcripts*, June 28, 2009.

[79] "Honduras: Ties with US return to normal," *Latin News Weekly Report*, April 22, 2010.

[80] For more information on CAFTA-DR, see CRS Report RL3 1870, *The Dominican Republic-Central America-United States Free Trade Agreement (CAFTA-DR)*, by J. F. Hornbeck.

[81] U.S. Department of Commerce data, as presented by *Global Trade Atlas*, February 2011.

[82] U.S. Department of Commerce, "U. S. Direct Investment Abroad Tables," *Survey of Current Business*, September 2010.

[83] U.S. Department of State, "Background Note: Honduras," November 2009.

[84] Brian Wagner, "Honduran Businesses Suffer as Political Crisis Continues," *Voice of America*, October 16, 2009; Kevin Bogardus, "U.S. Business sees Honduran elections as solution to crisis ," *The Hill*, October 28, 2009.

[85] Kathleen Schalch, "Hondurans Brace for Pros, Cons of CAFTA," *National Public Radio (NPR)*, May 19, 2005.

[86] U.S. Department of State, Bureau of Democracy, Human Rights, and Labor, "2009 Country Reports on Human Rights Practices," March 11, 2010.

[87] For more details, see 75 *Federal Register* 24734-24737, May 5, 2010.

[88] "18-Month Extension of Temporary Protected Status for Honduras, Questions and Answers," *States News Service*, May 5, 2010. See CRS Report RS20844, *Temporary Protected Status: Current Immigration Policy and Issues*, by Ruth Ellen Wasem and Karma Ester.

[89] "Honduras: Country Report," *Economist Intelligence Unit*, November 2010; "Roundtable Discussion: Outlook for Remittances to Latin America in 2010," *Inter American Dialogue*, April 12, 2010; "Latin America: Remittances slide," *Economist Intelligence Unit*, January 26, 2009; "Country Profile: Honduras," *Economist Intelligence Unit*, 2008.

[90] Department of State, Office of the Spokesman, "U.S. BRIDGE Initiative Commitments with El Salvador and Honduras," September 22, 2010.

[91] Clare Ribando Seelke, Specialist in Latin American Affairs, contributed information to this section.

[92] Information provided to CRS by the Department of Homeland Security, Immigration and Customs Enforcement, Office of Congressional Relations.

[93] Pamela Constable, "Deportees' Bittersweet Homecoming; Migration is Boon, Bane for Honduras," *Washington Post*, June 27, 2007.

[94] "CN Pide a EEUU que Cesen las Deportaciones de Compatriotas," *La Tribuna* (Honduras), March 14, 2007.

[95] Ana Arana, "How the Street Gangs Took Central America," *Foreign Affairs*, May/June 2005.

[96] United Nations Office on Drugs and Crime (UNODC), *Crime and Development in Central America: Caught in the Crossfire*, May 2007.

[97] Information Provided to CRS by the Department of Homeland Security, Immigration and Customs Enforcement, Office of Congressional Relations.

[98] For more information see CRS Report RL341 12, *Gangs in Central America* and CRS Report R40 135, *Mérida Initiative for Mexico and Central America: Funding and Policy Issues*, by Clare Ribando Seelke.

[99] House Armed Services Committee, Posture Statement of Gen. Bantz Craddock, Commander, U.S. Southern Command, March 9, 2005.

[100] "65% satisfecho con democracia," *La Prensa* (Honduras), November 23, 2010.

[101] U.S. Department of State, Bureau for International Narcotics and Law Enforcement Affairs, "International Narcotics Control Strategy Report," March 2010; "Gang massacre appalls Honduras," *Latin News Daily*, September 8, 2010, "Buss massacre in Honduras," *Latin News Daily*, January 7, 2011.

[102] This is four times the average homicide rate in Latin America of 18 per 100,000 inhabitants. "Honduras report signals rising violence," *Latin News Daily*, February 22, 2009; "Honduras has highest murder rate in Central America," *EFE News Service*, March 30, 2010; "Honduras posts startling homicide rate," *Latin News Daily*, January 18, 2011.

[103] Steven S. Dudley, *Drug Trafficking Organizations in Central America: Transportistas, Mexican Cartels and Maras*, Woodrow Wilson International Center for Scholars, May 2010.

[104] "Honduran Government Reaches Out to Rehabilitate Gangs," *ACAN-EFE*, January 30, 2006.

[105] Marion Barbel, "Homicide Rate Confirms Honduras as One of Region's Most Violent Nations," *Global Insight Daily Analysis*, September 11, 2008.

[106] "Honduras: Lobo seeks to unseat the PL," *Latin American Special Reports: Election Watch*, 2009.

[107] Gustavo Palencia "Nuevo Gobierno Honduras busca aplacar violencia ligada al narco," *Reuters*, January 28, 2010; Freddy Cuevas, "Honduras to send soldiers into streets to aid police in combatting wave of violent crime," *Associated Press*, April 13, 2010; "Militares a reforzar las operaciones policiales durante gobierno de Lobo," *La Tribuna* (Honduras), June 11, 2010.

[108] "Honduras denounces internal armed groups," *Latin News Daily*, November 24, 2010.

[109] CARSI is a package of counternarcotics and anticrime assistance for Central America, for which Congress appropriated $248 million from FY2008-2010.

[110] USAID, "Central American Regional Security Initiative (CARSI)," May 26, 2010.

[111] U.S. Department of State, Bureau for International Narcotics and Law Enforcement Affairs, "International Narcotics Control Strategy Report," March 2010.

[112] U.S. Department of State, Office to Monitor and Combat Trafficking in Persons, "Trafficking in Persons Report," June 2010.

[113] U.S. Department of Homeland Security, "DHS and DOE Launch Secure Freight Initiative," Press Release, December 7, 2006, and "Secure Freight Initiative Becomes Fully Operational in United Kingdom, Pakistan, and Honduras," Press Release, October 12, 2007.

In: Central America: Profiles and U.S. Relations
Editor: Brian J. Durham

ISBN: 978-1-61470-122-4
© 2011 Nova Science Publishers, Inc.

Chapter 9

HONDURAN POLITICAL CRISIS, JUNE 2009 - JANUARY 2010

Peter J. Meyer

SUMMARY

On June 28, 2009, the Honduran military detained President Manuel Zelaya and flew him to exile in Costa Rica, ending 27 years of uninterrupted democratic, constitutional governance. Honduran governmental institutions had become increasingly polarized in the preceding months as a result of Zelaya's intention to hold a non-binding referendum and eventually amend the constitution. After the ouster, the Honduran Supreme Court asserted that an arrest warrant had been issued for Zelaya as a result of his noncompliance with judicial decisions that had declared the non-binding referendum unconstitutional. However, the military's actions halted the judicial process before a trial could be held. The Honduran National Congress then adopted a resolution to replace Zelaya with the President of Congress, Roberto Micheletti.

Micheletti insisted that he took power through a "constitutional succession" throughout the seven months between Zelaya's forced removal and the inauguration of new President Porfirio "Pepe" Lobo Sosa. He also maintained tight control of Honduran society, severely restricting political activity that opposed his government. President Lobo, who won a November 2009 election that had been scheduled prior to the ouster, took office on January 27, 2010. Some Hondurans declared the election illegitimate, however, as a result of the conditions in the country at the time it was held. The political crisis has left Lobo with a number of challenges, including considerable domestic political polarization, a lack of international recognition, and a faltering economy.

The United States and the rest of the international community universally condemned Zelaya's ouster. They leveled a series of diplomatic and economic sanctions against the Micheletti government and pushed for a negotiated agreement to end the crisis. Although an accord was signed roughly one month before the November 2009 election, it quickly fell apart. The unity of the international community crumbled along with the agreement, as some countries—such as the United States—agreed to recognize the results of the election despite Zelaya never being restored to office, while others refused to do so.

Members demonstrated considerable interest in the Honduran political crisis during the first session of the 111th Congress. A number of resolutions were introduced regarding the situation. On July 8, 2009, H.Res. 619 (Mack) and H.Res. 620 (Serrano) were introduced in the House. H.Res. 619 condemned Zelaya for his "unconstitutional and illegal" actions and called for a peaceful resolution. H.Res. 620 called upon the Micheletti government to end its "illegal seizure of power." On July 10, 2009, H.Res. 630 (Delahunt) was introduced in the House. It condemned the "coup d'état" in Honduras; refused to recognize the Micheletti government; urged the Obama Administration to suspend non-humanitarian aid; and called for international observation of the November 2009 elections. On September 17, 2009, H.Res. 749 (Ros-Lehtinen) was introduced in the House. It called for the Secretary of State to work with Honduran authorities to ensure free and fair elections and for President Obama to recognize the November elections "as an important step in the consolidation of democracy and rule of law in Honduras."

This report examines the political crisis in Honduras, with specific focus on the events between June 2009 and January 2010. It concludes with the inauguration of President Lobo.

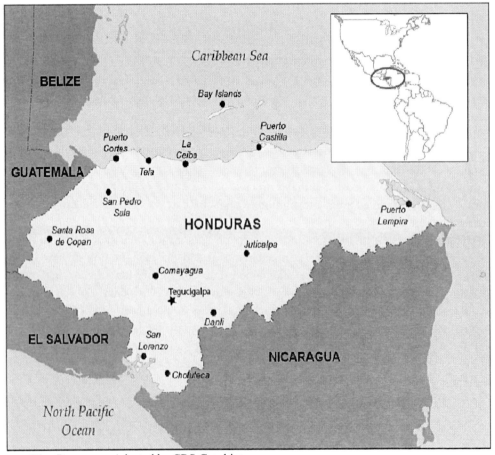

Source: Map Resources. Adapted by CRS Graphics.

Figure 1. Map of Honduras.

POLITICAL CONTEXT

Prior to the military-imposed exile of President Manuel Zelaya, Honduras, a Central American nation of 7.4 million people, enjoyed 27 years of uninterrupted elected civilian democratic rule. The Liberal (PL) and National (PN) parties have been Honduras' two dominant political parties since the military relinquished control of the country in 1982. Both are considered to be ideologically center-right, and there appear to be few major differences between the two. Manuel Zelaya of the PL was elected president in November 2005, narrowly defeating his PN rival, Porfirio Lobo Sosa. Zelaya—a wealthy landowner with considerable investments in the timber and cattle industries—was generally regarded as a moderate when he was inaugurated to a four- year term in January 2006.[1] As his term progressed, however, Zelaya advanced a number of populist policies, including free school enrollment, an increase in teachers' pay, and a 60% increase in the minimum wage.[2] Zelaya also forged closer relations with Venezuelan President Hugo Chávez, joining PetroCaribe and the Bolivarian Alternative for the Americas (ALBA) in 2008.[3] Although Zelaya's populist policies allowed him to maintain considerable support among certain sectors of Honduran society, they alienated many within the traditional economic and political elite. Likewise, his Administration's inability to achieve concrete results on a number of issues of importance— such as poverty and violent crime—significantly weakened his public standing. Opinion polls indicated that Zelaya's approval rating had fallen to about 30% prior to his ouster.[4]

PROPOSED CONSTITUTIONAL REFERENDUM

In March 2009, President Zelaya issued an executive decree introducing a process that eventually could have led to changes to the Honduran constitution. The decree called on the National Statistics Institute (INE) to hold a popular referendum on June 28, 2009, to determine if the country should include a fourth ballot box[5] during the general elections in November 2009. The fourth ballot would consult Hondurans about whether the country should convoke a national constituent assembly to approve a new constitution. In May 2009, Zelaya repealed the March decree and issued a new decree—not published until June 25, 2009—that made the referendum non-binding and removed the reference to a new constitution. The non-binding referendum would have asked Hondurans, "Do you agree that in the general elections of 2009, a fourth ballot box should be installed in which the people decide on the convocation of a National Constituent Assembly?"[6] Zelaya argued that the constitution—drafted in 1982—should be amended to reflect the "substantial and significant changes" that have taken place in Honduran society in recent years.[7]

Opposition

The proposal was immediately criticized by a number of officials. President of Congress Roberto Micheletti expressed ardent opposition, the 2009 presidential nominees of the PL and the PN— both of whom later indicated that they were open to a constitutional assembly[8]— accused Zelaya of trying to perpetuate himself in power, the Attorney General's office accused Zelaya of violating the constitution, and the Honduran judiciary[9] declared Zelaya's proposal unconstitutional.[10] Nonetheless, Zelaya pushed forward, maintaining that the law of citizen participation approved shortly after he took office allowed him to consult the people of Honduras in a non-binding poll. Zelaya also noted that the referendum did not propose specific constitutional changes, and any changes arising from an eventual assembly would take place after he left office. President Zelaya's refusal to accept the court rulings, however, sparked rumors that he was planning an institutional coup that would dissolve Congress and immediately call a constitutional assembly.[11]

Deterioration of Political Situation

The political situation in the country deteriorated considerably the week before the non-binding referendum was to be held as Honduran society and the country's governmental institutions became increasingly polarized. On June 23, 2009, the National Congress created an additional legal obstacle to the referendum, passing a law preventing referenda from occurring 180 days before or after general elections. A day later, Zelaya ordered the resignations of Honduran Defense Minister Edmundo Orellana Mercado and Chairman of the Joint Chiefs of Staff Romeo Vasquez Velasquez after they informed him that the Honduran military would not provide logistical support for the non-binding referendum since the courts had ruled it unconstitutional. The removal of Orellana and Vasquez prompted the resignation of 36 other Honduran military commanders, including the heads of the army, navy, and air force. [12] On June 25, 2009, the Supreme Court ordered that the Defense Minister and Armed Forces Chief should be restored to their positions, and the National Congress began debate on the possibility of censuring Zelaya. In response, Zelaya declared that the legislature and courts were working with the country's oligarchy to carry out a technical coup.[13]

By the day the non-binding referendum was to be held, Honduras was extremely divided. The legislature, the judiciary, the Attorney General, the Human Rights Ombudsman, the hierarchy of the Catholic Church, evangelical groups, business associations, and four of the five political parties represented in the National Congress—including Zelaya's own PL—opposed the referendum. Nearly all of these political and social actors called on the people of Honduras to boycott the vote. Proponents of the referendum—who saw it as a mechanism to overcome political and economic exclusion—included unions, peasants, women's groups, groups of ethnic minorities, and the small leftist Democratic Unification party (DU).[14]

DETENTION AND EXPULSION OF ZELAYA

On June 28, 2009, shortly before the polls were to open for the non-binding referendum, the Honduran military surrounded the presidential residence, arrested President Zelaya, and flew him to exile in Costa Rica. The military also confiscated all referendum materials from polling places across the country. In the aftermath of the ouster, the Honduran Supreme Court produced documents asserting that an arrest warrant for President Zelaya had been issued in secrecy on June 26, 2009, as a result of the executive branch's noncompliance with judicial rulings that had declared the non-binding referendum unconstitutional. Zelaya was charged with crimes against the form of government, treason, abuse of authority, and usurpation of functions for calling a referendum without the approval of the National Congress and intending to use the INE to supervise the vote rather than the Supreme Electoral Tribunal.[15] The judicial process was halted before a trial could be held, however, as a result of the Honduran military's actions.

The Honduran National Congress ratified the ouster soon after the military forced Zelaya from the country. The Congress accepted a letter of resignation allegedly signed by the exiled president, which Zelaya immediately declared to be fraudulent. [16] It then passed[17] a decree that disapproved of Zelaya's conduct for "repeated violations against the Constitution and laws of the Republic and nonobservance of the resolutions and rulings of the judicial organs," removed Zelaya from office, and named Roberto Micheletti—the President of Congress and the next in line constitutionally—the President of Honduras for the remainder of Zelaya's term, which ended on January 27, 2010.[18]

Although some maintain that Zelaya's removal was done through legal means,[19] others assert that the actions of the military and Congress were unconstitutional. According to most analysts, the Honduran military's decision to force Zelaya into exile directly violated the Honduran Constitution, which forbids the expatriation of Honduran citizens. Those involved in the ouster maintain that their actions were necessary to avoid chaos.[20] On January 26, 2010, a Honduran Supreme Court judge dismissed charges against members of the joint command of the Honduran military for their role in Zelaya's expatriation, asserting that the Honduran military had acted to "preserve democracy" and "avoid bloodshed."[21]

Some Honduran legal observers also have asserted that the actions of the Honduran National Congress were unconstitutional.[22] They maintain that the power to remove a president is reserved for the judicial branch. They also note that since Zelaya never resigned and the judicial process against him was terminated prematurely by the military's actions, Zelaya was still president and there was no vacancy to be filled. Nevertheless, the Honduran Supreme Court appears to have accepted the legality of the actions of Congress. On June 29, 2009, it ordered Zelaya's legal proceedings to continue through the ordinary judicial process since he "no longer holds high office;"[23] however, the Court has never directly ruled on the legality of Congress's actions.[24]

MICHELETTI GOVERNMENT

Governance

Roberto Micheletti assumed the office of the presidency following Zelaya's removal. Throughout the seven months between the ouster and the inauguration of President Lobo, Micheletti maintained that he was the legitimate president of Honduras as a result of a "constitutional substitution."[25] Upon assuming office, he named a new cabinet, announced a plan of governance, and assured the public that general elections would be held in November 2009, as previously planned.[26] Micheletti and the Honduran National Congress passed a 2009 budget, which included a 10% cut to the central government and a 20% cut to decentralized state bodies as a result of the loss of international support.[27] They also annulled more than a dozen decrees and reforms approved under Zelaya, including Honduras' accession to the Venezuelan-led trade bloc known as ALBA.[28]

Micheletti received strong support from some sectors of Honduran society throughout his government. On various occasions, Hondurans held large demonstrations in support of his government.[29] Likewise, prior to adjourning in mid-January 2010, the Honduran National Congress named Micheletti a "deputy-for-life," and offered life-long security to Micheletti and some 50 other Honduran officials involved in his government or the ouster of Zelaya.[30] Nonetheless, an October 2009 poll found that just 36% of Hondurans approved of Micheletti's job in office and 59% believed he rarely or never did what was in the interest of the Honduran people. The same poll found that 42% of Hondurans recognized Zelaya as president, while 36% recognized Micheletti.[31]

Repression

During his government, Micheletti implemented a number of measures that placed Honduran society under strict control. On the day of the ouster, security forces patrolled the streets, a curfew was put in place, and a number of local and international television and radio stations were shut down or intimidated.[32] Likewise, members of Zelaya's Administration, other political and social leaders, and some members of the press were detained or forced to go into hiding.[33] Over the next several months, the Micheletti government periodically implemented curfews—often arbitrarily and with little or no prior notification—and issued decrees restricting civil liberties.[34]

Micheletti declared a 45-day state of siege following Zelaya's September 21, 2009, announcement that he had clandestinely returned to Honduras and taken refuge in the Brazilian Embassy in Tegucigalpa.[35] The decree suspended freedom of the press and freedom of movement, required police or military authorization for public meetings, allowed detention without a warrant, and led to the government shutdown of two of the leading sources of media opposition to the Micheletti government.[36] Although criticism from the country's presidential candidates, members of the National Congress, and the Supreme Electoral Tribunal ultimately led Micheletti to revoke the decree three weeks later, repressive actions continued.[37]

The Inter-American Commission on Human Rights (IACHR), an autonomous organ of the Organization of American States, monitored the human rights situation in Honduras during the Micheletti government. The IACHR asserts that serious violations of human rights occurred, including "deaths, an arbitrary declaration of a state of emergency, suppression of public demonstrations through disproportionate use of force, criminalization of public protest, arbitrary detentions of thousands of persons, cruel, inhuman and degrading treatment and grossly inadequate conditions of detention, militarization of Honduran territory, a surge in incidents of racial discrimination, violations of women's rights, serious and arbitrary restrictions on the right to freedom of expression, and grave violations of political rights." The IACHR also asserts that the Honduran judicial system failed to investigate, prosecute, and punish those responsible for human rights violations.[38]

INTERNATIONAL RESPONSE TO OUSTER

Sanctions

The international community reacted quickly and forcefully to the events of June 28, 2009. The United States,[39] European Union, and United Nations condemned the ouster and called for Zelaya's immediate return, as did every regional grouping in the hemisphere from the System of Central American Integration (SICA) to the Caribbean Community (CARICOM) to the Union of South American Nations (UNASUR). On July 4, 2009, in accordance with Article 21 of the Inter- American Democratic Charter, the member states of the Organization of American States (OAS) unanimously voted to suspend Honduras from the organization for an unconstitutional interruption of the democratic order.[40] Moreover, countries throughout Latin America and Europe withdrew their ambassadors, diplomatically isolating the Micheletti government, which was not recognized by a single country.

Economic pressure was also placed on Honduras, which was already suffering as a result of the global financial crisis and U.S. recession. Some Central American countries imposed a 48-hour commercial blockade, international financial institutions withheld access to some $485 million in loans and other transfers, the European Union suspended an estimated $93 million in budget support, the United States terminated nearly $33 million in economic and military aid, and Venezuela—which provided 50% of Honduras' petroleum imports in 2008—stopped supplying the country with oil.[41]

Mediation Attempts

After the initial sanctions failed to return Zelaya to power, the international community focused its efforts on facilitating a negotiated solution to the political crisis. In July 2009, Zelaya and Micheletti agreed to participate in talks mediated by Costa Rican President Oscar Arias, who won a Nobel Peace Prize in 1987 for his efforts to end conflicts in Central America during his previous administration (1986-1990). Following initial meetings with President Arias, both leaders designated groups of negotiators to continue on their behalves. President Arias eventually proposed a 12-point plan known as the "San José Accord." Among other provisions, the proposal called for President Zelaya's reinstatement, the creation of a national unity government, a general amnesty for all political crimes committed before and after Zelaya's removal, an agreement not to pursue constitutional reform, and the creation of a verification commission to guarantee compliance with the accord.[42] Although Zelaya initially declared the negotiation process a failure, he later signaled that he would accept the Arias proposal.[43] Micheletti's negotiators said they would take the proposal back to the independent branches of the government to consider. They subsequently rejected the accord.[44] Nonetheless, the international community continued to push all of the parties involved to accept the San José Accord.

Following a new round of talks supported by the OAS and the United States, Zelaya and Micheletti signed an agreement on October 30, 2009. Based largely on the San José Accord, the "Tegucigalpa/San José Accord" called for (1) the formation of a national unity and reconciliation government; (2) a renunciation of any attempts to reform the non-amendable provisions of the constitution; (3) a recognition of the November elections with international observation; (4) the transfer of supervision of the armed forces (who traditionally assist in election logistics) to the Supreme Electoral Tribunal one month prior to the election; (5) a congressional vote— considering the input of the Supreme Court—on Zelaya's restitution to the presidency; (6) the creation of a verification commission to ensure the accord's implementation, and a truth commission to investigate the events before, during, and after the June 28 ouster; and (7) international recognition of Honduras and the removal of all sanctions against the country. The agreement also set a timeline for implementation: transfer of the agreement to Congress to consider Zelaya's restitution was to occur on October 30, 2009, the verification commission was to be formed by November 2, 2009, the national unity government was supposed to take office by November 5, 2009, and the formation of the truth commission was scheduled to occur in the first half of 2010.[45]

Despite proclamations by some in the international community that the accord signaled the end of the political crisis in Honduras,[46] little changed in the country following the agreement. Although a verification committee was created according to schedule, a national unity government was never formed.[47] Likewise, the accord was immediately sent to the legislative branch, yet the National Congress did not consider Zelaya's reinstatement until December 2, 2009—three days after the presidential election—at which point it reaffirmed his ouster.[48] As a result, Zelaya and members of the "National Resistance Front Against the Coup d'état" boycotted the November 2009 elections and refused to recognize the results.[49] Moreover, Micheletti refused to allow Zelaya to leave the Brazilian embassy, maintaining that the deposed president had to renounce his claim to the presidency and request refugee status in order to be given safe passage.[50]

NOVEMBER 2009 ELECTIONS

Results

On November 29, 2009, Honduras held general elections to fill nearly 3,000 posts nationwide, including the presidency and all 128 seats in the unicameral National Congress.[51] Former President of Congress and 2005 National Party (PN) presidential nominee Porfirio Lobo easily defeated his closest rival, former Vice President Elvin Santos of the Liberal Party (PL), 5 6.6% to 38.1%.[52] Lobo's PN also won 71 of the 128 seats in Congress, up from 55 in the 2005 election. The PL won just 45 seats in Congress, down from 62 in 2005.[53] A number of analysts have interpreted the vote as a clear rejection of the PL, which Hondurans saw as responsible for the country's political crisis as a result of Zelaya and Micheletti both belonging to the party.[54] A poll taken prior to the election found that 63% of Hondurans thought the election would help end the country's political crisis.[55]

Legitimacy

There has been considerable debate—both in Honduras and the international community— concerning the legitimacy of the November 2009 elections. Supporters of the elections note that the electoral process was initiated, and the members of the autonomous Supreme Electoral Tribunal (TSE) were chosen, prior to Zelaya's ouster. They also note that the candidates were selected in internationally observed primary elections in November 2008, and that election day was largely[56] free of political violence.[57] Nonetheless, some Hondurans and international observers have argued that the Micheletti government's suppression of opposition media and demonstrators prevented a fair electoral campaign from taking place. This led to election boycotts and a number of candidates for a variety of offices withdrawing from the elections, including an independent presidential candidate and some incumbent Members of Congress.[58] It also led organizations that traditionally observe elections in the hemisphere, such as the OAS, the EU, and the Carter Center, to cancel their electoral observation missions.[59] Critics of the elections also assert that the electoral turnout, which was just under 50% (5 points lower than 2005), demonstrated a rejection of the elections by the Honduran people. Supporters of the elections counter this assertion by arguing that Lobo won more absolute votes in 2009 than Zelaya did in 2005, and that the electoral rolls are artificially inflated—distorting the turnout rate—as a result of Honduras not purging the rolls of those who have died or migrated overseas.[60] Although a growing number of Hondurans and members of the international community have recognized Lobo as the legitimate President of Honduras, some have refused to do so.[61]

Challenges for the Lobo Administration

Political Polarization

President Lobo has already taken a number of steps to ease the political polarization in Honduras. Since his election, Lobo has called for a government of national unity and pledged to engage in dialogue with all sectors of Honduran society. [62] He intends to create two outside advisory councils: one composed of former presidents and another composed of members of the business community, the churches, unions, peasant organizations, and the media.[63] Lobo has included three of his presidential rivals in his administration, and the new Honduran National Congress, which is controlled by Lobo's National Party, incorporated members of each of the political parties into the leadership committee.[64] Moreover, Lobo arranged safe passage out of the country for Zelaya and immediately signed a bill providing political amnesty to Zelaya and those who removed him from office. The amnesty covers political and common crimes committed prior to and after the removal of President Zelaya, but does not include acts of corruption or violations of human rights.[65]

Although these actions have partially reduced the polarization of Honduran society, a number of analysts caution that the underlying cause of the crisis—the failure of the political elite to respond to the interests of the majority of the population—remains.[66] They assert that those who made up the "National Resistance Front Against the Coup d'état," an umbrella group of those opposed to Zelaya's removal, are still fully committed to reforming the Honduran constitution and pushing for greater political, economic, and social rights for traditionally excluded sectors of the Honduran population. These analysts maintain that Honduras will continue to be susceptible to political instability if Honduran leaders simply revert to that status quo that existed prior to the political crisis and largely ignore the basic needs of the 70% of the population that lives below the poverty line.

Lack of International Recognition

President Lobo faces a challenge in winning support from the international community. Following the ouster of President Zelaya, many nations expressed concern about the state of democracy in Latin America and the possibility that the events of June 28, 2009, could serve as an example for other countries. Not a single nation recognized the Micheletti government, and since Zelaya was not returned to office prior to the November 2009 election, a number of countries refused to recognize the result.[67] Lobo has called on the international community to stop "punishing" the people of Honduras for Zelaya's ouster.[68] Although the United States and several other countries in the region have indicated that they will support Lobo, he still needs to win the support of others—such as Brazil—in order to reintegrate Honduras into the international community and end the diplomatic and economic sanctions that have been leveled against the country.[69]

According to a number of analysts, the international community is likely to slowly restore relations with Honduras.[70] They assert that several countries have responded positively to Lobo's preliminary attempts at national reconciliation and have softened their positions. They also assert that countries that have yet to recognize Lobo have few remaining options since a growing number of nations and the majority of Hondurans have already recognized the new government.

Faltering Economy

Lobo's third major challenge is Honduras' faltering economy. The political crisis exacerbated economic problems that were already present as a result of the global financial crisis and U.S. recession. Steep declines in tourism and investment were added to already significant declines in exports and remittances. Likewise, steep declines in international loans and assistance were added to already significant declines in government revenue. As a result, Micheletti and the Honduran Congress were forced to slash central government spending by 10% and decentralized state bodies by 20%, and the Honduran economy contracted by an estimated 4.4% in 2009.[71]

According to some analysts, Lobo will need to re-establish flows of bilateral and multilateral aid in order to turn the economy around. This will allow Lobo to address Honduras' growing fiscal deficit and restore some of the spending that was cut in 2009. Although analysts suggest that the improving international economy should aid Honduras' recovery, they caution that it will be years before Honduras regains what was lost as a result of the political crisis.[72]

U.S. POLICY

Support for Democratic Solution to Political Impasse

In the weeks and months leading up to President Zelaya's proposed non-binding referendum, the United States expressed its support for a democratic solution to the political impasse in Honduras. The U.S. embassy repeatedly asserted that the referendum was a matter for Hondurans to resolve and that whatever was decided should comply with Honduran law.[73] As the situation deteriorated in the days before the proposed referendum was to take place, the United States continued to "urge all sides to seek a consensual democratic resolution."[74] The efforts of U.S. officials, however, failed to prevent Zelaya's forced removal.

Reaction to Ouster and Introduction of Sanctions

The United States government quickly responded to Zelaya's ouster. President Obama initially expressed deep concern about the situation and called on all Hondurans to respect democratic norms and resolve the dispute peacefully.[75] The Obama Administration later condemned the events more forcefully, declared them illegal, and asserted that the United States viewed Zelaya as the legitimate president of Honduras.[76]

Following its preliminary statements, the United States addressed the situation in Honduras in a variety of ways. In the days after Zelaya's forced removal, U.S. Southern Command minimized cooperation with the Honduran military, the U.S. State Department suspended some non- humanitarian foreign assistance, the U.S. embassy provided security and refuge for Zelaya's family, and U.S. officials met with President Zelaya in Washington, DC.[77] The United States also strongly supported the mediation of Costa Rican President Oscar Arias, advising both Zelaya and Micheletti to accept the proposed San José Accord. In order to place pressure on Honduran officials to accept the accord, the State Department revoked the visas of members and supporters of the Micheletti government, suspended non-emergency and non-immigrant visa services in the consular section of the U.S. embassy in Honduras, and announced that it would not recognize the results of the November 2009 general election in Honduras unless the situation changed. [78]

In September 2009, the United States terminated $32.7 million in foreign assistance appropriated for Honduras for FY2009. Some $10.3 million was intended for security assistance. Another $11.4 million was intended for economic and social development programs administered by the government of Honduras, including funds for anti-gang activities, trade capacity building, and aid to small farmers.[79] The final $11 million was intended for two transportation projects, and was all that remained of the $215 million MCC compact that Honduras signed in 2005.[80] Nonetheless, Honduras still received an estimated $42.5 million in U.S. foreign aid in FY2009, which provided direct assistance to the Honduran people. The assistance included funds for education, disease prevention, and democracy promotion.[81] The U.S. government would have been legally required to terminate some foreign assistance if it had declared Zelaya's ouster a "military coup."[82] Although the United States never made such a declaration, it terminated the foreign assistance that it would have been required to discontinue had it done so.

Recognition of Elections

Upon the signing of the ill-fated Tegucigalpa-San José Accord in late October 2009, the United States announced that it would support the November 2009 elections in Honduras. Although the agreement began to fall apart almost immediately, the United States continued to urge compliance with the accord's provisions. U.S. officials also announced that they would support the Honduran elections no matter what happened with the accord, maintaining elections represented a "significant step in Honduras' return to the democratic and constitutional order."[83]

Following the elections, the United States commended the Honduran people for "peacefully exercising their democratic right to select their leaders;" however, the United States noted that "significant work" remained to be done in order to end the political crisis.[84] The U.S. State Department then urged Honduran officials to implement the remaining provisions of the Tegucigalpa-San José Accord, including the vote on Zelaya's restitution, the creation of a national unity government, and the formation of a truth commission. U.S. officials expressed disappointment over the Honduran National Congress vote against Zelaya's restitution as well as Micheletti's refusal to step down in favor of a unity government. Nonetheless, U.S. officials have been encouraged by President Lobo's decision to form a unity government and his willingness to appoint a truth commission. As a result, the United States has offered its full support to Lobo and has called on other nations to do the same. [85]

CONGRESSIONAL ACTION

Congress has expressed considerable interest in the situation in Honduras since Zelaya's forced removal on June 28, 2009. On July 10, 2009, the House Committee on Foreign Affairs Subcommittee on the Western Hemisphere held a hearing on the crisis in Honduras. Over the course of the following months, a number of congressional delegations traveled to the country to observe the conditions on the ground and meet with Hondurans. Some Members of the Senate also placed temporary holds on the nominations of Arturo Valenzuela to be Assistant Secretary of State for Western Hemisphere Affairs and Thomas Shannon to be Ambassador to Brazil in protest of the Obama Administration's punitive policies toward Honduras and the Micheletti government.[86]

Several resolutions were introduced in the first session of the 111th Congress regarding the political crisis. On July 8, 2009, H.Res. 619 (Mack) and H.Res. 620 (Serrano) were introduced in the House. H.Res. 619 condemned Zelaya for his "unconstitutional and illegal" actions and called on all parties to seek a peaceful resolution. H.Res. 620 called upon the Micheletti government to end its "illegal seizure of power" and work within the rule of law to resolve the situation. On July 10, H.Res. 630 (Delahunt) was introduced in the House. It condemned the "coup d'etat" in Honduras; refused to recognize the Micheletti government; called for the reinstatement of Zelaya; urged the Obama Administration to suspend non-humanitarian assistance to Honduras; called for international observation of the November 2009 elections; and welcomed the mediation efforts of Costa Rican President Oscar Arias. On September 17, H.Res. 749 (Ros-Lehtinen) was introduced in the House. The resolution called for the Secretary of State to work with Honduran authorities to ensure free and fair elections in Honduras. It also called on President Obama to recognize the November elections "as an important step in the consolidation of democracy and rule of law in Honduras."

The Honduran political crisis also influenced a change to one of the provisions of the FY20 10 Consolidated Appropriations Act (P.L. 111-117). The heading of section 7008 of the "Department of State, Foreign Operations, and Related Programs Appropriations Act, 2010" (Division F) was changed from "Military Coups" to "Coups d'État." Section 7008 requires the U.S. government to terminate some foreign assistance to any country "whose duly elected head of government is deposed by military coup or decree." The U.S. Department of State has asserted that although Zelaya's ouster could be considered a "coup d'état," it was not a "military coup" and a termination of assistance was not legally required.[87] The House report to the appropriations bill (H.Rept. 111-366) notes that there are no substantive changes to section 7008, but conferees are "concerned that the previous title implied an unintended limitation of the provision's application." The House report also directs the Department of State's Office of the Legal Advisor to "undertake a review of events necessary to trigger the provisions of this section and submit a report on such events to the Committees on Appropriations not later than 45 days after enactment" of the bill.

APPENDIX. CHRONOLOGY OF THE POLITICAL CRISIS

On March 23, 2009, President Zelaya announced an executive decree—which was never officially published—calling for a popular referendum on June 28 on whether to include a fourth ballot box during the November 2009 general elections. The fourth ballot would have consulted Hondurans about whether the country should convoke a national constituent assembly to approve a new constitution.

On May 26, 2009, President Zelaya issued two executive decrees that were officially published on June 25, 2009. One annulled the March 23 decree. The other called for a non-binding referendum on June 28 on whether to include a fourth ballot box during the November 2009 general elections in which Hondurans could choose to convoke a national constituent assembly.

On May 27, 2009, a Honduran lower court judge ordered the suspension of the referendum that President Zelaya proposed on March 23.

On May 29, 2009, a Honduran lower court judge issued an order clarifying that the May 27 ruling applied to any other executive decree that would lead to the same ends as the suspended decree. On the same day, President Zelaya ordered the Honduran military and police to provide logistical support for the proposed referendum.

On June 16, 2009, a Honduran Appeals Court upheld the lower court ruling that declared President Zelaya's proposed non-binding referendum illegal.

On June 19, 2009, the Honduran Supreme Court ordered the Honduran security forces not to provide any support for the proposed non-binding referendum.

On June 23, 2009, the Honduran Congress passed a plebiscite and referendum law that prevents referenda from occurring within 180 days of a general election.

On June 24, 2009, President Zelaya asked for the resignations of the Chairman of the Joint Chiefs of Staff and the Defense Minister after they refused to provide logistical support for the proposed non-binding referendum.

On June 25, 2009, the Honduran Supreme Court ruled that the Chairman of the Joint Chiefs of Staff and the Defense Minister should remain in their positions despite Zelaya's request for their resignations. On the same day, Zelaya and a group of supporters removed referendum materials from an air force base in Tegucigalpa.

On June 26, 2009, the Organization of American States (OAS) adopted a resolution that offered support for the preservation of democratic institutions and the rule of law in Honduras and called on all social and political actors to maintain social peace and prevent the rupture of the constitutional order.

On June 28, 2009, shortly before the polls were to open for the non-binding referendum, the Honduran military arrested President Zelaya, flew him to Costa Rica, and seized all referendum materials. The Honduran Supreme Court indicated that an arrest warrant had previously been issued for the deposed president, and the National Congress replaced Zelaya with the President of Congress, Roberto Micheletti. The United States and governments around the world condemned the action and called for President Zelaya's reinstatement.

On July 1, 2009, the OAS adopted a resolution that would suspend Honduras' membership in the organization if the country failed to restore President Zelaya to power within three days. On the same day, the United Nations General Assembly adopted a resolution that condemned Zelaya's ouster and called for his immediate return, U.S. Southern Command ordered U.S. troops to minimize contact with the Honduran military, and the Honduran National Congress suspended a number of constitutional rights—such as the freedom of association and the freedom of movement—during curfew hours.

On July 2, 2009, the U.S. State Department announced it would suspend foreign assistance programs to Honduras that it would be legally required to terminate should it declare the events in Honduras a "military coup."

On July 4, 2009, the OAS unanimously voted to suspend Honduras for an unconstitutional interruption of the democratic order in accordance with Article 21 of the Inter-American Democratic Charter and the OAS resolution adopted three days earlier.

On July 5, 2009, Zelaya attempted to return to Honduras but the Micheletti government prevented his plane from landing.

On July 7, 2009, Zelaya met with U.S. Secretary of State Hillary Clinton in Washington, DC. Following their meeting, Secretary Clinton announced that Zelaya and Micheletti had agreed to engage in negotiations mediated by Costa Rican President Oscar Arias.

On July 9, 2009, Zelaya and Micheletti met separately with President Arias in Costa Rica to discuss a solution to the situation in Honduras. Zelaya and Micheletti never spoke face to face, and left the country after the meetings, designating representatives to continue negotiations.

On July 18, 2009, Costa Rican President Oscar Arias proposed a seven-point plan to end the political conflict in Honduras. Although the plan was agreed to in principle by Zelaya's representatives, it was rejected by Micheletti.

On July 22, 2009, Costa Rican President Oscar Arias modified his previously rejected proposal and offered a 12-point plan, known as the "San José Accord," to resolve the Honduran political crisis. Zelaya accepted the plan. Micheletti's negotiation team said it would take the proposal back to the independent branches of government in Honduras to consider. It later rejected the accord.

On July 24, 2009, exiled President Manuel Zelaya briefly crossed the Nicaraguan border, entering Honduras for the first time since his June 28, 2009 forced removal.

On July 28, 2009, the U.S. Department of State announced that it had revoked the diplomatic visas of four members of the Honduran government and was reviewing the visas of others.

On August 21, 2009, the Inter-American Commission on Human Rights (IACHR) concluded a five-day visit to Honduras. The Commission—which met with representatives of the Micheletti government, representatives of various sectors of civil society, and more than 100 individuals— "confirmed the existence of a pattern of disproportionate use of public force on the part of police and military forces, arbitrary detentions, and the control of information aimed at limiting political participation by a sector of the citizenry."

On August 25, 2009, a delegation of foreign ministers from the OAS left Honduras after a three- day mission that failed to convince the Micheletti government to accept the San José Accord. On the same day, the U.S. State Department announced that it was suspending non-emergency, nonimmigrant visa services in the consular section of the embassy in Honduras.

On September 3, 2009, exiled President Manuel Zelaya met with U.S. Secretary of State Hillary Clinton. On the same day, the U.S. State Department announced that it was terminating nearly $22 million in previously suspended foreign assistance to Honduras, revoking the visas of some members and supporters of the Micheletti government, and would be unable to support the outcome of the November elections under the existing conditions

On September 9, 2009, the Millennium Challenge Corporation terminated two transportation projects totaling $11 million from its compact with Honduras and put another $4 million on hold.

On September 21, 2009, President Manuel Zelaya revealed that he had returned to Honduras and was sheltered in the Brazilian embassy in the capital, Tegucigalpa.

On September 25, 2009, the United Nations Security Council condemned acts of intimidation against the Brazilian embassy by the Honduran military.

On September 26, 2009, the Micheletti government published a decree—dated September 22, 2009—that declared a state of siege and suspended a number of basic civil liberties for 45 days. The decree suspended freedom of the press and freedom of movement, required police or military authorization for public meetings, and allowed for detention without a warrant.

On September 27, 2009, Honduras expelled four diplomats from the OAS who formed part of an advance team planning a visit of foreign ministers from the region. On the same day, the Micheletti government warned Brazil that it would strip its embassy of diplomatic status if Brazil did not grant Zelaya political asylum or hand him over to Honduran authorities within 10 days.

On September 28, 2009, the Honduran military shut down Radio Globo and television Channel 36, two of the principal sources of media opposition to the Micheletti government.

On October 7, 2009, the Micheletti government issued a decree allowing it to revoke or cancel the licenses of any media outlet "fomenting social anarchy." On the same day, a new round of talks between Micheletti and Zelaya were initiated under the guidance of the OAS.

On October 19, 2009, the Micheletti government formally revoked the state of siege that entered into force on September 26, allowing Radio Globo and television Channel 36 to return to the air.

On October 28, 2009, then U.S. Assistant Secretary of State for Western Hemisphere Affairs, Thomas Shannon, and the National Security Council's director for the Western Hemisphere, Dan Restrepo, traveled to Honduras to restart dialogue between Zelaya and Micheletti.

On October 30, 2009, Micheletti and Zelaya signed an agreement designed to end the political crisis in Honduras known as the "Tegucigalpa/San José Accord."

On November 2, 2009, a four-member verification commission intended to ensure implementation of the accord, including two members appointed by the OAS and two members appointed by Zelaya and Micheletti, was created.

On November 4, 2009, the executive council of the Honduran National Congress voted to solicit non-binding legal opinions on Zelaya's restitution from the Supreme Court and other Honduran institutions and postponed convening an extraordinary session of Congress to consider the matter until it received the responses.

On November 5, 2009, Micheletti named a "national unity and reconciliation government" headed by himself, which Zelaya and his supporters refused to recognize.

On November 8, 2009, members of the "National Resistance Front Against the Coup d'état," including independent presidential candidate Carlos Reyes, announced that they would boycott the elections on November 29, 2009. They asserted that a fair election could not be held given the conditions under which the campaign had been conducted and the fact that Zelaya had not been restored to office.

On November 14, 2009, Zelaya released a letter to President Obama that announced that he was no longer willing to recognize the November 29, 2009, elections nor accept any reinstatement deal that would serve to legitimize the June 28, 2009, ouster.

On November 17, 2009, the President of the Honduran National Congress announced that a special legislative session would be convoked on December 2, 2009 (three days after the election), to consider the restoration of Zelaya.

On November 19, 2009, Micheletti announced that he would temporarily halt the "exercise of [his] public duties" between November 25 and December 2, in order to ensure that the attention of all Hondurans was "concentrated on the electoral process and not the political crisis."

On November 29, 2009, Porfirio Lobo of the National Party was elected president of Honduras. Lobo defeated his closest rival, Elvin Santos of the Liberal Party, 56.6% to 38.1%.

On December 2, 2009, 111 of the 128 deputies in the Honduran National Congress voted against restoring Zelaya to the Honduran presidency.

On December 9, 2009, Micheletti refused to allow Zelaya safe passage from the Brazilian embassy in Tegucigalpa to Mexico unless the deposed president renounced his claim to the presidency and requested political refugee status.

On January 6, 2010, the attorney general and anti-corruption prosecutor in Honduras filed charges against six members of the joint command of the Honduran military for their forced expatriation of Zelaya on June 28, 2009.

On January 13, 2010, the Honduran National Congress named Roberto Micheletti a "deputy-forlife" and approved a decree providing life-long security to Micheletti and some 50 other Honduran officials involved in his government or the ouster of Zelaya

On January 19, 2010, the U.S. State Department revoked the visas of five additional members of the Micheletti government.

On January 20, 2010, President-elect Lobo reached an agreement with President Leonel Fernández of the Dominican Republic to provide Zelaya safe passage from the Brazilian embassy in Tegucigalpa to the Dominican Republic.

On January 21, 2010, Roberto Micheletti took a leave of absence from his public functions in order to avoid a distraction from the transfer of power to the new president. Nevertheless, Micheletti continued to exercise the powers of the presidency until the inauguration of President Lobo.

On January 25, 2010, the new Honduran National Congress took office for its four-year term.

On January 26, 2010, a Honduran Supreme Court judge dismissed charges against members of the joint command of the Honduran military for their forced expatriation of Zelaya. The judge asserted that the Honduran military had acted to "preserve democracy and avoid bloodshed."

On January 27, 2010, Porfirio "Pepe" Lobo Sosa was inaugurated President of Honduras. On the same day, Zelaya was granted safe passage from the Brazilian embassy in Tegucigalpa to the Dominican Republic, and the Honduran National Congress approved a political amnesty for Zelaya and those involved in his ouster.

End Notes

[1] "People Profile: Manuel 'Mel' Zelaya," *Latin News Daily*, November 15, 2005; "Manuel Zelaya: empresario conservador que transitó a la izquierda," *Agencia Mexicana de Noticias*, June 29, 2009.

[2] The minimum wage decree—which did not affect the maquila sector's monthly minimum wage that fluctuates between 6,000 and 7,000 Lempiras ($318-$370)—increased the rural monthly minimum wage to 4,055 Lempiras ($215) and the urban monthly minimum wage to 5,500 Lempiras ($291). Calculations are based on an exchange rate of $1 U.S. dollar to 18.9 Honduran lempiras. "Elevan a L.5,500 el salario mínimo en Honduras," *El Heraldo* (Honduras), December 24, 2008.

[3] PetroCaribe is a Venezuelan program that provides oil at preferential discounted rates to Caribbean countries. ALBA is a socially oriented trade block that includes cooperation in a range of areas such as health, education, culture, investment, and finance. ALBA members include Bolivia, Cuba, Ecuador, Nicaragua, and Venezuela. The National Congress ratified Honduras' entrance into both PetroCaribe and ALBA. "Honduras: Congress signs up to Petrocaribe" *Latin American Caribbean & Central America Report*, March 2008; "Honduras: Congress approves Alba, with caveats," *Latin American Caribbean & Central America Report*, October 2008.

[4] Mica Rosenberg, "Protests erupt, gunshots heard after Honduras coup," *Reuters*, June 28, 2009.

[5] There are generally three ballot boxes at Honduran voting places: one for the presidential election, another for congressional elections, and a third for municipal elections.

[6] "Llegó el día de verdad," *El Tiempo* (Honduras), June 28, 2009.

[7] "Constitutional reform or power grab," *Latin American Weekly Report*, March 26, 2009.

[8] "Lobo the front runner in Honduras," *Latin News Daily*, July 15, 2009.

[9] It should be noted that the Honduran judiciary "is seen as neither effective nor fair" and "in practice, the judicial system is open to political influence." "Honduras Country Profile," *Economist Intelligence Unit*, 2008.

[10] "Honduras: Fiscalía dice Zelaya no puede llamar a consulta popular," *Associated Press*, March 25, 2009; Poder Judicial de Honduras, "Expediente Judicial Relación Documentada Caso Zelaya Rosales," available at http://www.poderjudicial.gob.hn/.

[11] "Honduras: Zelaya denies coup rumors," *Latin American Weekly Report*, June 11, 2009.

[12] "Consulta ciudadana genera crisis en Honduras," *Agencia Mexicana de Noticias*, June 25, 2009; "Honduras lurches," *Latin News Daily*, June 25, 2009.

[13] "Zelaya claims coup," *Latin News Daily*, June 26, 2009.

[14] "Llegó el día de verdad," *El Tiempo* (Honduras), June 28, 2009; "Partidos políticos advirtieron de crisis," *El Heraldo* (Honduras), June 28, 2009.

[15] Poder Judicial de Honduras, "Expediente Judicial Relación Documentada Caso Zelaya Rosales," available at http://www.poderjudicial.gob.hn/.

[16] "Diputados hondureños aceptan una supuesta renuncia del presidente Zelaya," *El Tiempo* (Honduras), June 28, 2009; "Zelaya ofrece conferencia en Costa Rica," *La Prensa* (Honduras), June 28, 2009.

[17] 122 of the 128 members of the National Congress reportedly voted for the resolution, with an independent and the five deputies of the DU not present for the vote. Some members of the Liberal Party maintain they were not present for the vote and that the reported vote count is inaccurate. "Zelaya planificaba disolver el Congreso," *El Heraldo* (Honduras), June 28, 2009; "Aparecen más diputados declarando que hubo golpe," *El Tiempo* (Honduras), July 3, 2009.

[18] "El decreto de la separación de Zelaya," *El Heraldo* (Honduras), June 28, 2009.

[19] Octavio Sánchez, "A 'coup' in Honduras? Nonsense," *Christian Science Monitor*, July 2, 2009; Miguel A. Estrada, "When a coup isn't; Under Honduras' Constitution, the ouster of President Manuel Zelaya was legal," *Los Angeles Times*, July 10, 2009; U.S. House Committee on International Relations, Subcommittee on the Western Hemisphere, Statement of Guillermo Perez-Cadalso, July 10, 2009.

[20] Frances Robles, "Top Honduran military lawyer: We broke the law," *Miami Herald*, July 3, 2009; Ginger Thompson, "On TV, Honduran Generals Explain Their Role in Coup," *New York Times*, August 5, 2009.

[21] "Juez exime a militares involucrados en golpe de Estado en Honduras," *Agence France Presse*, January 26, 2010.

[22] Edmundo Orellana, "El 28 de junio y la Constitución," *La Tribuna* (Honduras), August 1, 2009; Ramón Enrique Barrios, "No hubo sucesión constitucional," *El Tiempo* (Honduras), August 28, 2009.

[23] Poder Judicial de Honduras, "Expediente Judicial Relación Documentada Caso Zelaya Rosales," available at http://www.poderjudicial.gob.hn/.

[24] In August 2009, the Supreme Court accepted an amparo petition that called for the congressional decree removing Zelaya to be declared null and void. It has since ordered the National Congress to deliver the congressional decree and all other information relating to Zelaya's ouster to the Court to be reviewed. It has yet to issue a decision. "Por recurso de amparo: Corte le pide al Congreso decreto que derrocó a Mel," *El Tiempo* (Honduras), September 18, 2009.

[25] "Honduran interim gov't battles international isolation," *EFE News Service*, June 30, 2009.

[26] "Micheletti: promete combatir el hambre y la inseguridad," *La Prensa* (Honduras), June 29, 2009.

[27] "Honduras: Country Report," *Economist Intelligence Unit*, August 2009.

[28] "Honduras: Micheletti prepares to leave on high note," *Latin American Weekly Report*, January 21, 2010.

[29] "Hondureños cierran filas en favor de nuevo Gobierno de Honduras," *La Prensa* (Honduras), June 30, 2009.

[30] "Congreso de Honduras designa a Micheletti 'diputado vitalicio'," *Agence France Presse*, January 13, 2010; "Más de 50 funcionarios gozarán de seguridad vitalicia," *El Tiempo* (Honduras), January 15, 2010.

[31] "Hondureños ven solución en presidente alternativo y elecciones, según sondeo," *EFE News Service*, October 27, 2009; "Honduras: 42% reconoce a Zelaya como presidente, 36% a Micheletti (encuesta)," *Agence France Presse*, October 28, 2009.

[32] "Honduras: Decretan toque de queda por 48 horas," *La Prensa* (Honduras), June 28, 2009; "Honduras: Media Blackout, Protests Reported," *Stratfor*, June 29, 2009.

[33] "Al menos ocho ministros están detenidos," *La Prensa* (Honduras), June 28, 2009; "En la clandestinidad ministros de Zelaya," *El Tiempo* (Honduras), June 30, 2009; "Denuncian violaciones a la libertad de expresión," *El Tiempo* (Honduras), June 30, 2009.

[34] "Honduras suspende derechos constitucionales durante toque queda," *Reuters*, July 1, 2009; Amnesty International, "Honduras: human rights crisis threatens as repression increases," August 2009.

[35] Zelaya had attempted to return to the country on two previous occasions, but the Micheletti government prevented his plane from landing on July 5, 2009 and soldiers prohibited him from walking more than a few feet across the Nicaraguan border on July 24 and July 25, 2009.

[36] "Gobierno ordena suspender garantías constitucionales," *El Tiempo* (Honduras), September 28, 2009; Elisabeth Malkin & Ginger Thompson, "Honduras Shuts Down 2 Media Outlets, Then Relents," *New York Times*, September 29, 2009.

[37] "Pepe Lobo: Suspensión de garantías daña la imagen del país," *El Tiempo* (Honduras), September 28, 2009; Elisabeth Malkin & Ginger Thompson, "Honduras Shuts Down 2 Media Outlets, Then Relents," *New York Times*, September 29, 2009; Faustino Ordóñez Baca, "Decreto entorpece el proceso electoral," *El Heraldo* (Honduras), September 28, 2009; "Micheletti publica revocación restricciones Honduras," *Reuters*, October 19, 2009.

[38] Inter-American Commission on Human Rights, *Honduras: Human Rights and the Coup D'état*, Organization of American States, OEA/Ser.L/V/II. Doc. 55, December 30, 2009.

[39] For more on the U.S. response, see "U.S. Policy."

[40] Lesley Clark & Laura Figueroa, "OAS suspends Honduras over president's ouster," *Miami Herald*, July 5, 2009. This was the first time the OAS suspended a country since Cuba was suspended in 1962.

[41] Robin Emmott, "Aid freeze in post-coup Honduras hurting poor," *Reuters*, November 12, 2009; "Honduras can't touch IMF resources—IMF" *Reuters*, September 9, 2009; "Unión Europea suspende ayuda financiera a Honduras," *Reuters*, July 20, 2009; "Senior State Department Officials Hold Background News Teleconference on Honduras," *CQ Newsmaker Transcripts*, September 3, 2009; "Venezuela halts oil deliveries

to Honduras," *EFE News Service*, July 8, 2009; "Negociación solo es para que Zelaya enfrente la justicia," *El Heraldo* (Honduras), July 7, 2009.

[42] Juan Pablo Carranza, "Arias presentó el 'Acuerdo de San José' para buscar reconciliación en Honduras," *La Nación* (Costa Rica), July 22, 2009.

[43] "Zelaya reafirma apoyo a Plan Arias para ser restituido como presidente," *Agence France Presse*, August 4, 2009.

[44] "Honduras: De Facto Leader Rejects Part of a Deal," *New York Times*, August 1, 2009; "Corte Suprema opuesta a la restitución de Manuel Zelaya," *El Tiempo* (Honduras), August 24, 2009.

[45] "El próximo jueves debe estar formado el gobierno de unidad," *El Tiempo* (Honduras), October 30, 2009.

[46] Secretary of State Hillary Rodham Clinton, "Breakthrough in Honduras," *U.S. Department of State*, October 30, 2009; Jordi Zamora, "Fin de crisis en Honduras, un espaldarazo a la política multilateral de EEUU," *Agence France Presse*, October 30, 2009; "La comunidad internacional celebra el acuerdo alcanzado en Honduras," *Agence France Presse*, October 30, 2009.

[47] The verification committee was composed of four members: former Chilean President Ricardo Lagos (2000-2006) and U.S. Secretary of Labor Hilda Solís, appointed by the OAS; Jorge Reina, appointed by Zelaya; and Arturo Corrales, appointed by Micheletti. "Comisión de Verificación se instala y el Congreso consulta al Poder Judicial," *EFE News Service*, November 3, 2009; "Micheletti pretende seguir en Gobierno de Honduras mientras Congreso decide," *EFE News Service*, November 4, 2009.

[48] The National Resistance Front Against the Coup d'état is an umbrella group of Hondurans who opposed Zelaya's forced removal. Its members include Hondurans from a variety of backgrounds, political parties, and social organizations. "Rechazan restitución de Zelaya," *La Prensa* (Honduras), December 3, 2009.

[49] Noé Leiva, "Zelaya impugnará elecciones mientras militares se entrenen contra boicot," *Agence France Presse*, November 19, 2009; Noé Leiva, "Honduras: Resistencia contra el Golpe se organiza para boicotear elecciones," *Agence France Presse*, November 23, 2009.

[50] "Micheletti says no to Mexico," *Latin News Daily*, December 10, 2009.

[51] "Elecciones, incierto antídoto contra la crisis socio política," *El Tiempo* (Honduras), August 31, 2009.

[52] "TSE confirma el triunfo de 'Pepe' en las elecciones," *El Heraldo* (Honduras), December 21, 2009.

[53] "Final results in Honduras," *Latin News Daily*, December 22, 2009.

[54] Noé Leiva, "El Partido Liberal de Zelaya, el gran perdedor de los comicios hondureños," *Agence France Presse*, November 30, 2009; "Partido Liberal sacrificó el poder para salvar democracia," *La Tribuna* (Honduras), December 3, 2009.

[55] "Hondureños ven solución en presidente alternativo y elecciones, según sondeo," *EFE News Service*, October 27, 2009.

[56] A demonstration in San Pedro Sula by those opposed to the government of Roberto Micheletti was forcefully dispersed on election day. "Police fire tear gas on Honduras poll protesters," *Agence France Presse*, November 29, 2009.

[57] José Saúl Escobar Andrade, Enrique Ortez Sequeira, and David Andrés Matamoros Batso, "Honduran Elections," Remarks at the Inter-American Dialogue, Washington, DC, October 22, 2009; International Republican Institute, "Hondurans Turn Out to Polls in Credible Elections: IRI's Preliminary Statement on Honduras' 2009 National Elections," November 30, 2009.

[58] "Seguidores de Zelaya no particparán en elecciones aunque haya restitución," *EFE News Service*, November 8, 2009; "Renuncian importantes dirigentes del liberalismo," *El Tiempo* (Honduras), November 22, 2009; "Zelayistas dicen que hay incongruencias en la UD," *El Tiempo* (Honduras), November 23, 2009.

[59] Gustavo Palencia, "Honduras busca convencer observadores para cuestionada elección," *Reuters*, November 12, 2009; "La CE dice que no hay tiempo para una misión electoral y envía dos expertos," *EFE News Service*, November 11, 2009.

[60] "Honduras: Tug of War Between Opposition and De Facto Regime Regarding Flow of Voters," *Latin America Data Base NotiCen*, December 3, 2009; "Final results in Honduras," *Latin News Daily*, December 22, 2009.

[61] Frente Nacional de Resistencia Contra el Golpe de Estado, "Comunicado No. 41," November 30, 2009; "El Mercosur anuncia 'pleno desconocimiento' de nuevo gobierno de Honduras," *EFE News Service*, December 8, 2009.

[62] "Gobierno de austeridad y unidad anuncia Lobo," *El Heraldo* (Honduras), January 12, 2010.

[63] "Nueva administración creará y desaparecerá ministerios," *El Tiempo* (Honduras), January 18, 2010.

[64] "UD, DC y el Pinu aceptan formar parte del gobierno," *El Tiempo* (Honduras), January 26, 2010; "Congreso hondureño elige directiva que incluye a la izquierda por primera vez," *EFE News Service*, January 23, 2010.

[65] "Lobo secures exit from Honduras for Zelaya," *Latin News Daily*, January 21, 2010; "Congreso aprueba amnistía para delitos políticos comunes conexos," *El Tiempo* (Honduras), January 27, 2010.

[66] Kevin Casas-Zamora, "A Discussion on the Honduran Elections," Remarks at the Inter-American Dialogue, Washington, DC, December 9, 2009; "¿Renovarse o morir? (Editorial)," *El Tiempo* (Honduras), January 26, 2010.

[67] "El Mercosur anuncia 'pleno desconocimiento' de nuevo gobierno de Honduras," *EFE News Service*, December 8, 2009.

[68] "Lobo pide a la comunidad internacional que no siga 'castigando' a su pueblo," *EFE News Service*, November 30, 2009.

[69] "Brasil sin representantes en investidura de Lobo en Honduras," *Agence France Presse*, January 27, 2010.

[70] "Insulza confía que OEA reanude diálogo con Honduras tras investidura de Lobo," *EFE News Service*, January 14, 2010; Diego Urdaneta, "Comunidad internacional recompondrá relaciones con la Honduras de Lobo," *Agence France Presse*, January 26, 2010; "Honduras politics: Lobo takes charge," *Economist Intelligence Unit*, January 26, 2010.

[71] "Honduras: Country Report," *Economist Intelligence Unit*, August 2009 & January 2010.

[72] "Honduras politics: Lobo takes charge," *Economist Intelligence Unit*, January 26, 2010.

[73] "'El presidente Zelaya está equivocado': Micheletti," *La Prensa* (Honduras), March 23, 2009; "'Uno no puede violar la Constitución': Llorens," *La Prensa* (Honduras), June 4, 2009.

[74] "State Department Regular News Briefing," *CQ Newsmaker Transcripts*, June 26, 2009.

[75] White House, Office of the Press Secretary, "Statement from President on the situation in Honduras," June 28, 2009.

[76] "Senior Administration Officials Hold State Department Background Briefing via Teleconference on Honduras," *CQ Newsmaker Transcripts*, June 28, 2009.

[77] U.S. Department of State, Office of the Spokesman, "U.S. Assistance to Honduras," July 7, 2009; "State Department Regular News Briefing," *CQ Newsmaker Transcripts*, July 6, 2009; Secretary of State Hillary Rodham Clinton, "Remarks at the Top of the Daily Press Briefing," U.S. Department of State, July 7, 2009.

[78] U.S. Department of State, Office of the Spokesman, "Revocation of Diplomatic Visas," July 28, 2009; U.S. Department of State, Office of the Spokesman, "Temporary Suspension of Non-Immigrant Visa Services in Honduras," August 25, 2009; U.S. Department of State, Office of the Spokesman, "Termination of Assistance and Other Measures Affecting the De Facto Regime in Honduras," September 3, 2009; "Senior State Department Officials Hold Background News Teleconference on Honduras," *CQ Newsmaker Transcripts*, September 3, 2009.

[79] U.S. Department of State, Office of the Spokesman, "U.S. Assistance to Honduras," July 7, 2009; U.S. Department of State, Office of the Spokesman, "Termination of Assistance and Other Measures Affecting the De Facto Regime in Honduras," September 3, 2009; "Senior State Department Officials Hold Background News Teleconference on Honduras," *CQ Newsmaker Transcripts*, September 3, 2009.

[80] Prior to Zelaya's ouster, $80 million of the MCC compact had been dispersed and contracts worth an additional $124 million had been signed. Information Provided to CRS by the Millennium Challenge Corporation; Millennium Challenge Corporation, "MCC Board of Directors Upholds Importance of Country-Led Development and Accountability," September 9, 2009.

[81] U.S. Agency for International Development, "Congressional Notification #7," December 18, 2009; U.S. Department of State, Executive Budget Summary, Function 150 and Other International Programs, FY2011.

[82] Section 7008 of the 2009 Omnibus Appropriations Act (P.L. 111-8) states: "None of the funds appropriated or otherwise made available" for bilateral economic assistance or international security assistance "shall be obligated or expended to finance directly any assistance to the government of any country whose duly elected head of government is deposed by military coup or decree."

[83] Assistant Secretary of State Arturo Valenzuela, "Briefing on the Honduran Elections," U.S. Department of State, November 30, 2009.

[84] Ian Kelly, "Honduran Election," U.S. Department of State, November 29, 2009.

[85] Assistant Secretary of State Arturo Valenzuela, "Remarks on Recent Developments in Honduras," U.S. Department of State, December 3, 2009; U.S. Ambassador Hugo Llorens, Remarks at the Inter-American Dialogue, Washington, DC, January 19, 2010.

[86] Caitlin Webber, "GOP, Protesting Honduras Policy, Eyes Nominations," *CQ Today*, July 28, 2009.

[87] "Senior State Department Officials Hold Background News Teleconference on Honduras," *CQ Newsmaker Transcripts*, September 3, 2009.

In: Central America: Profiles and U.S. Relations
Editor: Brian J. Durham

ISBN: 978-1-61470-122-4
© 2011 Nova Science Publishers, Inc.

Chapter 10

NICARAGUA PROFILE

U.S. Department of State

Official Name: Republic of Nicaragua

GEOGRAPHY

Area: 129,494 sq. km. (59,998 sq. mi.); slightly larger than New York State.

Cities: *Capital*--Managua (pop. 1.6 million). *Other major cities*--Bluefields, Chinandega, Granada, Jinotega, Leon, Masaya, Matagalpa, and Rivas.

Terrain: Extensive Atlantic coastal plains rising to central interior mountains; narrow Pacific coastal plain interrupted by volcanoes.

Climate: Tropical in lowlands; cooler in highlands.

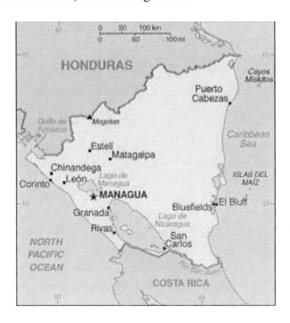

Flag of Nicaragua

PEOPLE

Nationality: *Noun and adjective*--Nicaraguan(s).
Population (July 2010 est.): 5,955,928; *density*--42 per sq. km.
Annual population growth rate (2009 est.): 1.784%.
Ethnic groups: Mestizo (mixed Amerindian and white) 69%, white 17%, black 9%, and Amerindian 5%.
Religion: Predominantly Roman Catholic, with rapidly growing Protestant congregations.
Languages: Spanish (official), English and indigenous languages on Caribbean coast.
Education: *Years compulsory*--none enforced (28% of first graders eventually finish sixth grade). *Literacy*--81%.
Health: *Life expectancy*--71.5 yrs. *Infant mortality rate* (2009 est.)--25 deaths/1,000 live births.
Work force (2010 est.): 2.3 million.

GOVERNMENT

Type: Republic.
Independence: 1821.
Constitution: The 1987 Sandinista-era constitution was amended in 1995 to provide for a more even distribution of power among the four branches of government and again in 2000 to increase the size of the Supreme Court and the Controller General's Office and to make changes to the electoral laws. The changes in 2000 allowed for the president to be elected with 35% of the popular vote so long as there was at least a five percentage point difference between the first and second place candidates in order to avoid a second round of voting.
Branches: *Executive*--president and vice president. *Legislative*--National Assembly (unicameral).
Judicial--Supreme Court and subordinate appeals, district, and local courts, as well as separate labor and administrative tribunals. *Electoral*--Supreme Electoral Council, responsible for organizing and holding elections.
Administrative subdivisions: 15 departments and two autonomous regions on the Atlantic coast; 153 municipalities.
National political parties and leaders: Conservative Party or PC (Bolanos Davis); Independent Liberal Party or PLI (whose presidency is currently in dispute); Liberal Constitutionalist Party or PLC (Jorge Castillo-Quant); Nicaraguan Liberal Alliance or ALN (Alejandro Mejia-Ferreti); Sandinista National Liberation Front or FSLN (Daniel Ortega-

Saavedra); Sandinista Renovation Movement or MRS (Enrique Saenz-Navarrete). Suffrage: Universal at 16.

ECONOMY

GDP (2009): $6.2 billion.
GDP real growth rate (2009): -1.5%.
Per capita GDP (2009): $1,071.
Components of GDP (2009): *Manufacturing*--17.7% of GDP; *agriculture, cattle, forestry and fishing*--16.8% of GDP; *retail, hotels, and restaurants*--14.2% of GDP; *government*--12.6% of GDP; *real estate*--7.5% of GDP; *personal services*--6.6% of GDP; *telecommunications and transportation*--5.5% of GDP; *financial services*--5.1% of GDP; *construction*--4.7% of GDP; *utilities*--2.6% of GDP; *mining*--1.1% of GDP. Inflation rate (2009): 0.93%.
Natural resources: arable land, fresh water, fisheries, gold, timber, hydro and geothermal power potential.
Trade (2009): *National exports*--$2.363 billion (f.o.b.): coffee, shrimp and lobster, beef, sugar, industrial goods, gold, bananas. *Free trade zone exports*--$972.2 million: mostly textiles and apparel, automobile wiring harnesses, cigars. *Markets*--United States, Central American Common Market, European Union (EU), Mexico, Japan. *Imports*--$3.47 billion (2009), primarily consumer goods, machinery and equipment, raw materials, and petroleum products. *Free trade zone imports*--$830.6 million. *Suppliers*--United States, Mexico, Costa Rica, Venezuela, Guatemala, El Salvador.

PEOPLE

Most Nicaraguans are of both European and indigenous ancestry, and the culture of the country reflects the mixed Ibero-European and indigenous heritage of its people. Only the indigenous of the eastern half of the country remain ethnically distinct and retain their tribal customs and languages. A large black minority, of Afro-Caribbean origin, is concentrated along the Caribbean coast. In the mid-1980s, the central government divided the eastern half of the country--the former department of Zelaya--into two autonomous regions and granted the people of the region limited self-rule under an elected regional council of 45 deputies and an indirectly-elected governor.

Roman Catholicism is the dominant religion, but Evangelical Protestantism has experienced rapid growth over the past 10 years. There are strong Anglican and Moravian communities on the Caribbean coast, and a small Muslim population exists in Managua and in the larger cities along the Pacific coast. Buddhist and Jewish communities are small. Most Nicaraguans live in the Pacific lowlands and the adjacent interior highlands. The population is 58% urban.

HISTORY

Nicaragua takes its name from Nicarao, chief of the indigenous tribe that lived around present-day Lake Nicaragua during the late 1400s and early 1500s. In 1524, Hernandez de Cordoba founded the first Spanish permanent settlements in the region, including two of Nicaragua's principal towns: Granada on Lake Nicaragua, and Leon, located west of Lake Managua. Nicaragua gained independence from Spain in 1821, briefly becoming a part of the Mexican Empire and then a member of a federation of independent Central American provinces. In 1838, Nicaragua became an independent republic.

Much of Nicaragua's political history since independence has been characterized by the rivalry between the Liberal elite of Leon and the Conservative elite of Granada, which frequently led to civil war. Initially invited by the Liberals in 1855 to join their struggle against the Conservatives, an American named William Walker and his "Filibusterers" seized the presidency in 1856. Walker's troops and Nicaraguan troops fought a historic battle at San Jacinto hacienda on September 14, 1856, which is now celebrated as a national holiday. In 1857, the Liberals and Conservatives united to drive Walker out of office. Three decades of Conservative rule followed. In 1893, Jose Santos Zelaya took advantage of divisions within the Conservative ranks and led a Liberal revolt that carried him to power. Zelaya ended a longstanding dispute with Britain over the Atlantic coast in 1894, and formally reincorporated that region into Nicaragua, establishing Nicaragua's present-day boundaries.

By 1909, political differences and rivalries again emerged over plans for a trans-isthmian canal and concessions granted to American investors in Nicaragua. In 1909 the United States provided political support to Conservative-led forces rebelling against President Zelaya and intervened militarily to protect American lives and property. With the exception of a 9-month period in 1925-26, the United States maintained troops in Nicaragua from 1912 until 1933. From 1927 until 1933, U.S. Marines stationed in Nicaragua engaged in an effort to capture rebel forces led by Augusto Sandino, a Liberal general who had rejected a 1927 negotiated agreement brokered by the United States to end the conflict between Liberals and Conservatives.

After the departure of U.S. troops in 1933, National Guard Commander Anastasio Somoza Garcia outmaneuvered his political opponents--including Sandino, who was assassinated by National Guard officers--and took over the presidency in 1936. Somoza and his two sons who succeeded him sought to maintain close ties with the United States. The Somoza dynasty, beset by corruption, ended in 1979 with a massive uprising led by the Sandinista National Liberation Front (FSLN), which had conducted a low-scale guerrilla war against the Somoza regime since the early 1960s.

Soon after taking power the FSLN pushed out rival factions and established an authoritarian dictatorship under leadership of Daniel Ortega. U.S.-Nicaraguan relations deteriorated rapidly as the regime nationalized many private industries, confiscated private property, supported Central American guerrilla movements, and maintained links to international terrorists, including the Colombian guerrilla group Revolutionary Armed Forces of Colombia (FARC), the Basque Homeland and Freedom (ETA) separatist group, and the Palestine Liberation Organization (PLO). The United States suspended aid to Nicaragua in 1981. Later the Ronald Reagan administration provided assistance to the Nicaraguan resistance (Contras) and in 1985 imposed an embargo on U.S.-Nicaraguan trade.

In response to both domestic and international pressure, Ortega's Sandinista regime entered into negotiations with the Nicaraguan resistance leaders and ultimately agreed to nationwide elections in February 1990. In these elections, Nicaraguans elected as their President the National Opposition Union (UNO) candidate, Violeta Barrios de Chamorro, widow of the slain journalist and editor of the daily newspaper La Prensa, Pedro Joaquin Chamorro. She defeated Ortega, the Sandinista Party candidate.

During President Chamorro's nearly 7 years in office, her government achieved major progress toward consolidating democratic institutions, advancing national reconciliation, stabilizing the economy, privatizing state-owned enterprises, and reducing human rights violations. Despite a number of irregularities--which were due largely to logistical difficulties and a complicated electoral law--the October 20, 1996 presidential, legislative, and mayoral elections were judged free and fair by international observers and by the groundbreaking national electoral observer group Etica y Transparencia (Ethics and Transparency). This time Nicaraguans elected former Managua Mayor Arnoldo Aleman, leader of the center-right Liberal Alliance. Aleman defeated Sandinista Party candidate Daniel Ortega.

The first transfer of power in modern Nicaraguan history from one democratically-elected president to another took place on January 10, 1997, when the Aleman government was inaugurated. Aleman's administration was marred by graft and corruption. At the end of his term, Aleman entered into a political pact (el Pacto) with Daniel Ortega to divide control of state institutions between them and perpetuate themselves in power.

Nicaragua held presidential and legislative elections in November 2001. Enrique Bolanos of the Liberal Constitutional Party was elected to the Nicaraguan presidency on November 4, 2001, defeating Sandinista candidate Daniel Ortega by 14 percentage points. President Bolanos was inaugurated on January 10, 2002. His administration sought to deliver on campaign promises to reinvigorate the economy, create jobs, fight corruption, and support efforts against terrorism. However, political attacks from both the left and the right severely blunted his administration's efforts to shrink traditional sources and bases of political patronage and corruption.

FSLN candidate Daniel Ortega won the presidential elections of November 5, 2006, with 38% of the vote, defeating a divided opposition. ALN candidate Eduardo Montealegre garnered 29%; Jose Rizo of the PLC received 26%; and MRS' Edmundo Jarquin polled fourth with 6%. Ortega was inaugurated on January 10, 2007.

In early 2008, Eduardo Montealegre was forced out of the ALN and formed his own movement, Vamos con Eduardo (VCE), and ran for mayor of Managua. The VCE and PLC formed an electoral alliance to compete under the same banner during the November 2008 municipal elections. Those elections were marred by a number of serious irregularities and were universally denounced domestically and internationally as severely flawed. Official results released by the Supreme Electoral Council awarded 105 of Nicaragua's 153 municipalities to the ruling FSLN. As a result of the electoral fraud, over $100 million in international assistance was lost beginning in 2009. A subsequent regional council election in March 2010 on Nicaragua's Caribbean coast was also marred by election fraud that favored the FSLN.

Government and Political Conditions

Nicaragua is a constitutional democracy with executive, legislative, judicial, and electoral branches of government. In 1995, the executive and legislative branches negotiated a reform of the 1987 Sandinista constitution, which gave extensive new powers and independence to the legislature--the National Assembly--including permitting the Assembly to override a presidential veto with a simple majority vote and eliminating the president's ability to pocket-veto a bill.

Nicaragua's constitution guarantees freedom of speech, peaceful assembly and association, religion, and movement within the country, as well as foreign travel, emigration, and repatriation. In the run-up to the November 2008 municipal elections the government made attempts to limit some of these rights, including limiting free and open discussion in the media and academia, and peaceful assembly. The constitution prohibits discrimination based on birth, nationality, political belief, race, gender, language, religion, opinion, national origin, and economic or social condition. All public and private sector workers, except the military, public safety workers, and police, are entitled to form and join unions of their own choosing. Most of Nicaragua's labor force is involved in the informal service and agricultural sectors and is not unionized. However, the formal manufacturing and government/public sectors are heavily unionized. About 65% of unions are affiliated with the Sandinistas. Workers have the right to strike. Collective bargaining is becoming more common in the private sector.

The president and the members of the unicameral National Assembly are elected to concurrent 5-year terms. The National Assembly consists of 92 total deputies (90 elected from party lists drawn at the regional and national levels, plus the outgoing president and the second place finisher in the most recent presidential election).

The Supreme Court supervises the functioning of the still largely ineffective, often partisan, and overburdened judicial system. In 2000, the Ortega-Aleman pact orchestrated expansion of the Supreme Court from 12 to 16 justices. The National Assembly elects Supreme Court justices to staggered 5-year terms. Led by a council of seven magistrates, the Supreme Electoral Council (CSE) is the co-equal branch of government responsible for organizing and conducting elections, plebiscites, and referendums. The National Assembly elects the CSE magistrates and their alternates to 5-year terms. A 2000 constitutional amendment expanded the number of CSE magistrates from five to seven and gave the PLC and the FSLN a freer hand to name party activists to the Council, prompting allegations that both parties were politicizing electoral institutions and processes and excluding smaller political parties.

The constitution provides the Assembly with sole power to elect Supreme Court judges, CSE magistrates, and other national level public officials. However, in January 2010 President Ortega issued a decree that indefinitely extended the terms of these incumbent officials. As a result, as of May 2010 about two dozen of these officials remained in their positions despite the fact that their terms had expired, including several Supreme Court judges. After Liberal judges boycotted the Supreme Court for several months, Ortega replaced them in August 2010 with five Sandinista and two Liberal justices.

Political Parties

The 2006 national elections resulted in the following distribution of the 92 seats in the National Assembly (installed January 9, 2007): FSLN--38; PLC--25; ALN--24; MRS--5. The political parties have since reorganized and the makeup of the Assembly is now FSLN--37; PLC--20; BDN--13; ALN--7; MRS--4; BUN--5; and Independent--6.

Principal Government Officials

President--Jose Daniel Ortega Saavedra
Vice President--Jaime Morales Carazo
Minister of Foreign Affairs--Samuel Santos
Minister of Finance--Alberto Jose Guevara Obregon
Minister of Industry and Commerce--Orlando Solorzano Delgadillo
Minister of Government--Ana Isabel Morales
Secretary General of the Ministry of Defense--Ruth Tapia Roa
Chief of the Armed Forces--General Julio Cesar Aviles Castillo
Chief of Naval Forces--Captain Roger Antonio Gonzalez Diaz
Ambassador to the United States--Francisco Obadiah Campbell Hooker
Ambassador to the United Nations--Maria Eugenia Rubiales de Chamorro
Ambassador to the Organization of American States--Denis Ronaldo Moncada Colindres
Nicaragua maintains an embassy in the United States at 1627 New Hampshire Avenue, NW, Washington, DC 20009 (tel. 202-939-6570). Nicaragua has consulates in Houston, Los Angeles, Miami, New York, and San Francisco. Contact information: http://www.state

ECONOMY

With a gross domestic product (GDP) of $6.2 billion and a per capita income of $1,071 in 2009, Nicaragua is the second-poorest country in the Western Hemisphere. The economy contracted by 1.5% in 2009, largely as a result of falling demand for Nicaraguan exports and decreased domestic investment. Official sources estimate GDP growth of 3%-4% for 2010, mainly due to an increase in commodity prices and Venezuelan-funded stimulus spending. Official unemployment in 2009 was 8%, but 65% of all workers earn a living in the informal sector, where underemployment is high. In 2009, Nicaraguans received $768 million in remittances from abroad, the majority from the United States. Total exports are equivalent to 39% of GDP.

Because Nicaragua has abundant arable land and water resources, agriculture will always be an important component of the economy. About a third of GDP is derived from agriculture, timber, and fishing. Opportunities exist in food and timber processing and preparation for export. Currently, most agriculture is small-scale and labor intensive. Livestock and dairy production have seen steady growth over the past decade and have taken the greatest advantage of free trade agreements. Many export products, especially coffee, have benefited from the recent rise in international commodity prices.

Social indicators for Nicaragua have improved since 1991. The current population of Nicaragua is 5.9 million; life expectancy at birth is 71.5 years. Prenatal care coverage has steadily improved and infant mortality has dropped from 52 deaths per 1,000 live births in 1991 to 25 per 1,000. The country has achieved 85% vaccination coverage, and since 2004, infectious disease has fallen from fourth to fifth place among the leading causes of death, with the number of such deaths down nearly 50% since 1996. In 2007, the Minister of Education reported school enrollment as 86.5%. Nicaragua's score on the United Nations Human Development Index rose by 25% from 1990 to 2010 (from 0.454 to 0.565). Despite these statistical gains, the benefits of economic development have been uneven. Blackouts, water shortages, and high energy prices disproportionately affect the poorest in the population. About 46% of the population lives on less than $1.15 a day.

President Ortega's stated objective is to implement socialism in Nicaragua, which he further defines as a mixed economy, guided by Christian and socialist ideals. He has used funds provided by Venezuela through the Bolivarian Alliance for the Americas (ALBA) to increase the role of the FSLN party in the economy, including the purchase of a hotel, cattle ranch, television station, gasoline filling stations, construction equipment, and electricity generators. At the same time, President Ortega has maintained many of the legal and regulatory underpinnings of the market-based economic model of his predecessors, despite rhetoric decrying the "neo-liberal economic model," and along with it capitalism and the United States, which he refers to as the imperial power.

Nicaragua signed a 3-year Poverty Reduction and Growth Facility (PRGF) with the International Monetary Fund (IMF) in October 2007. As part of the IMF program, the Government of Nicaragua agreed to implement free market policies linked to targets on fiscal discipline, poverty spending, and energy regulation. The lack of transparency surrounding ALBA funds, channeled through state-run enterprises rather than the official budget, has become a serious issue for the IMF and international donors. In November 2010, the IMF approved a 1-year extension of the arrangement. The extension allows for the disbursement of the remaining $36 million dollars in 2011, but the program is contingent on the publication of additional information about off-budget expenditures.

Nicaragua has stayed current with the U.S.-Central America-Dominican Republic Free Trade Agreement (CAFTA-DR), which entered into force for Nicaragua on April 1, 2006. Nicaraguan exports to the United States, which account for two-thirds of Nicaragua's total exports, were $1.6 billion in 2009, up 37% since 2005. Textiles and apparel account for about half of all exports to the United States, while automobile wiring harnesses add another 10%. Other leading export products are coffee, meat, cigars, sugar, ethanol, and fresh fruit and vegetables, all of which have seen remarkable growth since CAFTA-DR went into effect. U.S. exports to Nicaragua, meanwhile, were $680 million in 2009, up 15% from 2005.

Despite important protections for investment included in CAFTA-DR, the investment climate has steadily worsened since Ortega took office. President Ortega's decision to support radical regimes such as Iran and Cuba, his harsh rhetoric against the United States and capitalism, and his use of government institutions to persecute political enemies and their businesses have had a negative effect on perceptions of country risk. The government reported foreign investment inflows of $432 million in 2009, mostly in energy and telecommunications. There are over 100 companies operating in Nicaragua with some relation to a U.S. company, either as wholly or partly-owned subsidiaries, franchisees, or exclusive distributors of U.S. products. The largest are in energy, financial services, textiles/apparel, manufacturing, and fisheries.

Poor enforcement of property rights deters both foreign and domestic investment, especially in real estate development and tourism. Conflicting claims and weak enforcement of property rights has invited property disputes and litigation. The court system is widely believed to be corrupt and subject to political influence. Establishing verifiable title history is often entangled in legalities relating to the expropriation of 28,000 properties by the revolutionary government that Ortega led in the 1980s. Authorities seldom challenge illegal property seizures by private parties, occasionally undertaken in collaboration with corrupt municipal officials.

The U.S. Embassy's Economic and Commercial Section advances U.S. economic and business interests by briefing U.S. firms on opportunities and challenges to trade and investment in Nicaragua, encouraging key Nicaraguan decision makers to work with U.S. firms, helping to resolve problems that affect U.S. commercial interests, and working to change local economic and trade ground rules in order to afford U.S. firms a level playing field on which to compete. U.S. businesses may access key Embassy economic reports at http://nicaragua.usembassy.gov/econ.html.

FOREIGN RELATIONS

Nicaragua traditionally pursues an independent foreign policy. Since returning to power in 2007, Daniel Ortega has sought to build closer ties with Iran, Russia, and the ALBA states, especially Venezuela. Immediately after his inauguration Ortega formally joined ALBA. In 2008, Ortega made Nicaragua the second country (of only four) to grant diplomatic recognition to South Ossetia and Abkhazia, the breakaway "independent republics" of Georgia.

Nicaragua submitted three territorial disputes--one with Honduras, one with Costa Rica, and the other with Colombia--to the International Court at The Hague for resolution. The dispute with Honduras was resolved by The Hague in October 2007, and President Ortega and Honduran President Jose Manuel Zelaya Rosales met on October 8, 2007 to recognize the finality of the decision. Also in 2007, Nicaragua, Honduras, and El Salvador reached an agreement on fishing rights in the Gulf of Fonseca, though the actual border demarcation remains unresolved, by mutual agreement. In December 2007, The Hague issued an interim decision on the Colombia-Nicaragua dispute that granted sovereignty of the San Andres archipelago to Colombia, but urged both parties to work toward a mutually satisfactory resolution regarding the surrounding waters. As of mid-2010, no action had been taken toward that end.

Costa Rica and Nicaragua have long-disputed issues related to their boundary. An 1858 treaty fixed the boundary on the river's southern bank, and a subsequent arbitration finding validated that treaty. A 2009 International Court of Justice (ICJ) decision also accepted the river's southern bank as the boundary.

In October 2010, Costa Rica accused Nicaraguan troops of invading Costa Rican territory after Costa Rica protested Nicaragua's dredging operations in the San Juan River, claiming that the dredging was causing irreparable environmental damage. The Permanent Council of the Organization of American States (OAS) and attendees of the Meeting of Consultation of the Ministers of Foreign Affairs of the OAS adopted separate resolutions to support OAS Secretary General's recommendations, which included the removal of armed military and civilian security forces from the disputed area. Nicaragua claims its troops are on its soil, refused to remove them, and continued dredging operations. Costa Rica filed a provisional injunction with the International Court of Justice to be considered in January 2011.

At the 1994 Summit of the Americas, Nicaragua joined six Central American neighbors in signing the Alliance for Sustainable Development, known as the Conjunta Centroamerica-USA, or CONCAUSA, to promote sustainable economic development in the region.

Nicaragua belongs to the United Nations and several specialized and related agencies, including the World Bank, the International Monetary Fund (IMF), World Trade Organization (WTO), UN Educational, Scientific, and Cultural Organization (UNESCO), World Health Organization (WHO), Food and Agriculture Organization (FAO), International Labor Organization (ILO), and UN Human Rights Commission (UNHRC). Nicaragua also is a member of the Organization of American States (OAS), the Pan-American Health Organization (PAHO), the International Civil Aviation Organization (ICAO), the Central American Armed Forces Conference (CFAC), the Non-aligned Movement (NAM), the International Atomic Energy Commission (IAEA), the Inter-American Development Bank (IDB), and the Central American Bank for Economic Integration (CABEI).

U.S.-NICARAGUAN RELATIONS

U.S. policy supports the preservation of the democratic process initiated in Nicaragua with the 1990 election of President Chamorro. The United States has promoted national reconciliation, encouraging Nicaraguans to resolve their problems through dialogue and compromise. It recognizes as legitimate all political forces that abide by the democratic process and eschew violence. U.S. assistance is focused on strengthening democratic institutions, stimulating sustainable economic growth, and supporting the health and basic education sectors.

Section 527 of the Foreign Relations Authorization Act, Fiscal Years 1994 and 1995, prohibits U.S. assistance and support to any country in which U.S. citizens have not received adequate and effective compensation for outstanding claims against the government for confiscated property, as is the case in Nicaragua. The law provides authority to the President, which is delegated to the Secretary of State, to waive the prohibition when it is in the national interest. In 2010, the Secretary issued the 17th waiver of the Section 527 prohibition based upon Nicaragua's progress in resolving U.S. citizen claims.

Other key U.S. policy goals for Nicaragua are:

- Improving respect for human rights and resolving outstanding high-profile human rights cases;
- Developing a free market economy with respect for property and intellectual property rights; and

- Increasing the effectiveness of Nicaragua's efforts to combat transnational crimes, including narcotics trafficking, money laundering, illegal alien smuggling, international terrorist and criminal organizations, and trafficking in persons.

Since 1990, the United States has provided over \$2 billion in assistance to Nicaragua. About \$489 million of that was for debt relief, and another \$488 million was for balance-of-payments support. The United States also provided \$94 million in 1999, 2000, and 2001 as part of its overall response to Hurricane Mitch. In response to Hurricane Felix, the United States provided over \$15 million in direct aid to Nicaragua to support humanitarian relief and recovery operations from the damage inflicted in September 2007. Aside from funding for Hurricanes Mitch and Felix, the levels of assistance have fallen incrementally to reflect the improvements in Nicaragua. Assistance has been focused on promoting more citizen political participation, compromise, and government transparency; stimulating sustainable growth and income; and fostering better-educated and healthier families.

The Millennium Challenge Corporation's (MCC) 5-year, \$175 million compact with the Republic of Nicaragua entered into force on May 26, 2006. The Millennium Challenge Compact sought to reduce poverty and spur economic growth by funding projects in the regions of Leon and Chinandega aimed at reducing transportation costs and improving access to markets for rural communities; increasing wages and profits from farming and related enterprises in the region; and attracting investment by strengthening property rights. In June 2009, the MCC Board terminated portions of the compact when the Government of Nicaragua refused to address credible accusations of fraud related to the November 2008 municipal elections.

In: Central America: Profiles and U.S. Relations
Editor: Brian J. Durham

ISBN: 978-1-61470-122-4
© 2011 Nova Science Publishers, Inc.

Chapter 11

NICARAGUA: POLITICAL SITUATION AND U.S. RELATIONS

Clare Ribando Seelke

SUMMARY

Nicaragua, the second poorest country in Latin America after Haiti, has had a difficult path to democracy, characterized by ongoing struggles between rival caudillos (strongmen), generations of dictatorial rule, and civil war. Since 1990, Nicaragua has been developing democratic institutions and a framework for economic development. Nonetheless, the country remains extremely poor and its institutions are weak. Former revolutionary Sandinista leader, Daniel Ortega, was inaugurated to a new five-year presidential term in January 2007 and appears to be governing generally democratically and implementing market-friendly economic policies. The United States, though concerned about Ortega's ties to Venezuela and Iran and his authoritarian tendencies, has remained actively engaged with the Ortega Administration. The two countries are working together to implement the U.S.-Dominican Republic-Central America Free Trade Agreement (CAFTA-DR), control narcotics and crime, and promote economic development through the Millennium Challenge Account (MCA). Nicaragua is receiving some $28.6 million in U.S. assistance in FY2008 and could benefit from the proposed Mérida Initiative for Mexico and Central America.

BACKGROUND

Nicaragua is a Central American nation bordering both the Caribbean sea and the Pacific ocean between Costa Rica and Honduras. Slightly smaller than the state of New York, Nicaragua has a population of roughly 5.4 million. With a per capita income level of $1000 (2006), Nicaragua is classified by the World Bank as a lower middle income developing country.[1] Nicaragua is still largely an agricultural country, but its nontraditional exports (textiles, tobacco products, vegetables, gold) have expanded rapidly in the last few years.

Nicaragua's key development challenge is to boost growth rates to a level that can reduce poverty, which is especially severe in rural areas.

Nicaragua has had a conflicted and anti-democratic past, dominated from 1936 until 1979 by the Somoza dictatorship. Anastasio Somoza and his two sons who succeeded him, though corrupt and authoritarian, were staunch anti-communists who maintained good relations with the United States. In 1979, the Somoza government was toppled by a revolution led by the Sandinista National Liberation Front (FSLN), a leftist guerrilla group that had opposed the regime since the early 1 960s. That revolution resulted in the loss of some 50,000 lives. During the 1 980s, Nicaragua was embroiled in a decade-long struggle between its leftist Sandinista government, which confiscated private property and maintained ties with rebel forces in neighboring El Salvador, and U.S.-backed counterrevolutionary forces. Since democratic elections were held in 1990, Nicaragua has adopted pro-market economic reforms, held free and fair elections, and worked toward building democratic institutions. Despite progress on those fronts, successive governments have made limited inroads in combating corruption and addressing the country's high levels of poverty and inequality.[2]

POLITICAL SITUATION

On January 10, 2007, Sandinista leader and former President Daniel Ortega was inaugurated to a five-year presidential term. Ortega's previous presidency (1985-1991) was marked by a civil conflict pitting the government against U.S.-backed "contras." Ortega, who had lost the last three presidential elections, won only 37.9% of the vote in the November 2006 elections, but Nicaraguan law allowed him to avoid a run-off vote since he was more than 5% ahead of the next closest candidate, Eduardo Montealegre, then head of the Nicaraguan Liberal Alliance (ALN).

Ongoing disputes between powerful leaders, endemic corruption, and weak institutions have undermined the consolidation of democracy in Nicaragua. The 2006 elections followed more than a year of political tensions among then-President Enrique Bolaños, Ortega and the leftist Sandinista party, and allies of rightist former President Arnoldo Alemán. Alemán and Ortega, once longtime political foes, negotiated a power- sharing pact ("El Pacto") in 1998 that has since influenced national politics. In addition to a tendency to have caudillos like Ortega and Alemán dominate national politics, Nicaragua is known to have high levels of corruption. According to Transparency International's 2007 Corruption Perception Index, Nicaragua is one of ten Latin American countries where corruption is perceived as rampant. Currently, some opposition leaders are urging the Ortega government to publicly disclose how it is using the aid Nicaragua receives from Venezuela, including funds earned through the re-sale of Venezuelan oil bought on preferential terms through Petrocaribe. They are concerned that the president of Nicaragua's state-owned oil company, which distributes the Venezuelan oil, is also the treasurer of the Sandinista party.[3] Finally, the politicization of government entities, including party influence over the judiciary, is an obstacle to governance in Nicaragua.

Since no single party won an outright majority in Nicaragua's 90-member National Assembly in the November 2006 legislative elections, President Ortega and the Sandinistas (FSLN) must form alliances in order to enact legislation The FSLN has generally relied on an informal alliance with the Constitutionalist Liberal Party (PLC), dominated by jailed former President Alemán, to pass legislation. In December 2007, however, the PLC broke with the Ortega government by voting against its plan to increase the power of the country's Citizen Power Councils (CPCs), which are funded by the executive branch, over the existing municipal authorities.[4] The PLC has since aligned with Eduardo Montealegre, who, until recently was head of the ALN, to contest the ruling FSLN and its allies in the November 2008 municipal elections. Those elections will test the strength of the FSLN, which currently holds 87 of the country's 153 municipalities.[5]

Economic and Social Policy

In 2008, the Ortega government faces the challenges of boosting the country's moderate growth rates (GDP growth was 2.9% in 2007) and reducing poverty. According to the World Bank, although overall poverty has declined in Nicaragua since the country's return to democracy (from 50.3% in 1993 to roughly 46% today), more than two-thirds of the rural population is impoverished. While Nicaragua made some progress towards development in the 1 990s, much of those gains were reversed by the devastation wrought by Hurricane Mitch in 1998. As a result of sluggish growth rates, some social indicators for Nicaragua have shown little or no improvement since 1993. Nicaragua is highly dependent on foreign aid, which contributed 26% of its budget in 2006. It is also dependent on remittances sent from Nicaraguans living abroad, which totaled some $656 million in 2006 and accounted for 17% of the country's GDP. The official unemployment rate is about 5%, but underemployment is a major problem and some 60% of workers are employed in the informal sector, which doesn't provide social security and other benefits.[6]

The Ortega government has adopted a poverty reduction strategy and a 2008 budget in line with International Monetary Fund (IMF) recommendations. As a result, the IMF and the World Bank have cancelled roughly $200 million and $1.5 billion respectively in foreign debt owed by Nicaragua. President Ortega is expected to announce a development plan by mid-2008 that is likely to emphasize sustainable agro-industrial development. Obstacles to Nicaragua's growth prospects in 2008 will be the rising price of oil and the economic slowdown in the United States, which could affect trade and remittance flows.

Some economists have also warned that if Ortega should engage in an increasingly radical or authoritarian manner, foreign investment in Nicaragua could decline.[7]

Foreign Relations

President Ortega is working with the United States and the IMF to boost the country's long-term prospects for economic development, but is also seeking aid from Iran and Venezuela to meet more immediate needs. Iran has pledged to invest in Nicaragua's ports, agricultural sector, and energy network, with Venezuela co- financing many infrastructure projects. Venezuela has promised to build a $3.5 billion oil refinery and to provide up to 10 million barrels of oil at preferential prices annually through the PetroCaribe program.[8] Ortega shares an ideological affinity with President Hugo Chávez of Venezuela and the other countries comprising the Bolivarian Alternative for the Americas (ALBA) trade block (Cuba and Bolivia). President Ortega generally maintains good relations with neighboring countries in Central America, but his government has been embroiled in a serious border dispute with Colombia. In December 2007, the International Court of Justice (ICJ) upheld Colombia's sovereignty over the islands of San Andrés and Providencia, but the ICJ is still determining the official maritime boundaries between the two countries.

U.S.-NICARAGUAN RELATIONS

Despite initial concerns about the impact of Ortega's November 2006 re-election on U.S.-Nicaraguan relations, the bilateral relationship, though tense at times, appears to be generally intact. One cause of tension has been President Ortega's tendency to vacillate between anti-U.S. rhetoric and reassurances that he will respect private property and pursue free-trade policies. In September 2007, Ortega denounced the United States in a speech before the United Nations as "the imperialist global empire."[9] Rhetoric aside, Ortega's interest in cooperating with the United States has been reflected in his pledge to hand over 651 Soviet-made surface-to-air missiles in exchange for military and medical equipment. Ortega has continued cooperating with the IMF, which approved a new three- year poverty reduction package for Nicaragua in October 2007. His government is also implementing the CAFTA-DR. The United States provides significant foreign assistance to Nicaragua, and the two countries cooperate on counternarcotics, trade, and security matters. The United States responded to Hurricane Mitch in 1998 by granting Temporary Protected Status (TPS) to eligible Nicaraguan migrants living in the United States. In May 2007, the U.S. government extended the TPS of an estimated 4,000 eligible Nicaraguans through January 5, 2009. In response to Hurricane Felix, a category 5 hurricane that hit Nicaragua in September 2007, the United States provided hurricane assistance to Nicaragua to help with the recovery efforts.

U.S. Aid

The United States provided Nicaragua with $50.2 million in foreign aid in FY2006 and $36.9 million in FY2007, while an estimated $28.6 million is being provided in FY2008. The Administration has also requested, but Congress has not yet considered, some $2 million in FY2008 supplemental assistance for Nicaragua as part of the Administration's Mérida Initiative to boost the region's capabilities to interdict the smuggling of drugs, arms, and people, and to support a regional anti-gang strategy. For FY2009, the Administration has requested $38 million for Nicaragua, not including P.L. 480 food aid. Nicaragua could also receive roughly $6.7 million of the $100 million in Mérida Initiative funds for Central America included in the FY2009 budget request.[10] The FY2009 request includes increases in funds for security reform and combating transnational crime, democracy and civil society programs, and trade capacity building programs to help Nicaragua benefit from CAFTA-DR.

Millennium Challenge Account (MCA)

In addition to traditional development assistance, Nicaragua benefits from its participation in the MCA, a presidential initiative that increases foreign assistance to countries below a certain income threshold that are pursuing policies to promote democracy, social development, and sustainable economic growth. In 2005, the Bush Administration signed a five-year, $175 million compact with Nicaragua to promote rural development. The compact, which entered into force in May 2006, includes three major projects in the northwestern regions of León and Chinandega. Those projects aim to promote investment by strengthening property rights, boost the competitiveness of farmers and other rural businesses by providing technical and market access assistance, and reduce transportation costs by improving road infrastructure. During a recent visit to Nicaragua, John Danilovich, director of the Millennium Challenge Corporation, asserted that, despite some political differences, he believes that the United States and Nicaragua can work together to combat poverty.[11]

Consolidating Democracy

U.S. democracy programs aim to reform government institutions to make them more transparent, accountable and professional; combat corruption; and promote the rule of law. The United States provided some $13 million to support the November 2006 elections in Nicaragua. Some 18,000 observers monitored the elections. Following the November 2008 municipal elections, USAID is expected to help increase the capacity and transparency of local governments. Other ongoing programs seek to increase citizen advocacy and the role of the media.

Human Rights

U.S. officials have expressed some concerns regarding respect for human rights in Nicaragua. According to the State Department's March 2008 human rights report on Nicaragua, civilian authorities generally maintained effective control of security forces, but there were some reports of unlawful killings involving the police. Some of the most significant human rights abuses included harsh prison conditions, arbitrary arrests and detentions, and widespread corruption in and politicization of government entities, including the judiciary and the Supreme Electoral Council. Human rights problems related to labor issues include child labor and violation of worker rights in some free trade zones. In October 2007, Human Rights Watch asserted that Nicaragua's current ban on all abortions, which includes cases where the mother's life is at risk, has put pregnant women's health at risk.[12]

Counternarcotics Cooperation

Nicaragua is a significant sea and land transshipment point for cocaine and heroin being shipped from South America to the United States, according to the State Department's

February 2008 International Narcotics Control Strategy Report (INCSR). Trafficking occurs on both the country's Atlantic and Pacific coasts, with increasing trafficking occurring on the Pacific Coast since 2006. The INCSR report asserts that Nicaraguan law enforcement were "very successful" in their counternarcotics efforts in 2007. Seizures and arrests increased dramatically, with 153 kilograms of heroin and 13 metric tons of cocaine seized (compared to 23.4 kilograms of heroin and 9.72 metric tons of cocaine in 2006) and 192 traffickers arrested (up from 67). It also asserts that corruption, particularly within the judiciary, has been an obstacle to Nicaragua's counterdrug efforts. The Ortega Administration has asked the United States for more assistance to deal with drug gangs.[13] The FY2009 budget request includes an increase in U.S. counternarcotics aid to Nicaragua. As noted above, other assistance could be provided through the proposed Mérida Initiative.

Trade

Nicaragua's National Assembly approved the CAFTA-DR in October 2005 and passed related intellectual property and other reforms in March 2006. The agreement went into effect in Nicaragua on April 1, 2006. Compared to other CAFTA-DR countries, Nicaragua has attracted textile and apparel investors because of its relatively low wage costs. In addition, Nicaragua is the only CAFTA-DR country allowed to export a certain amount of apparel products composed of third country fabric to the United States duty- free. Foreign Direct Investment (FDI) in Nicaragua totaled roughly $282 million in 2006, an 18.5% increase over 2005. In 2007, FDI rose again to some $335 million. CAFTADR has also helped to accelerate U.S.-Nicaraguan trade. In 2006, Nicaraguan exports to the United States totaled about $1.53 billion, up 29.2% from 2005. They rose again in 2007 to roughly $1.6 billion, with particularly strong growth in exports of apparel, sugar, coffee, cigars, cheese, and fruits and vegetables. For the same period, Nicaraguan imports from the United States rose 20.6% in 2006 to $752 million as compared to 2005, and by 18.5% in 2007 to $890 million. Key Nicaragua imports from the United States include machinery, grains, fuel oil, textile fabric, plastics, pharmaceuticals, and motor vehicles.[14]

Property Claims

Resolution of property claims by U.S. citizens has been a contentious issue in U.S.-Nicaraguan relations since the Sandinista regime expropriated property in the 1980s. The Nicaraguan government has gradually settled many claims through compensation, including the claims of 4,500 U.S. citizens. Fewer than 700 claims registered with the U.S. Embassy remain unresolved. The Ortega government's willingness to continue processing those claims was rewarded in July 2007 by the Administration's renewal of a waiver that allows Nicaragua to continue receiving U.S. foreign assistance despite the past expropriation of property owned by U.S. citizens.

End Notes

[1] World Bank, World Development Report, 2008 and "Nicaragua Country Brief,"December 2007.

[2] U.S. Department of State, "Background Note: Nicaragua," January 2008; *Nicaragua: A Country Study*, Tim Merrill, ed. Washington D.C.: Federal Research Division, Library of Congress, 1994.

[3] "Opposition Accuses FSLN of 'Privatizing' Venezuelan Aid," *Central America Report*, Feb 1. 2008.

[4] "Government-Opposition Relations Deteriorate in Nicaragua," *Global Insight Daily Analysis*, December 10, 2007. In January 2008, the Nicaraguan Supreme Court upheld the legality of the CPCS, which are backed by President Ortega and organized by his wife, Rosario Murillo. See "Nicaraguan Politics: Sparring Abroad, Calm at Home," *Economist Intelligence Unit (EIU)* , February 20, 2008.

[5] "Alliances Ready for Nicaraguan Elections," *Latinnews Daily*, March 4, 2008; "Nicaragua: Country Report," *EIU*, March 2008.

[6] Poverty is defined as living on less than $2 a day. Historical data is from World Bank, *Nicaragua Poverty Assessment*, June 2004. See World Bank, World Development Report, 2008; U.S. Department of State, "Background Note: Nicaragua," January 2008; "Remittances to Central America up to $12.1 billion in 2007," *Latin America News Digest*, November 7, 2007.

[7] "Nicaragua: Country Report," *EIU*, March 2008.

[8] "Iran's Push Into Nicaragua," *San Antonio Express-News*, December 17, 2007; "Nicaragua, Esso Standard Oil Sign Accord," *Latin America News Digest*, January 11, 2008.

[9] "Nicaragua's Ortega Rips U.S. 'Tyranny,'" *Miami Herald*, September 26, 2007; "Ortega's Statements Put U.S. Ties to the Test," *Miami Herald*, September 15, 2007.

[10] U.S. Department of State Mérida briefing paper provided to Congressional offices. Country breakdowns for proposed Mérida funding were not included in the FY2009 budget request.

[11] "U.S. Official: Washington Can Work on Poverty With Nicaraguan President Ortega," *Associated Press*, January 24, 2008.

[12] Human Rights Watch, "Nicaragua: Over Their Dead Bodies,"October 2007.

[13] "Nicaragua Asks U.S. For Help in Drug War," *El País*, February 6, 2008; Data on seizure and arrests for 2007 provided by the U.S. Department of State.

[14] Trade figures are drawn from the World Trade Atlas; U.S. Department of Commerce, Fact Sheet, "Nicaragua: Trade and Investment Impact of CAFTA-DR," February 2008;

In: Central America: Profiles and U.S. Relations
Editor: Brian J. Durham

ISBN: 978-1-61470-122-4
© 2011 Nova Science Publishers, Inc.

Chapter 12

PANAMA PROFILE

U.S. Department of State

Official Name: Republic of Panama

GEOGRAPHY

Area: 78,200 sq. km. (30,193 sq. mi.); slightly smaller than South Carolina. Panama occupies the southeastern end of the isthmus forming the land bridge between North and South America.

Cities: *Capital*--Panama City (1.7 million, metropolitan area). *Other cities*--Colon (204,000), David (179,674).

Terrain: Mountainous (highest elevation Cerro Volcan Baru, 3,475 m.--11,468 ft.); coastline 2,857 km. (1,786 mi.).

Climate: Tropical, with average daily rainfall 28 mm. (1 in.) in winter.

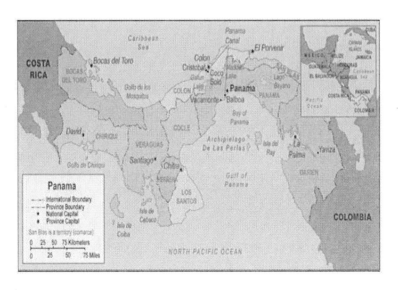

Flag of Panama

PEOPLE

Nationality: *Noun and adjective*--Panamanian(s).
Population (May 2010): 3,322,576.
Annual population growth rate: 1.503%.
Ethnic groups: Mestizo (mixed African, Amerindian, and European ancestry) 70%, Amerindian and mixed (West Indian) 14%, Caucasian 10%, Amerindian 6%. *Origins*--36.5% African, 37.6% indigenous, and 25.9% Caucasian.
Religions: Roman Catholic 84%, Protestant 15%, other 1%.
Languages: Spanish (official); 14% speak English as their native tongue; various indigenous languages. Many Panamanians have a working knowledge of English and many professional college-educated Panamanians in Panama City are bilingual.
Education: *Years compulsory*--primary grades 1-6, or through age 15. *Attendance*--95% for primary school-age children, 62.2% for secondary, 34.9% for tertiary. *Literacy*--92.6% overall; urban 94%; rural 62%.
Health: *Infant mortality rate* (2010)--11.97 deaths/1,000 live births. *Life expectancy*--77.61 yrs.
Work force: 1.392 million: Commerce (wholesale and retail)--17.9%; agriculture, cattle, hunting, silviculture--15%; construction--9.8%; industries (manufactures)--18%; transportation, storage, communications--6.9%; private home domestic services--5.8%; public and defense administration--5.6%; hotels and restaurants--5.4%; other community and social activities, teaching--4.9%; real estate activities, business, and rentals--4.8%; social and health services--3.5%; financial intermediation--2.0%.
Unemployment (2009): 7%.
Poverty rate (2006): 28.6%.

GOVERNMENT

Type: Constitutional democracy.
Independence: November 3, 1903.
Constitution: October 11, 1972; amended 1983 and 1994 and reformed in 2004.
Branches: *Executive*--president (chief of state), vice president. (A second vice presidential slot was abolished starting with the 2009 electoral cycle.) *Legislative*--National Assembly (unicameral; 71 members, reduced from 78 to 71 members for May 2009 elections). *Judicial*--Supreme Court.
Subdivisions: Nine provinces and five (indigenous) territories.

Political parties: Panamenista Party (formerly the Arnulfista Party (PA); Democratic Change (CD); National Liberal Republican Movement (MOLIRENA); Democratic Revolutionary Party (PRD); Patriotic Union (UP).

Suffrage: Universal at 18.

ECONOMY

GDP (2008 est.): $25.04 billion.

Annual growth rate: 5.6% (2010 projected); 2.4% (2009); 11% (2008); 12% (2007).

Per capita GDP: $11,900 (2009 est., purchasing power parity); $10,900 (2007); $9,900 (2006).

Natural resources: Timber, copper, gold.

Services (67% of GDP): Finance, insurance, health and medical, transportation, telecommunications, Canal and maritime services, tourism, Colon Free Zone, public administration, and general commerce.

Agriculture (6.2% of GDP): *Products*--bananas, corn, sugarcane, rice, coffee, shrimp, timber, vegetables, livestock.

Industry/manufacturing (14.2% of GDP): construction, brewing, cement and other construction materials, sugar milling.

Trade (2009): *Exports (goods)*--$821 million in exports, with salmon/tuna as the largest dollar amount, followed by beef, watermelon, shrimp, and pineapples. *Export partners* (as a percentage of total export value in 2009)--U.S. 42%, China (P.R.C.) and Taiwan 5.3%, Costa Rica 7.3%, Sweden 5.4%, Netherlands 6.5%, Spain 6.2%. *Imports (goods)*--$7.8 billion was imported in 2009: petrol and fuel oils capture the largest percentage by weight (21%) and in dollar amount (8.5%). Capital goods, foodstuffs, chemicals, and consumer and intermediate goods are the remaining imports. *Import partners* (2009)--the top five countries include the U.S. 29%, Costa Rica 5.2%, Mexico 4.5%, China 4.2%, and Japan 3.6%. *U.S. exports to Panama* (2009)--$4.3 billion: primarily oil and capital- and technology-intensive manufactured goods. *Panama exports to U.S.* (2009)--$350 million: primarily seafood and repaired goods.

Foreign direct investment (2009): $1.8 billion.

PEOPLE

Panamanians' culture, customs, and language are predominantly Caribbean Spanish. The majority of the population is ethnically mestizo or mixed Spanish, indigenous, Chinese, and West Indian. Spanish is the official and dominant language; English is a common second language spoken by the West Indians and by many businesspeople and professionals. More than half the population lives in the Panama City-Colon metropolitan corridor.

Panama is rich in folklore and popular traditions. Lively salsa--a mixture of Latin American popular music, rhythm and blues, jazz, and rock--is a Panamanian specialty, and Ruben Blades its best-known performer. Indigenous influences dominate handicrafts such as the famous Kuna textile *molas*. Artist Roberto Lewis' Presidential Palace murals and his restoration work and ceiling in the National Theater are widely admired.

As of 2009, more than 105,000 Panamanian students attended the University of Panama, the Technological University, the Autonomous University of Chiriqui (third-largest in the country), and the University of Santa Maria La Antigua, a private Catholic institution. Including smaller colleges, there are 88 institutions of higher education in Panama. The first 6 years of primary education are compulsory. As of 2007, there were there were about 445,000 students enrolled in grades one through six. The total enrollment in the six secondary grades for the same period was about 260,000. More than 90% of Panamanians are literate.

HISTORY

Panama's history has been shaped by the evolution of the world economy and the ambitions of great powers. The earliest known inhabitants of Panama were the Cuevas and the Coclé tribes, but they were decimated by disease and fighting when the Spanish arrived in the 1500s.

Rodrigo de Bastidas, sailing westward from Venezuela in 1501 in search of gold, was the first European to explore the Isthmus of Panama. A year later, Christopher Columbus visited the Isthmus and established a short-lived settlement in the Darien. Vasco Nunez de Balboa's tortuous trek from the Atlantic to the Pacific in 1513 demonstrated that the Isthmus was, indeed, the path between the seas, and Panama quickly became the crossroads and marketplace of Spain's empire in the New World. Gold and silver were brought by ship from South America, hauled across the Isthmus, and loaded aboard ships for Spain. The route became known as the Camino Real, or Royal Road, although it was more commonly known as *Camino de Cruces* (Road of the Crosses) because of the abundance of gravesites along the way.

Panama was part of the Spanish empire for 300 years (1538-1821). From the outset, Panamanian identity was based on a sense of "geographic destiny," and Panamanian fortunes fluctuated with the geopolitical importance of the Isthmus. The colonial experience also spawned Panamanian nationalism as well as a racially complex and highly stratified society, the source of internal conflicts that ran counter to the unifying force of nationalism.

Building the Canal

Modern Panamanian history has been shaped by its trans-isthmian canal, which had been a dream since the beginning of Spanish colonization. From 1880 to 1890, a French company under Ferdinand de Lesseps attempted unsuccessfully to construct a sea-level canal on the site of the present Panama Canal. In November 1903, with U.S. encouragement, Panama proclaimed its independence and concluded the Hay/Bunau-Varilla Treaty with the United States.

The treaty granted rights to the United States "as if it were sovereign" in a zone roughly 10 miles wide and 50 miles long. In that zone, the U.S. would build a canal, then administer, fortify, and defend it "in perpetuity." In 1914, the United States completed the existing 83-

kilometer (52 mile) canal, which is one of the world's greatest feats of engineering. The early 1960s saw the beginning of sustained pressure in Panama for the renegotiation of this treaty.

Military Coups and Coalitions

From 1903 until 1968, Panama was a constitutional democracy dominated by a commercially oriented oligarchy. During the 1950s, the Panamanian military began to challenge the oligarchy's political hegemony. In October 1968, Dr. Arnulfo Arias Madrid, twice elected president and twice ousted by the Panamanian military, was ousted for a third time as president by the National Guard after only 10 days in office. A military government was established, and the commander of the National Guard, Brigadier General Omar Torrijos, soon emerged as the principal power in Panamanian political life. Torrijos' regime was harsh and corrupt, but his charisma, populist domestic programs, and nationalist (anti-U.S.) foreign policy appealed to the rural and urban constituencies largely ignored by the oligarchy.

Torrijos' death in 1981 altered the tone but not the direction of Panama's political evolution. Despite the 1983 constitutional amendments, which appeared to proscribe a political role for the military, the Panama Defense Forces (PDF), as they were then known, continued to dominate Panamanian political life behind a facade of civilian government. By this time, General Manuel Noriega was firmly in control of both the PDF and the civilian government.

The United States froze economic and military assistance to Panama in the summer of 1987 in response to the domestic political crisis in Panama and an attack on the U.S. Embassy. In April 1988, President Reagan invoked the International Emergency Economic Powers Act, freezing Panamanian Government assets in all U.S. organizations. In May 1989 Panamanians voted overwhelmingly for the anti-Noriega candidates. The Noriega regime promptly annulled the election, and embarked on a new round of repression. By the fall of 1989 the regime was barely clinging to power, and the regime's paranoia made daily existence unsafe for American citizens.

On December 20, 1989, President George H.W. Bush ordered the U.S. military into Panama to protect U.S. lives and property, to fulfill U.S. treaty responsibilities to operate and defend the Canal, to assist the Panamanian people in restoring democracy, and to bring Noriega to justice. The U.S. troops involved in Operation Just Cause achieved their primary objectives quickly, and Noriega eventually surrendered to U.S. authorities. He completed his sentence for drug trafficking charges in September 2007. In August 2007, a U.S. federal court in Miami found Noriega extraditable to France to serve a sentence imposed there after an *in absentia* conviction for money laundering. Noriega was extradited to France in 2010 after exhausting all his appeals in U.S. courts, and was sentenced to a 10-year prison term.

Rebuilding Democracy

Panama's Electoral Tribunal moved quickly to rebuild the civilian constitutional government, reinstated the results of the May 1989 election on December 27, 1989, and confirmed the victory of President Guillermo Endara and Vice Presidents Guillermo Ford and Ricardo Arias Calderon.

During its 5-year term, the often-fractious Endara government struggled to meet the public's high expectations. Its new police force was a major improvement over its predecessor but was not fully able to deter crime. Ernesto Perez Balladares was sworn in as President on September 1, 1994, after an internationally monitored election campaign.

Perez Balladares ran as the candidate for a three-party coalition dominated by the Democratic Revolutionary Party (PRD), the erstwhile political arm of military dictatorships. Perez Balladares worked skillfully during the campaign to rehabilitate the PRD's image, emphasizing the party's populist Torrijos roots rather than its association with Noriega. He won the election with only 33% of the vote when the major non-PRD forces splintered into competing factions. His administration carried out economic reforms and often worked closely with the U.S. on implementation of the Canal treaties.

On September 1, 1999, Mireya Moscoso, the widow of former President Arnulfo Arias Madrid, took office after defeating PRD candidate Martin Torrijos, son of the late dictator, in a free and fair election. During her administration, Moscoso attempted to strengthen social programs, especially for child and youth development, protection, and general welfare. Moscoso's administration successfully handled the Panama Canal transfer and was effective in the administration of the Canal.

The PRD's Martin Torrijos won the presidency and a legislative majority in the National Assembly in 2004. Under Torrijos, Panama continued strong economic growth and initiated the Panama Canal expansion project.

In May 2009, Panama held general elections and selected Ricardo Martinelli as president. President Martinelli assumed the presidency on July 1, 2009 and promised to promote free trade, establish a Panama City metro system, reform the health care system, and complete the expansion plan for the Panama Canal.

GOVERNMENT AND POLITICAL CONDITIONS

Panama is a representative democracy with three branches of government: executive and legislative branches elected by direct vote for 5-year terms, and an appointed judiciary. The judicial branch is organized under a nine-member Supreme Court (each judge is appointed for a 10-year term) and includes all tribunals and municipal courts. An autonomous Electoral Tribunal supervises voter registration, the election process, and the activities of political parties. Anyone over the age of 18 may vote.

Principal Government Officials

President--Ricardo MARTINELLI
Vice President and Minister of Foreign Affairs--Juan Carlos VARELA
Ambassador to the United States--Jaime E. ALEMAN
Ambassador to the Organization of American States--Guillermo COCHEZ

Panama maintains an **embassy** in the United States at 2862 McGill Terrace, NW, Washington, DC 20008 (tel: 202-483-1407), and consulates in Washington DC, Honolulu, Houston, Miami, New Orleans, New York, Philadelphia, San Juan, San Diego, and Tampa.

NATIONAL SECURITY

As of July 2010, the Panamanian Security Forces consisted of the Panamanian National Police (PNP), the National Frontier Service (Servicio Nacional de Fronteras or SENAFRONT), the National Aero-Naval Service (Servicio Nacional Aero-Naval or SENAN), and the Institutional Protection Service (SPI--a secret service equivalent). A constitutional amendment passed in 1994 permanently abolished the military.

The lead criminal investigative entity is the Judicial Investigative Directorate (DIJ). Previously under the nominal direction of the autonomous Attorney General and known as the Technical Judicial Police (PTJ), the DIJ is now part of the PNP though it maintains investigative links with the Attorney General's office.

ECONOMY

Panama's economy is based primarily on a well-developed services sector that accounts for nearly 70% of GDP. Services include the Panama Canal, banking, the Colon Free Zone, insurance, container ports, flagship registry, tourism, and medical and healthcare.

In October 2006, Panamanians voted overwhelmingly in favor of a $5.25 billion Canal expansion project to construct a third set of locks, which is expected to be completed in 2014. The Government of Panama expects the project to be a transforming event for Panama that will provide 7,000-9,000 direct new jobs during the peak construction period of 2009-2011 and increase economic opportunities for years to come. The expansion is financed through a combination of loans from multilateral institutions and current revenues. In July 2009, the Panama Canal Authority (ACP) awarded the contract to build the locks to an international consortium led by Spain's Sacyr Vallehermoso. The locks will be 60% wider and 40% longer than the existing locks so the Canal can handle all but eight of the world's container vessels, along with supersize tankers and bulk carriers of ores and grains.

GDP growth in 2009 was 2.4%, reflecting a slowing of the robust growth of 11.0% seen in 2008. Although growth slowed in 2009, due to the global economic downturn, it has improved in 2010 and is still one of the most positive growth rates in the region. Growth has been fueled by the construction, transportation, maritime, and tourism sectors and Panama Canal-related activities. As a result of this growth, government deficit as a percentage of GDP dropped to 43% in 2009, and government-issued debt is classified as the lowest rung of investment grade. A recent United Nations report highlighted progress in poverty reduction from 2001 to 2007--overall poverty fell from 37% to 29%, and extreme poverty fell from 19% to 12%.

Panama has bilateral free trade agreements (FTAs) in force with Chile, El Salvador, Taiwan, Singapore, Guatemala, Honduras, Nicaragua, and Costa Rica. Panama signed an FTA with Canada in May 2010, but it has not yet entered into force. Panama is exploring free trade negotiations with Mexico, Colombia, the Mercosur countries, the Andean Community, the European Union, and CARICOM. The U.S. and Panama signed a Trade Promotion Agreement (TPA) in June 2007. The agreement was overwhelmingly approved in July 2007 by the Panamanian National Assembly, but has yet to be ratified by the United States Congress. Once implemented, the agreement will promote economic opportunity by eliminating tariffs and other barriers to trade of goods and services and will provide a framework for any trade disputes.

FOREIGN RELATIONS

Panama is a member of the UN General Assembly and most major UN agencies. It maintains membership in several international financial institutions, including the World Bank, the Inter-American Development Bank, and the International Monetary Fund.

Panama is a member of the Organization of American States and was a founding member of the Rio Group. Although it was suspended from the Latin American Economic System--known informally both as the Group of Eight and the Rio Group--in 1988 due to its internal political system under Noriega, Panama was readmitted in 1994 as an acknowledgment of its democratic credentials.

Panama is a member of the Central American Integration System (SICA). It is in the process of withdrawing from the Central American Parliament (Parlacen). Panama joined its six Central American neighbors at the 1994 Summit of the Americas in signing the Alliance for Sustainable Development, known as the Conjunta Centroamerica-USA or CONCAUSA, to promote sustainable economic development in the region.

U.S.-PANAMANIAN RELATIONS

The United States cooperates with the Panamanian Government in promoting economic, democratic, security, and social development through U.S. and international agencies. Cultural ties between the two countries are strong, and many Panamanians come to the United States for higher education and advanced training. In 2007, the U.S. and Panama partnered to launch a regional health worker training center. The center provides training to community healthcare workers in Panama and throughout Central America. About 27,000 American citizens reside in Panama, many retirees from the Panama Canal Commission and individuals who hold dual nationality. There is also a rapidly growing enclave of American retirees in the Chiriqui Province in western Panama.

In the economic investment arena, the Panamanian Government has been successful in the enforcement of intellectual property rights and has concluded a Bilateral Investment Treaty Amendment with the United States and an agreement with the Overseas Private Investment Corporation. Although money laundering remains a problem, Panama passed significant reforms in 2000 intended to strengthen its cooperation against international financial crimes.

The Panama Canal Treaties

The 1977 Panama Canal Treaties entered into force on October 1, 1979. They replaced the 1903 Hay/Bunau-Varilla Treaty between the United States and Panama (modified in 1936 and 1955), and all other U.S.-Panama agreements concerning the Panama Canal, which were in force on that date. The treaties comprise a basic treaty governing the operation and defense of the Canal from October 1, 1979 to December 31, 1999 (Panama Canal Treaty) and a treaty guaranteeing the permanent neutrality of the Canal (Neutrality Treaty).

The details of the arrangements for U.S. operation and defense of the Canal under the Panama Canal Treaty are spelled out in separate implementing agreements. The Canal Zone and its government ceased to exist when the treaties entered into force and Panama assumed jurisdiction over Canal Zone territories and functions, a process that was finalized on December 31, 1999.

In: Central America: Profiles and U.S. Relations
Editor: Brian J. Durham

ISBN: 978-1-61470-122-4
© 2011 Nova Science Publishers, Inc.

Chapter 13

PANAMA: POLITICAL AND ECONOMIC CONDITIONS AND U.S. RELATIONS

Mark P. Sullivan

SUMMARY

With five successive elected civilian governments, the Central American nation of Panama has made notable political and economic progress since the 1989 U.S. military intervention that ousted the regime of General Manuel Noriega from power. Current President Ricardo Martinelli of the center-right Democratic Change (CD) party was elected in May 2009, defeating the ruling center-left Democratic Revolutionary Party (PRD) in a landslide. Martinelli was inaugurated to a five-year term on July 1, 2009. Martinelli's Alliance for Change coalition also captured a majority of seats in Panama's National Assembly. Panama's service-based economy has been booming in recent years, largely because of the ongoing Panama Canal expansion project (slated for completion in 2014), but economic growth slowed in 2009 because of the global financial crisis and U.S. economic recession. Nevertheless, the economy rebounded in 2010, with a growth rate approaching 7%, and strong growth is continuing in 2011.

President Martinelli still retains high approval ratings, but he has been criticized by some civil society groups for taking a heavy-handed approach toward governing and for not being more consultative. The country experienced labor unrest in July 2010 after the government approved legislation that would have allowed companies to suspend contracts of striking workers and hire replacement workers during strikes, but the government ultimately agreed to repeal the provisions. In February 2011, the government amended the country's mining law to allow foreign investment. Indigenous groups have protested the change even though President Martinelli has vowed that his administration would not approve any mining concessions in indigenous areas.

The United States has close relations with Panama, stemming in large part from the extensive linkages developed when the Canal was under U.S. control and Panama hosted major U.S. military installations. The current relationship is characterized by extensive counternarcotics cooperation, assistance to help Panama assure the security of the Canal, and a proposed bilateral free trade agreement (FTA). U.S. bilateral assistance amounted to $7.6 million in FY2009 and $7.3 million in FY2010. The FY2011 request is for $10.6 million, while the FY2012 request is for $2.6 million. This funding does not include assistance in FY2008 and FY2009 under the Mérida Initiative to assist Central American countries in their efforts to combat drug trafficking, gangs, and organized crime; beginning in FY2010, Panama has been receiving assistance under the successor Central America Regional Security Initiative.

The United States and Panama signed a bilateral FTA in June 2007, and Panama's National Assembly overwhelmingly approved the agreement in July 2007. Neither the 110th nor the 111th Congress considered the agreement. Issues that have raised congressional concern relate to worker rights and to Panama's tax transparency. On November 30, 2010, Panama and the United States signed a Tax Information Exchange Agreement that had been a prerequisite of some Members of Congress for the consideration of the FTA. In the 112th Congress, several measures have been introduced that would express support for the FTA with Panama: S.Res. 20 (Johanns) and S. 98 (Portman), both introduced January 25, 2011; and H.Res. 86 (Frelinghuysen), introduced February 11, 2011.

POLITICAL AND ECONOMIC CONDITIONS

Panama has made notable political and economic progress since the December 1989 U.S. military intervention that ousted the military regime of General Manuel Antonio Noriega from power. The intervention was the culmination of two and a half years of strong U.S. pressure against the de facto political rule of Noriega, commander of the Panama Defense Forces. Since that time, the country has had five successive civilian governments, with the current government of President Ricardo Martinelli of the center-right Democratic Change (CD) party elected in May 2009 to a five-year term. Inaugurated on July 1, 2009, Martinelli is a businessman and former government minister. His electoral alliance, known as the Alliance for Change, also won a majority of seats in the unicameral National Assembly. Panama's largely service-based economy has been booming in recent years, spurred on by the Panama Canal expansion project that begun in 2007 that is expected to be completed in 2014.

From the Endara to the Torrijos Administration

Endara Government (1989-1994)

Before the U.S. intervention, Panama had held national elections in May 1989, and in the presence of a large number of international observers, the anti-Noriega coalition, headed by Guillermo Endara, prevailed by a three-to-one margin. The Noriega regime annulled the election, however, and held on to power. By the fall, the military regime was losing political power and relied increasingly on irregular paramilitary units, making the country unsafe for U.S. forces and U.S. citizens. On December 20, 1989, President George H. W. Bush ordered the U.S. military into Panama "to safeguard the lives of Americans, to defend democracy in Panama, to combat drug trafficking, and to protect the integrity of the Panama Canal Treaty."

Noriega was arrested on January 3, 1990, and brought to the United States to stand trial on drug trafficking charges. (Also see "Status of Manuel Noriega" below.)

As a result of the intervention, the opposition coalition headed by Guillermo Endara that had won the May 1989 election was sworn into office. During his term, President Endara made great progress in restoring functioning political institutions after 21 years of military-controlled government, and under his administration, a new civilian Public Force replaced Noriega's Panama Defense Forces. But Endara had difficulties in meeting high public expectations, and the demilitarization process was difficult, with some police and former military members at times plotting to destabilize, if not overthrow, the government.

Pérez Balladares Government (1994-1999)

In May 1994, Panamanians went to the polls to vote in presidential and legislative elections that observers called the freest in almost three decades. Ernesto Pérez Balladares, candidate of the former pro-Noriega Democratic Revolutionary Party (PRD), who led a coalition known as "United People," won with 33% of the vote. Placing a surprisingly strong second, with 29% of the vote, was the Arnulfista Party (PA) candidate, Mireya Moscoso de Gruber, heading a coalition known as the "Democratic Alliance."

In the electoral race, Pérez Balladares campaigned as a populist and advocated greater social spending and attention to the poor. He stressed the need for addressing unemployment, which he termed Panama's fundamental problem. Pérez Balladares severely criticized the Endara government for corruption, and he was able to overcome attempts to portray him as someone closely associated with General Noriega. (Pérez Balladares served as campaign manager during the 1989 elections for candidate Carlos Duque, who the Noriega regime had tried to impose on the electorate through fraud.) Instead, Pérez Balladares focused on the PRD's ties to the populist policies of General Omar Torrijos, whose 12-year (1969-1981) military rule of Panama ended when he died in a plane crash in 1981.

President Pérez Balladares implemented an economic reform program that included liberalization of the trade regime, privatization of state-owned enterprises, the institution of fiscal reform, and labor code reform. Tariffs were reduced to an average of 8%.

Pérez Balladares also worked closely with the United States as the date of the Panama Canal turnover approached. Under his government, Panama and the United States held talks on the potential continuation of a U.S. military presence in Panama beyond the end of 1999 (the date Panama was to assume responsibility for defending the Canal). Ultimately negotiations ended without such an agreement.

Although Panama's constitution does not allow for presidential reelection, President Pérez Balladares actively sought a second term in 1999. In 1997, the PRD had begun studying the possibility of amending the constitution to allow a second bid for the presidency in the May 1999 elections. Ultimately, a referendum was held on the issue in August 1998 but failed by a large margin.

Late in his administration, Pérez Balladares became embroiled in a scandal involving the illegal sale of visas to Chinese immigrants attempting to enter the United States via Panama. As a result, U.S. officials cancelled the former president's U.S. tourist visa in November 1999.[1]

Moscoso Government (1999-2004)

In her second bid for the presidency, Arnulfista Party (PA) candidate Mireya Moscoso was victorious in the May 1999 elections. Moscoso, who was inaugurated September 1, 1999, for a five-year term, captured almost 45% of the vote and soundly defeated the ruling PRD's candidate Martin Torrijos (son of former populist leader Omar Torrijos), who received almost 38% of the vote. Until March 1999, Torrijos had been leading in opinion polls, but as the election neared, the two candidates were in a dead heat. A third candidate, Alberto Vallarino, heading a coalition known as Opposition Action, received about 17% of the vote.

President Moscoso, a coffee plantation owner and Panama's first female president, ran as a populist during the campaign, promising to end government corruption, slow the privatization of state enterprises, and reduce poverty. She also promised to ensure that politics and corruption did not interfere with the administration of the Canal. The memory of her husband Arnulfo Arias, a nationalist who was elected three times as president, but overthrown each time, was a factor in the campaign, particularly since Arias was last overthrown in 1968 by General Omar Torrijos, the father of the PRD's 1999 and 2004 presidential candidate.

Although Moscoso took the presidency, the PRD-led New Nation coalition won a majority of 41 seats in the 71-member unicameral Legislative Assembly. Just days before her inauguration, however, Moscoso was able to build a coalition, with the support of the Solidarity Party, the Christian Democratic Party (which later became the Popular Party), and the National Liberal Party, that gave her government a one-seat majority in the Assembly. In August 2000, the Christian Democrats deserted the coalition and formed an alliance with the principal opposition, the PRD. However, corruption scandals in 2002 led to five PRD legislators defecting to support the Moscoso government, once again giving the president majority support in the Legislative Assembly.

The Moscoso government partially reversed the trade liberalization process of the Pérez Balladares by raising tariffs on some agricultural products, some of which reached the maximum rate allowed under Panama's World Trade Organization obligations.[2]

As noted above, Moscoso was elected as a populist, with pledges to end government corruption and reduce poverty, but her campaign pledges proved difficult to fulfill amid high-profile corruption scandals and poor economic performance. As a result, the president's popularity declined significantly from a 70% approval rating when she first took office in 1999 to only 15% in 2004.[3]

Torrijos Government (2004-2009)

In the May 2004 presidential race, Martín Torrijos of the PRD won a decisive victory with 47.5% of the vote, defeating former President Guillermo Endara, who received 3 0.6% of the vote, and former Foreign Minister José Miguel Alemán, who received 16.4% of the vote. Torrijos' electoral alliance also won a majority of seats in the unicameral National Assembly (formerly known as the Legislative Assembly), 43 out of 78 seats, which should provide him with enough legislative support to enact his agenda. Elected at 40 years of age, Torrij os—the son of former populist leader General Omar Torrijos (1968-1981)—spent many years in the United States and studied political science and economics at Texas A&M University. He served four years under the Pérez Balladares government as deputy minister of interior and justice, and as noted above, became the PRD's presidential candidate in the 1999 elections.

Leading up to the election, Torrijos had been topping public opinion polls, with 42%-49% support. In the campaign, he emphasized anti-corruption measures as well as a national strategy to deal with poverty, unemployment, and underdevelopment. He was popular among younger voters and had a base of support in rural areas. Torrijos maintained that his first priority would be job creation.[4] He called for the widening of the Canal, a project that would cost several billion dollars, and would seek a referendum on the issue. During the campaign, all three major candidates supported negotiation of a free trade agreement with the United States, maintaining that it would be advantageous for Panama. Endara and Alemán appeared to emphasize the protection of some sensitive Panamanian sectors such as agriculture, while Torrijos stressed that such an agreement would make Panama's economy more competitive and productive.[5]

During his five years in office, President Torrijos faced such major challenges as dealing with the deficits of the country's social security fund (Caja de Seguro Social, CSS); developing plans for the expansion of the Panama Canal; combating unemployment, poverty, and increasing crime; and contending with the effects of the global financial crisis and U.S. recession on the Panamanian economy.

After protests and a protracted strike by construction workers, doctors, and teachers in June 2005, the Torrijos government was forced to modify its plans for reforming the social security fund. After a national dialogue on the issue, Panama's National Assembly approved a watered-down version of the original plan in December 2005. The enacted reform did not raise the retirement age but will gradually increase required monthly payments into the system and introduces a dual pension system that combines aspects of privatization with the current system.[6] In mid-December 2007, an almost six-week strike by doctors in the public healthcare system was resolved, with the government offering a 26.7% increase in salaries equivalent and a commitment not to privatize the system.[7]

In April 2006, the government unveiled its ambitious plans to build a third set of locks that would double the Canal's capacity, and allow larger post-Panamax ships to transit the Canal. Panama's Cabinet approved the expansion plan in June, and the National Assembly approved it in July 2006. A referendum on the expansion project took place on October 22, 2006, with 78% supporting the project. The referendum was viewed as a victory for the Torrijos government, which advanced the project as integral to Panama's future economic development and one that helped restore the president's popularity.[8]

The Torrijos government's agenda also included judicial, penal and anti-corruption reforms, as well as an economic development strategy to target poverty and unemployment. The government implemented a new penal code in May 2008 that took a tougher stance on crime by increasing sentences on serious crimes and other measures. In early July 2008, Panama's National Assembly gave President Torrijos powers to carry out security sector reforms over the next two months. In August 2008, President Torrijos enacted five decree laws reorganizing Panama's law enforcement and security services, including the establishment of a National Border Service and a National Intelligence and Security Service (SENIS). Some critics fear that the actions will lead to Panama's re-militarization, while Torrijos maintains that the new agencies are needed to combat growing drug crimes.[9] In mid-December 2008, the Torrijos government approved additional changes to the penal code that increased penalties for the illegal possession of firearms and introduced sentences for attacking a police official.[10]

In order to deal with the effects of the global financial crisis, President Torrijos announced the establishment of a $1.1 billion fund in January 2009 to allow for eased credit access and loans to financial institutions in Panama. The fund—financed with support from the Inter-American Development Bank, the Andean Development Corporation, and the National Bank of Panama— was established in order to counter the tightening of credit because of the global financial crisis.[11]

Martinelli Government (2009-2014)

May 2009 Elections

Because Panama's Constitution does not allow for immediate re-election, Torrijos was ineligible to run in the May 3, 2009, presidential election, which supermarket mogul and former government minister Ricardo Martinelli of the small center-right Democratic Change (CD) party won in a landslide. Despite strong economic growth and reductions in poverty, support for the Torrijos government in its last year in office eroded because of concerns about rising crime, the effects of the global financial crisis, and problems in improving infrastructure and public services. This contributed to the PRD's poor showing in the 2009 presidential and legislative elections.

While initially in 2008 it appeared that the candidate of the ruling PRD, former housing minister Balbina Herrera, was favored to win, opinion surveys late in the year reflected a significant shift in favor of Ricardo Martinelli. Polls in January 2009 showed Martinelli with 43% support compared to 25% for Herrera and almost 15% for Juan Carlos Varela of the center-right Panameñista Party (PP).[12] In late January 2009, Martinelli and Varela struck a deal to run together in a four-party coalition dubbed the Alliance for Change, with Martinelli leading the ticket and Varela as his running mate. The new alliance further widened Martinelli's lead in opinion polls. Ultimately, Martinelli captured 60% of the vote compared to almost 38% of the vote for Herrera.[13]

Martinelli's Alliance for Change also won a majority of seats in the unicameral National Assembly that will increase the chances that the president will be able to secure enough votes to enact his legislative agenda. The Alliance for Change parties captured 42 out of 71 seats in the legislature, with Martinelli's CD winning 15 and the PP winning 21 seats. The opposition PRD, however, still remains the largest single party in the legislature, with 26 seats although internal divisions could weaken its power. [14] The Alliance for Change coalition faces some internal divisions that could jeopardize its cohesion, especially if President Martinelli's popularity begins to falter.

Challenges for the Martinelli Government

President Martinelli still retains high approval ratings, measured at over 70% in December 2010,[15] although this strong popularity masks some of the difficulties that the president has faced since taking office. Moreover, the president has been criticized by civil society groups for taking a heavy-handed approach toward governing and not being consultative with civic groups.[16] In early January 2011, a bill initiated by a deputy from President Martinelli's CD that would have amended the constitution to allow for consecutive presidential re-election was rejected by a congressional committee. Panama's next presidential election is scheduled for May 2014. During the 2009 presidential race, Martinelli reportedly agreed that the Panameñista Party would head the coalition in 2014, although some reports indicate that there are concerns that President Martinelli will not adhere to this and might support another candidate.[17]

In 2009, a significant economic challenge facing the Martinelli government was dealing with the fallout stemming from the global financial crisis, but the economy weathered the storm and avoided the contraction experienced by many Latin American economies. Panama's service-based economy had been booming in recent years, largely because of the Panama Canal expansion project, but the global financial crisis and the related decline in U.S. import demand stemming from the U.S. recession slowed Panama's economic growth. The economy grew 12.1% in 2007 and 10.1% in 2008. Initially, some economists were predicting that the economy would contract in 2009, but the economy ended up growing an estimated 3.2%. This made Panama's economy one of the few in the region registering positive economic growth in 2009. In 2010, the economy grew even faster, with an estimated growth rate approaching 7%, and the forecast for 2011 is for growth over 6%.[18]

Although Panama is categorized by the World Bank as having an upper-middle-income economy because of its relatively high per capita income level of $6,180 (2008), one of the country's major challenges is highly skewed income distribution with large disparities between the rich and poor.[19] In order to tackle poverty, the previous Torrijos government initiated a social support program of conditional cash transfers to poor families (Red de Oportunidades) and in mid-2008, the government extended the program to include the elderly living in extreme poverty. Poverty rates have been reduced from almost 37% in 2002 to almost 26.4% in 2009. Extreme poverty or indigence in Panama declined from 18.6% in 2002 to 11.1% in 2009.[20] Since taking office, President Martinelli has fulfilled his campaign pledge to provide $100 a month to poor seniors.

During the 2009 presidential campaign, Martinelli pledged to simplify the tax system by the introduction of a flat tax for individuals and for corporations in order to discourage tax evasion. Instead, however, the government enacted two tax reform measures, the first in September 2009 and the second in March 2010, that increased reliance on indirect taxes, reduced income tax rates, and broadened the tax base. These measures are expected to increase government revenue by more than 2%, according to the International Monetary Fund.[21] The tax reform in March 2010 reduced corporate and personal income tax rates, and offset the loss of revenue by raising the sales tax from 5% to 7% (not including food) and raising other taxes on banks, casinos, airlines, and the free-trade zone, with a projected net increase in revenue. The government maintains that additional revenue from the reform will be used to augment social expenditures (such as scholarships and cash transfers to the elderly), but critics of the measure maintain that the poor will be hit by an increase in the cost of living. The tax measure in 2010 prompted protests against the government in March, with violent clashes between police and demonstrators, and some 200 people were detained.[22] The tax measure, however, also led to an upgrading of Panama's investment-grade credit rating that could improve the country's financing costs and its attractiveness for foreign investment.[23]

During the 2009 campaign, Martinelli also called for a number of large public infrastructure projects, including a subway system for Panama City, a light rail system on the outskirts of Panama City, regional airports and roads, and a third bridge over the Canal. The government has already begun to move ahead on some projects. It has set up a body to oversee a plan to construct a subway system in Panama City, and in October 2010 awarded the $1.4 billion project to a Brazilian and Spanish construction consortium.

Another challenge for the Martinelli government has been dealing with Panama's rising crime, which increased significantly in 2008 and 2009, but declined in 2010. From 2000-2006, the annual homicide rate averaged between 10 and 11 homicides per 100,000 inhabitants.[24] The rate subsequently increased from 13 per 100,000 in 2007 to 19 in 2008 and 24 in 2009. Panama had 806 murders in 2009, up 23% from 2008, with drug trafficking the driving force behind the increase.[25] During the 2009 electoral campaign, Martinelli proposed a safe streets program that included increasing the number of police and raising police pay. In February 2010, President Martinelli announced an expansion of the national police force with an additional 4,000 officers that would raise the total force to over 15,000.[26] In late 2010, Panama's minister of public security said that the number of murders in 2010 had declined about 15% to 692.[27]

The Martinelli government initiated a number of anti-corruption investigations against officials from the PRD who served in government, including former President Ernest Pérez Balladares (1994-1999), but the PRD maintains that Martinelli is using an anti-corruption crusade to prosecute its political opposition. In late January 2010, Panama's Supreme Court voted to suspend Attorney General Ana Matilde Gomez on allegations of abuse of authority. Gomez had been appointed by the Torrijos government in 2005 to a 10-year post, but the Martinelli government had criticized her for failing to act in cases involving former high-ranking PRD government officials. Gomez's interim successor, Giuseppe Bonissi (reportedly a close associate of Martinelli), resigned in December 2010 after accusations that some government prosecutors had given preferential treatment to suspected drug-traffickers. President Martinelli then appointed career official José Ayú Prado to finish out the rest of Gómez's term until 2015. The appointment reportedly was lauded by civic groups who had feared that President Martinelli would again designate a close ally.[28]

Some observers have criticized President Martinelli for undermining the independence of the judiciary because of his nomination of two political allies to the Supreme Court in December 2009. The National Assembly quickly approved the nominations, and the two justices took office in January 2010. A complaint on this and the broader issue of problems with Panama's judicial system was heard by the Inter-American Commission on Human Rights in March 2010, with representatives of the Citizens Alliance for Justice (Alianza Ciudadana Pro Justicia). The alliance represents 20 Panamanian civil society organizations dedicated to implementing judicial reform and improving the administration of justice.[29] In January 2011, Panama's Supreme Court revived legislation approved in 1999 under the Pérez Balladares government that expanded the court from 9 to 12 judges and established a "court of constitutional guarantees" within the Supreme Court. President Moscoso's government subsequently repealed the legislation expanding the court and the membership of the court returned to 9 members. But in January 2011, the Supreme Court declared the Moscoso government's action unconstitutional so that the court will return to 12 members. Critics maintain that it will give President Martinelli more influence over the court.[30]

In July 2010, Panama experienced labor unrest in response to controversial legislation that would have allowed companies to suspend contracts of striking workers, allowed companies to hire replacement workers during strikes, and ended the obligatory payment of union dues. Two striking workers in the banana sector were killed in clashes with police in Bocas del Toro and more than 120 people were injured. The strike was suspended after the

Martinelli government agreed to suspend some of the controversial aspects of the law. In October 2010, the government agreed to repeal the law altogether, including the controversial labor provisions as well as provisions that would have relaxed environmental standards. The law had included provisions that would have allowed the government to eliminate environmental-impact studies for public works deemed of "social interest."[31]

On February 10, 2011, Panama's National Assembly approved legislation initiated by the Martinelli government that amended the country's mining law to allow foreign government investment in the sector. Changes to the law were reportedly motivated by plans of Canada's Inmet Mining company to secure financing from Singapore and South Korea for a mining project known as Cobre Panama.[32] Indigenous and environmental groups have protested the amendment of the mining law and have called for its repeal. President Martinelli has vowed that his administration would not approve any mining concession in indigenous areas, including in the Cerro Colorado, believed to hold the country's largest copper reserves, which lies in the indigenous Ngöbe-Buglé comarca (semi-autonomous region) in Chiriquí province. Nevertheless, indigenous and environmental groups have vowed more protests, with some calling for a referendum to settle the dispute.[33]

Human Rights Issues

The Panamanian government generally respects human rights, but, as noted by the State Department in its 2009 human rights report (issued in March 2010), human rights problems continue in a number of areas. Prison conditions overall remain harsh, with reported abuse by prison guards, and prolonged pretrial detention remains a problem. According to the report, the judiciary is marred by corruption and ineffectiveness, and is subject to political manipulation. Other serious problems include discrimination and violence against women, trafficking in persons, discrimination against indigenous communities, and child labor.

Administration of Justice. As noted above, there has been some criticism in Panama regarding the administration of justice and the independence of the judicial branch. Some observers have criticized President Martinelli for undermining the independence of the judiciary because of his nomination of two political allies to the Supreme Court in December 2009. A complaint on the issue regarding the justice system was heard by the Inter-American Commission on Human Rights on March 23, 2010, with representatives of the Citizens Alliance for Justice (Alianza Ciudadana Pro Justicia). The alliance represents 20 Panamanian civil society organizations dedicated to implementing judicial reform and improving the administration of justice.[34]

Freedom of the Press. In past years, Panama had been criticized by the State Department and international human rights groups for vestiges of "gag laws" used by the government to silence those criticizing policies or officials, but the legislature repealed these laws in May 2005. Nevertheless, as noted in the State Department's human rights report, the legislature approved penal code amendments in May 2007 that allow for the prosecution of journalists who violate the privacy of public officials or who publish classified information. The new penal code went into effect in May 2008. Nongovernmental organizations assert that the new code threatens freedom of speech and press.

As noted in the State Department human rights report, there have been some official attempts to impede freedom of speech and the press. International press rights groups such as the Committee to Protect Journalists and Reporters Without Borders have expressed concern about several cases. In September 2008, a judge ordered the seizure of a local newspaper, *El Periódico*, because it published the tax returns of a prominent businessman. The paper subsequently went out of business, but the case remains under appeal. In February 2009, a Panamanian court sentenced Jean Marcel Chéry, the director of the daily *El Siglo*, to two years in prison for trespassing in connection with reporting on alleged corruption involving a Supreme Court Justice. Chéry has appealed the decision. In September 2009, a Panamanian court convicted a journalist from *La Prensa* of libel against a former vice president.

In October 2010, a Panamanian court convicted two television journalists of defamation and banned them from working as journalists for a year, but President Martinelli immediately issued a pardon after their conviction. Press rights groups welcomed Martinelli's action, but called for legal reforms to fully decriminalize defamation.[35] In early January 2011, a draft law that would have allowed anyone convicted of insulting the president or an elected official to be sentenced to prison was withdrawn from consideration in the National Assembly. The bill had been criticized by journalists and press rights groups, and President Martinelli had warned that he would veto the measure.[36]

Past Human Rights Abuses Under Military Rule. In an attempt to redress human rights abuses that occurred under military rule (1968-1989) and to prevent their recurrence, the Moscoso government established a Truth Commission in 2001 that documented 70 cases of murder and 40 disappearances, but progress has been slow in investigation and prosecution of these cases. In 2008, Panama's attorney general announced that investigations had either been opened or reopened in 47 of these cases because of new evidence. According to the State Department's 2009 human rights report, more than half of these cases have been temporarily dismissed or closed, but 19 are at various stages of the trial process.

In 2008, the Panamanian government opened an investigation into the alleged killings of more than 20 persons who reportedly were thrown from helicopters in the Darién region in 1982-1983. In November 2009, Panama's attorney general asked a court to call to trial former Minister of Government and Justice Daniel Delgado for a killing in 1970 when he was a member of Panama's National Guard.

In July 2006, just as a human rights trial was approaching an end, a former military officer implicated in the 1970 killing of activist Heliodoro Portugal died from an apparent heart attack. In September 2008, the Inter-American Commission on Human Rights ordered the Panamanian government to pay restitution to the family of Portugal.

Displaced Persons. In recent years, violence from the civil conflict in neighboring Colombia has resulted in hundreds of displaced persons seeking refuge in the neighboring Darién province of Panama. Many of the Colombians have lived in Panama for years, have given birth to children in Panama, and do not want to return to Colombia because of family and cultural ties to local Panamanian communities. While many of the displaced are Afro-Colombians, there have also been indigenous people from Colombia who have fled to Panama because of the violence.

The State Department's 2009 human rights report notes that there are around 1,000 officially recognized refugees in Panama, but also reports that the Office of the U.N. High

Commissioner for Refugees (UNHCR) classifies some 15,000 people in the country as "persons of concern" in need of international protection. UNHCR has a permanent office in Panama and was generally allowed access to provide services to refugees, internally displaced persons, and persons under temporary humanitarian protection.

In April 2008, UNHCR lauded Panama for the approval of a new law that allows long-standing refugees (those residing 10 years or more) the opportunity to apply for permanent residency. According to UNHCR, the new law will largely affect refugees from Nicaragua and El Salvador who arrived in Panama during the Central American conflicts of the 1 980s, and will not affect the more recent refugees from Colombia.[37] According to the State Department's 2009 human rights report, 41 cases have been approved under the law and another 140 cases are pending.

Worker Rights. With regard to worker rights in Panama, the State Department's 2009 human rights report notes that while Panamanian law recognizes the right of private-sector workers to form and join unions of their choice, the law requires a minimum of 40 persons to a form a union, and only one trade union is allowed per business. The International Labor Organization (ILO) Committee of Experts criticizes both provisions as violations of workers' rights to organize, according to the State Department human rights report. Public servants may not form unions, but they may form associations, which can bargain collectively, and there is a limited right to strike with the exception of those areas vital for public welfare and security. The National Federation of Public Servants (FENASEP), an umbrella organization of 21 public-sector worker associations, is not permitted to call strikes, and the ILO has expressed concerns about this. The State Department report also noted that child labor was a problem, with violations occurring most frequently in rural areas at harvest time and in the informal sector. (Also see "Remaining FTA Issues" below.)

Human Trafficking. According to the State Department's 2010 Trafficking in Persons (TIP) report, issued in June 2010, Panama is a source, transit, and destination country for women and children trafficked domestically for commercial sexual exploitation. Non-governmental organizations report that some Panamanian children are subjected to involuntary domestic servitude. The report maintained that the government showed little evidence of progress in combating human trafficking, with weak law enforcement, no penal code prohibition against forced labor, and failure to provide adequate assistance to trafficking victims and to identify trafficking victims among vulnerable populations. As a result, Panama was placed on the Tier 2 Watch List.[38]

Panama previously had been on the State Department's Tier 2 Watch List in 2008 for failing to show evidence of increasing efforts to combat human trafficking and for failing to provide adequate victim assistance. After the 2008 TIP report was issued, the government increased prevention efforts, enacted a legislative reform package to strengthen its anti-trafficking laws, and eliminated a special visa category that had been used to facilitate the trafficking of Colombian women into the sex trade. As a result in Panama was placed on the Tier 2 List in June 2009 because of the government's anti-trafficking efforts.

U.S.-PANAMA RELATIONS

Since the 1989 U.S. military intervention that ousted the regime of General Manuel Antonio Noriega from power (see "Background on the 1989 U.S. Military Intervention"), the United States has had close relations with Panama, stemming in large part from the extensive history of linkages developed when the Panama Canal was under U.S. control and Panama hosted major U.S. military installations. Today, about 27,000 U.S. citizens reside in Panama, many retirees of the former Panama Canal Commission, and there are growing numbers of other American retirees in the western part of the country.[39]

The current U.S. relationship with Panama is characterized by extensive cooperation on counternarcotics efforts, U.S. assistance to help Panama assure the security of the Canal, and a proposed bilateral free trade agreement (FTA) that was signed in 2007. Panama is seeking the FTA as a means of increasing U.S. investment in the country, while the United States has stressed that an FTA with Panama, in addition to enhancing trade, would further U.S. efforts to strengthen support for democracy and the rule of law.

The United States turned over control of the Canal to Panama at the end of 1999, according to the terms of the 1977 Panama Canal Treaty, at which point Panama assumed responsibility for operating and defending the Canal. All U.S. troops were withdrawn from Panama at that time and all U.S. military installations reverted to Panamanian control. However, under the terms of the Treaty on the Permanent Neutrality and Operation of the Panama Canal, or simply the Neutrality Treaty, the United States retains the right to use military force if necessary to reopen the Canal or restore its operations.

U.S. Foreign Aid and Other Support

Because of Panama's relatively high per capita income level, the United States has not provided large amounts of foreign aid to Panama in recent years. Nevertheless, aid has included development assistance to improve business competitiveness and trade-led economic growth; child, survival, and health assistance to help in the fight against HIV/AIDS; and security assistance to improve Panama's counterterrorism capabilities, security programs, and maritime interdiction. In recent years, U.S. bilateral assistance (not including Peace Corps assistance) amounted to $3.7 million in FY2008, $7.6 million in FY2009, and $7.3 million in FY2010.

For FY2011, the Obama Administration requested $10.6 million in assistance for Panama, including $7.5 million in Development Assistance and $2.1 million in Foreign Military Financing (FMF). According to the State Department's FY20 11 Congressional Budget Justification for Foreign Operations, the United States will work in partnership with Panama to advance common interests in improving citizen safety, strengthening democratic institutions, enhancing the health and education of all citizens, addressing income inequality, and supporting sustainable economic growth. Congressional action on FY20 11 assistance has not been completed. FY20 12, the Administration did not request any Development Assistance, but requested $2.6 million in military assistance, with $1.8 million in FMF and $800,000 in International Military Education and Training (IMET).

These aid figures do not reflect additional assistance that Panama has been receiving since FY2008 under the Mérida Initiative, a program providing assistance to Mexico and Central American countries in their efforts to combat drug trafficking, gangs, and organized crime. In March 2009, Panama and the United States signed a letter of agreement for $2 million in funding under the initiative; overall, Panama will receive an estimated $11 million in Mérida Initiative assistance for FY2008/2009. For FY20 10, instead of funding under the Mérida Initiative, Panama will receive a portion of the $83 million in assistance under the Central America Regional Security Initiative (CARSI), a successor to the Mérida Initiative for Central America. For each of FY20 11 and FY20 12, the Obama Administration requested $100 million in assistance for CARSI. The lack of details for actual and proposed country funding for Panama under the Mérida Initiative and CARSI makes it difficult to provide an overall picture of U.S. assistance going to Panama.

A number of U.S. agencies provide support to Panama. The U.S. Agency for International Development has a mission in Panama administering U.S. foreign aid programs, and the Peace Corps has over 180 volunteers in the country working on a range of development projects. The State Department, the Drug Enforcement Administration, the U.S. Coast Guard, and the Department of Homeland Security are involved in providing counternarcotics support to Panama. The Department of Health and Human Services provided support in 2007 to launch a Regional Training Center for health-care workers in Panama City that trains students from throughout Central America. The U.S. Southern Command (Southcom) also provides support to Panama through military exercises providing humanitarian and medical assistance, and at times provides emergency assistance in the case of natural disasters such as floods or droughts. Southcom also has sponsored annual multinational training exercises since 2003 focused on the defense of the Panama Canal. Panama also hosts the Smithsonian Tropical Research Institute dedicated to studying biological diversity.

Port Security and Other Counterterrorism Efforts

Panama also participates in the Container Security Initiative (CSI) operated by the U.S. Customs and Border Protection of the Department of Homeland Security, and the Megaports Initiative run by the National Nuclear Security Administration of the Department of Energy. Three Panamanian ports—Balboa, Colón, and Manzanillo—participate in the CSI, while those three ports plus the port of Cristobal participates in the Megaports Initiative. The CSI uses a security regime to ensure that containers that pose a potential risk for terrorism are identified and inspected at foreign ports before they are placed on vessels destined for the United States. The Megaports Initiative involves deploying radiation detection equipment in order to detect nuclear or radioactive materials.

The State Department's Country Reports on Terrorism, 2009, issued in August 2010, maintained the main terrorist concerns in Panama remained the presence of the Revolutionary Armed Forces of Colombia (FARC) in the Darién province bordering Colombia and potential actions against the Panama Canal. The report noted that Panama continued to work in both areas. A small number of FARC members from the guerrilla group's 57th Front were reported to operate in the Darién, using the area as a safe haven and drug trafficking base. The members also were responsible for the kidnapping of a U.S.-Cuban citizen near Panama City in April 2008 who was held until February 2009. Panama turned over several FARC members to the United States for prosecution in 2009. In January 2010, three FARC members were killed and two were captured in a clash with Panamanian forces in the Darién. In late 2010, Panama and Colombia agreed to establish police stations near each side of the border in order.

With regard to the Panama Canal, the United States and Panama have continued to work together to plan for potential incidents that could close the Canal. Since 2003, Panama has participated in annual PANAMAX exercises with the United States and a number of other Latin American countries focused on ensuring the security of the Canal. The most recent exercise was held in August 2010 involving 16 nations in the region in addition to the United States and Panama.

Drug Trafficking and Money Laundering

An important concern for U.S. policymakers over the years has been securing Panamanian cooperation to combat drug-trafficking and money-laundering. Panama is a major transit country for illicit drugs from South America to the U.S. market because of its geographic location and its large maritime industry and containerized seaports. Moreover, the country's service-based economy, with a large banking sector and trading center (Colón Free Zone, CFZ), makes Panama vulnerable to money laundering. The State Department's March 2010 *International Narcotics Control Strategy Report* (INCSR) maintains that there was increased narcotics trafficking by Colombian, Mexican, and other drug trafficking organizations through Panama. According to the report, the increased trafficking and the presence of Colombian illegally armed groups in the Darién region contributed to rising crime, violence, and gang presence throughout the country. The country's murder rate increased from 11.1 per 100,000 to 23.2 in 2009 according to the INCSR.[40] The report also maintains that the majority of money laundering in the country relates to proceeds from drug trafficking (especially the sale in the United States and Europe of cocaine produced in Colombia) or from the transshipment of smuggled, pirated, and counterfeit goods through the CFZ.

Drug traffickers use fishing vessels, cargo ships, small aircraft, and go-fast boats to move illicit drugs—primarily cocaine—through Panama. Some of the drugs are transferred to trucks for northbound travel or are placed in sea-freight containers for transport on cargo vessels. Traffickers also utilize hundreds of abandoned or unmonitored airstrips as well as couriers who transit Panama by commercial air flights. There also has been increasing domestic drug abuse, particularly among youth.

According to the 2010 INCSR, the Martinelli government "continued Panama's history of strong cooperation with the U.S. on counternarcotics operations." In 2009, according to the report, the government seized 54 metric tons of cocaine and over $11 million in cash linked to drug trafficking.

U.S. support has included programs to improve Panama's ability to intercept, investigate, and prosecute illegal drug trafficking; strengthen Panama's judicial system; improve Panama's border security; and promote stricter enforcement of existing laws. The United States also has provided resources to modernize and maintain vessels and bases of the National Aero-Naval Service (SENAN), the National Border Service (SENAFRONT), and the National Police (PNP); assisted with training and maintenance for aircraft involved in interdiction efforts; provided training and support for a multi-agency drug interdiction team at Tocumen Airport; trained a quick response motorcycle team; and continued support for a PNP law enforcement modernization program to develop police leadership and implement community-based policing procedures.

Looking ahead, the 2010 INCSR encourages Panama to devote more resources to the modernization of its security services and to continue with reform efforts that improve public sector accountability and transparency.

Panama has made significant progress in strengthening its anti-money-laundering regime since June 2000, when it was cited as a non-cooperative country in the fight against money laundering by the Financial Action Task Force (FATF), a multilateral anti-money-laundering body. Subsequently, the government undertook a comprehensive effort to improve its anti-moneylaundering regime by enacting two laws and issuing two decrees in 2000. As a result of these efforts, the FATF removed Panama from its non-cooperative country list in June 2001.

Nevertheless, the 2010 INCSR maintains that while Panama has a comprehensive legal framework against money laundering and financial crimes, it lacks the investigative and judicial infrastructure to prosecute cases. According to the report, Panama has not prosecuted a money laundering case in recent years. The report maintained that Panama should increase its efforts to detect, prevent, and combat money laundering and terrorist financing and pointed to the need for better training and pay for law enforcement personnel and customs officials. It also called on the government to devote more resources in order to combat bulk cash smuggling and trade-based money laundering in the CFZ. As in the past, the report expressed concern about the issuance of bearer shares, and maintained that the government should take steps to eliminate or immobilize these financial instruments. Panama subsequently acted on the issue of bearer shares when on February 1, 2011, President Martinelli signed into law bearer shares or "know your client" legislation.[41]

Panama has received small amounts of regular U.S. bilateral counternarcotics assistance in recent years. For example, Panama received almost $1 million in International Narcotics Control and Law Enforcement (INCLE) assistance in FY2008 and $2.2 million in FY2009. In addition, however, as noted above, Panama is receiving an estimated $11 million in FY2008/FY2009 assistance under the Mérida Initiative, and beginning in FY2010, Panama has been receiving funding under the successor CARSI.

As noted above, the Martinelli government has moved to establish 11 air and naval anti-drug bases in the country, six on the Pacific side of the country and five on the Caribbean side. The first air-naval base was established in late November 2009 on Chapera Island off Panama's Pacific coast, and several more have been have been opened so far in 2010, including one in the Darién region. U.S. officials maintain that the United States has no plans to establish U.S. bases in Panama, while Panamanian officials maintain that U.S. support for Panama's effort will consist of providing some training and equipment.[42]

Tax Haven Status[43]

While there is no single accepted definition for a tax haven, the Organization for Economic Co- Operation and Development (OECD) has stated four criteria can be used to identify tax haven jurisdictions.[44] The criteria are no or nominal taxes and three criteria related to transparency and the exchange of information.

Whereas the OECD recognized that the determination of appropriate tax policy is a national concern, the organization has stated that the areas of transparency and information exchange require a multilateral solution. Following this belief, the OECD has an ongoing project, the Global Forum on Transparency and Exchange of Information for Tax Purposes (the Global Forum), working to increase transparency and information exchange.[45] In April 2002, Panama committed itself to meet the OECD principles on transparency and information exchange, thus averting a designation as a non-cooperative tax haven.

As of February 2011, Panama remained on the OECD's so-called "gray list" as one of just six remaining jurisdictions worldwide that have committed to the internationally agreed tax standard to help prevent tax evasion, but that have not yet substantially implemented the standard.[46] To date, however, Panama has made significant progress in moving toward implementing that tax standard. Since late 2009, it has negotiated agreements with 10 countries for the exchange of tax information. These include double taxation agreements with nine countries,[47] and most significantly, a tax information exchange agreement (TIEA) with the United States signed in November 2010. Jurisdictions that have signed at least 12 such agreements for the exchange of tax information are considered by the OECD to have substantially implemented the tax standard and are removed from the "gray list." Panama has three additional double taxation agreements in the works and their conclusion could lead to the country being removed from the "gray list." It should be noted, however, that even if Panama is removed from the OECD's "gray list," the country would still be subject to Global Forum peer reviews of its legal and regulatory system for the exchange of information for tax purposes.[48]

As noted below (see "Remaining FTA Issues"), Panama's National Assembly approved "know your client" legislation in early February 2011 requiring the identification of the owners of bearer shares, an action set forth in the joint declaration to the U.S.-Panama TIEA, and is expected to approve the TIEA itself by the end of April 2011. In the meantime, Panama does have a Mutual Legal Assistance Treaty (MLAT) with the United States, which covers the exchange of tax information if the income is effectively tied to an illegal activity, such as unreported income from drug trafficking.

It is not clear the extent to which Panama is used as a corporate tax haven. According to the most recent IRS data, 159 U.S. corporations have subsidiaries in Panama. This accounts for less than 2% of all U.S. corporations. Focusing on larger corporations, 18 of the 100 largest publicly traded companies and 14 of the 100 largest federal contractors had subsidiaries in Panama.[49] The revenue cost of these subsidiaries to the United States is unknown.

Panama's corporate tax is more similar to the United States' than other possible tax havens. The Panamanian corporate tax rate of 27.5% is at nearly the level of the top U.S. corporate tax rate of 35%.[50] In comparison, other commonly cited tax havens, such as the Cayman Islands, do not levy a tax on corporate income. As a result, the corporate tax rate is unlikely the motivating factor for the location of U.S. subsidiaries in Panama.

Non-tax factors could provide motivation for U.S. corporations to have subsidiaries in Panama. In the case of Panama, it, along with Liberia, is commonly used as a flag of convenience. Traditional reasons for choosing a flag of convenience include protection from income taxes, wage scales, and regulations. A specific example of the type of advantage flying a flag of convenience offers is bypassing the 50% duty the United States government charges on repairs performed on American-flagged ships in foreign ports. Other non-tax factors could also motivate U.S. corporations to have subsidiaries in Panama.

Over the years, Panama's lack of tax transparency and information exchange agreements could have been factors in making the country a destination for tax evasion. In 2007 testimony before the Senate Committee on Finance, several speakers commented that a lack of transparency and strong bank secrecy laws were commonly found in tax evasion destinations.[51] Other commentators specifically identified Panama as being an ideal location for tax evasion activities.[52] However, Panama's recent negotiation of tax sharing agreements with a number of countries, including a TIEA with the United States in November 2010, and its recent passage of "know your client" legislation could be factors that deter the country from being used as a destination for tax evasion.

U.S. Trade Relations

Panama has largely a service-based economy, which historically has run a merchandise trade deficit with the United States. In 2010, the United States ran a $5.7 billion trade surplus with Panama, exporting almost $6.1 billion in goods and importing $379 million. Panama was the 36th- largest U.S. export market in 2010. Panama's major exports to the United States include fish and seafood, gold, sugar, and fresh fruits. Major imports include oil, machinery and other capital goods, consumer goods, and foodstuffs.[53] The stock of U.S. foreign investment in Panama was estimated at $7.8 billion in 2009, with over 60% concentrated in depository institutions and holding companies. This almost equaled the combined U.S. foreign investment in the five other Central American nations.[54]

With the exception of two years (1988-1989), when the United States was applying economic sanctions on Panama under General Noriega's rule, Panama has been a beneficiary of the U.S. preferential import program known as the Caribbean Basin Initiative (CBI), begun in 1984. The program was amended several times and made permanent in 1990. CBI benefits were expanded in 2000 with the enactment of the Caribbean Basin Trade Partnership Act (CBTPA) (Title II, P.L. 106-200), which provided NAFTA-equivalent trade benefits, including tariff preferences for textile and apparel goods, to certain CBI countries, including Panama. In May 2010, Congress approved an extension of CBTPA benefits through September 2020 (P.L. 111-17 1). The program continues in effect until then, or the date on which a free trade agreement enters into force between the United States and a CBTPA beneficiary country.

Potential Free Trade Agreement

Panama and the United States began negotiations for a free trade agreement in April 2004. There had been expectations that the negotiations would be completed in early 2005, but continued contention over several issues and a lengthy hiatus prolonged the negotiations until December 2006. Issues included market access for agricultural products, considered sensitive by Panama; procurement provisions for the Panama Canal Authority regarding expansion activities; and sanitary control systems governing the entry of U.S. products and animals to the Panamanian market. Negotiations were suspended for some time in 2006 until after Panama held its Canal expansion referendum in October, but a 10th round led to the conclusion of negotiations on December 19, 2006.

Under the proposed agreement, over 88% of U.S. exports of consumer and industrial goods would become duty-free immediately, while remaining tariffs would be phased out over 10 years. Over 50% of U.S. agricultural exports to Panama would become duty-free immediately, while tariffs on most remaining farm products would be phased out within 15 years. In December 2006, Panama and the United States also signed a bilateral agreement on sanitary and phytosanitary measures in which Panama will recognize the equivalence of the U.S. food safety inspection to those of Panama and will no longer require individual plant inspections. Under the FTA, U.S. companies would be guaranteed a fair and transparent process to sell goods and services to Panamanian government entities, including the Panama Canal Authority.[55]

When the negotiations were concluded, then-U.S. Trade Representative Susan Schwab stated that the agreement would be subject to additional discussions on labor, and that the Administration would work with both sides of the aisle in Congress to ensure strong bipartisan support before submitting it to Congress.[56] On May 10, 2007, congressional leaders and the Bush Administration announced a bipartisan trade deal whereby pending free trade agreements would include enforceable key labor and environmental standards. This included an obligation to adopt and maintain in practice five basic internationally recognized labor principles: freedom of association; recognition of the right to collective bargaining; elimination of forced or compulsory labor; abolition of child labor; and elimination of discrimination in respect of employment and occupation.

The United States and Panama ultimately signed the proposed FTA on June 28, 2007, with the enforceable labor and environmental standards outlined in the bipartisan trade deal. Panama's National Assembly ratified the agreement on July 11, 2007, by a vote of 58 to 3, with one abstention.

The U.S. Congress had been likely to consider implementing legislation for the agreement in the fall of 2007, but the September 1, 2007, election of Pedro Miguel González of the ruling PRD to head Panama's legislature for one year delayed consideration of the FTA. González is wanted in the United States for his alleged role in the murder of U.S. Army Sergeant Zak Hernández and the attempted murder of U.S. Army Sergeant Ronald Marshall in June 1992. The State Department issued a statement expressing deep disappointment about the election of González because of his October 1992 indictment in the United States for the murder of Sergeant Hernández. Although González was acquitted in Panama in 1997 for the Hernández murder, observers maintain that the trial was marred by jury rigging and witness intimidation. González denies his involvement, and his lawyer asserts that ballistic tests in the murder were inconclusive. While polls in Panama in 2007 showed that Panamanians believed that González should have stepped down, the case also energized the populist anti-American wing of the ruling PRD.[57] González did not seek a second term as president of the National Assembly when his term expired on September 1, 2008, and another PRD official, Raúl Rodríguez, was elected Assembly president. This essentially removed the issue as an impediment to U.S. congressional consideration of the FTA.

Remaining FTA Issues

The Obama Administration has focused on working out final issues with Panama related to labor rights and tax transparency.[58]

The United States has raised labor issues related to collective bargaining rights in Panama's export processing zones (EPZs) and the right to strike in companies less than two years old. In January 2011, legislation was introduced in Panama's National Assembly addressing both of these issues.[59] Another labor issue reportedly raised by the United States, according to some press reports, relates to labor rights in a special economic zone in Panama's Baru region in the western province of Chiriquí; the law that had established the special zone made collective bargaining discretionary for six years.[60]

In addition, as noted above (see "Human Rights Issues"), certain provisions of Panama's labor laws that restrict unions have been criticized by the ILO. These include a requirement that a minimum of 40 people are needed to form a union. The Martinelli government has not agreed to make changes to Panama's labor code to reduce the number of members needed to start a union from 40 to 20, reportedly because there is no support for such a change, even from Panama's labor sector.[61]

With regard to tax transparency issues, some Members of Congress had wanted to delay consideration of the Panama FTA until the United States and Panama signed a tax information exchange agreement (TIEA). This ultimately occurred on November 30, 2010, and led some Members of Congress to maintain that the TIEA could pave the way for action on the FTA. According to the Treasury Department, the agreement will provide the United States with access to information it needs to enforce U.S. tax laws, including information related to bank accounts in Panama. It will permit both countries to seek information from each other on all types of national taxes in both civil and criminal matters for tax years beginning on or after November 30, 2007.[62]

In a joint declaration at the signing of the TIEA, both countries agreed that the agreement would take effect as soon as practicable after Panama approves implementing legislation under its domestic laws, expected before the end of 2011, to comply fully with the terms of the agreement. As noted in the declaration, Panama maintained that it would enact legislation requiring the identification of the owners of bearer shares, an issue that U.S. officials have raised with Panama for a number of years.[63] Such legislation on bearer shares, also referred to as "know your client" legislation, was signed into law by President Martinelli on February 1, 2011.[64] Panamanian Vice President and Foreign Minister Juan Carlos Varela maintained during a mid-February 2011 visit to Washington, DC, that he expected Panama's National Assembly to approve the TIEA before the end of April 2011.

In the 112th Congress, several measures have been introduced in support of the FTA with Panama. S.Res. 20 (Johanns), introduced January 25, 2011, would express the sense of the Senate that the United States should immediately approve FTAs with Panama, Colombia, and South Korea. S. 98 (Portman), introduced January 25, 2011, would, among other provisions, express the sense of Congress that the President should submit the Panama, South Korea, and Colombia FTAs to Congress and that Congress should approve those agreements. H.Res. 86 (Frelinghuysen), introduced February 11, 2011, would express the sense of the House that the Panama, Colombia, and South Korea FTAs should be implemented immediately.

On January 25, 2011, the House Ways and Means Committee held a hearing on the pending FTAs with Colombia, Panama, and South Korea.[65] On February 8, 2011, a Senate Foreign Relations Committee minority staff report urged the Administration to invest the political capital needed to secure approval of the Panama and Colombia FTAs.[66]

For details on the bilateral FTA, see CRS Report RL32540, *The Proposed U.S.-Panama Free Trade Agreement*, by J. F. Hornbeck.

Operation and Security of the Panama Canal

Historical Background and the Panama Canal Treaties

When Panama proclaimed its independence from Colombia in 1903, it concluded a treaty with the United States for U.S. rights to build, administer, and defend a canal cutting across the country and linking the Pacific and Atlantic oceans. (See **Figure 1**, *Map of Panama*, at the end of this report.) The treaty gave the United States rights in the so-called Canal Zone (about 10 miles wide and 50 miles long) "as if it were sovereign" and "in perpetuity." Construction of the Canal was completed in 1914. In the 1 960s, growing resentment in Panama over the extent of U.S. rights in the country led to pressure to negotiate a new treaty arrangement for the operation of the Canal. Draft treaties were completed in 1967 but ultimately rejected by Panama in 1970.

New negotiations ultimately led to the September 1977 signing of the two Panama Canal Treaties by President Jimmy Carter and Panamanian head of government General Omar Torrijos. Under the Panama Canal Treaty, the United States was given primary responsibility for operating and defending the Canal until December 31, 1999. (Subsequent U.S. implementing legislation established the Panama Canal Commission to operate the Canal until the end of 1999.) Under the Treaty on the Permanent Neutrality and Operation of the Panama Canal, or simply the Neutrality Treaty, the two countries agreed to maintain a regime of neutrality, whereby the Canal would be open to ships of all nations. The U.S. Senate gave its advice and consent to the Neutrality Treaty on March 16, 1978, and to the Panama Canal Treaty on April 18, 1978, both by a vote of 68-32, with various amendments, conditions, understandings, and reservations. Panama and the United States exchanged instruments of ratification for the two treaties on June 16, 1978, and the two treaties entered into force on October 1, 1979.

Some treaty critics have argued that Panama did not accept the amendments, conditions, reservations, and understandings of the U.S. Senate, including the DeConcini condition to the Neutrality Treaty. That condition states: "if the Canal is closed, or its operations are interfered with, the United States of America and the Republic of Panama shall each independently have the right to take such steps as each deems necessary, in accordance with its constitutional processes, including the use of military force in the Republic of Panama, to reopen the Canal or restore the operations of the Canal, as the case may be." However, others argued that Panama, in fact, had accepted all U.S. Senate amendments. The State Department asserted that Panama expressly accepted all amendments, conditions, and understandings to the two treaties, including the DeConcini condition. The United States and Panama signed the instruments of ratification for both treaties, which incorporated all the Senate provisions. The two countries cooperated throughout the years on matters related to the Canal and established five binational bodies to handle these issues. Two of the bodies were set up to address defense affairs and conducted at least 16 joint military exercises between 1979 and 1985 involving Panamanian and U.S. forces.

Canal Transition and Current Status

Over the years, U.S. officials consistently affirmed a commitment to follow through with the Panama Canal Treaty and turn the Canal over to Panama at the end of 1999. That transition occurred smoothly on December 31, 1999. The Panama Canal Treaty terminated on that date, and the Panama Canal Commission (PCC), the U.S. agency operating the Canal, was succeeded by the Panama Canal Authority (ACP), a Panamanian government agency established in 1997.

Under the terms of the Neutrality Treaty, which has no termination date, Panama has had responsibility for operating and defending the Canal since the end of 1999. As noted above, both Panama and the United States, however, in exercising their responsibilities to maintain the regime of neutrality (keeping the Canal secure and open to all nations on equal terms) independently have the right to use military force to reopen the Canal or restore its operations. This is delineated in the first condition of the Neutrality Treaty.

The secure operation of the Panama Canal remains a U.S. interest since the Canal is important for U.S. ocean-borne trade. The Canal's largest trade route in FY20 10 for ocean-borne cargo was between the east coast of the United States and Asia, which comprised almost 41% of total Panama Canal long tons cargo traffic. The Canal's second-largest trade route in FY20 10 was between the east coast of the United States and the west coast of South America, which comprised almost 12% of total Panama Canal long tons cargo traffic. The United States provides assistance to Panama to improve its ability to provide security for the Canal and to enhance port and maritime security. U.S. officials have consistently expressed satisfaction that Panama is running the Canal efficiently, and since 2003, the U.S. military has conducted exercises with Panama and other countries to protect the Canal in case of attack.

Headed by Alberto Alemán Zubieta, the Panama Canal Authority has run the Canal for more than 10 years and has been lauded for increasing Canal safety and efficiency. In January 2006, the Martín Torrijos government established a social investment fund backed by Panama Canal revenues that invests in schools, hospitals, bridges, roads, and other social projects. The initiative, according to the government, was designed to show Panamanians that the Canal is contributing to economic development and improving the quality of life for Panamanians.[67]

Canal Expansion Project

In April 2006, the Panama Canal Authority presented to President Torrijos its recommendation to build a third channel and new set of locks (one on the Atlantic and one on the Pacific) that would double the capacity of the Canal and allow it to accommodate giant container cargo ships known as post-Panamax ships. The project would also widen and deepen existing channels and elevate Gatun Lake's maximum operating level. The estimated cost of the seven-year project is $5.25 billion, to be self-financed by the ACP through graduated toll increases and external bridge financing of about $2.3 billion that would be paid off in about 10 years. According to the ACP, the overall objectives of the expansion project are to (1) achieve long-term sustainability and growth for the Canal's financial contributions to the Panamanian national treasury; (2) maintain the Canal's competitiveness; (3) increase the Canal's capacity to capture the growing world tonnage demand; and (4) make the Canal more productive, safe, and efficient.[68]

President Torrijos and his Cabinet approved the expansion project in June 2006, and the Legislative Assembly overwhelmingly approved it in July 2006, with 72 out of 78 deputies voting for the project. Pursuant to Panama's Constitution (Article 319), the project had to be submitted to a national referendum. The Torrijos government chose to hold the referendum on October 22, 2006, close to the anniversary of October 23, 1977, the date when Panamanians approved the two Panama Canal treaties in a national plebiscite by a two-to-one margin. The expansion project was approved by 78% of the vote.

There had been some vocal opposition to the Canal expansion project. The organization known as the Peasant Coordinator Against the Dams (CCCE, *Coordinadora Campesina Contra los Embalses*), consisting of agricultural, civil, and environmental organizations, asserted that the expansion project would lead to flooding and would drive people from their homes. An umbrella protest group known as the National Front for the Defense of Economic and Social Rights (*Frenadeso*), which was formed in 2005 during protests against social security reforms, called for a "no" vote.[69] Former Presidents Jorge Illueca and Guillermo Endara, as well as former Panama Canal administrator Fernando Manfredo, also opposed the expansion project, maintaining that the price was too high and too much of a gamble. Critics feared that the total price tag could rise considerably and expressed concern that toll increases could make alternative routes more economically attractive.[70]

The ACP is moving ahead with the Canal expansion project. The Panamanian government officially launched the project on September 3, 2007, with a ceremony led by former President Jimmy Carter, whose Administration negotiated the Panama Canal Treaties. The project is expected to be completed by 2014. In March 2009, three multinational consortiums placed bids for the multi-billion dollar contract to build the new set of locks.[71] The ACP announced in July 2009 that the consortium *Grupo Unidos por el Canal* (United for the Canal) led by Spanish construction company Sacyr Vallehermoso was the winner of the contract after posting a bid of $3.12 billion. The consortium also includes Italian, Belgian, and Panamanian companies, as well as two U.S. companies—Montgomery Watson Harza and Tetra Tech—involved as design subcontractors.[72] In January 2010, the ACP awarded the fourth and final dry excavation contract to a consortium made up of Spanish, Mexican, and Costa Rican companies. The excavation work will create an access channel linking the new Pacific locks with the Gaillard Cut, which is the narrowest stretch of the Canal.

Background on the 1989 U.S. Military Intervention

The December 20, 1989, U.S. military intervention in Panama, known as Operation Just Cause, was the culmination of almost two and a half years of strong U.S. pressure, including economic sanctions, against the de facto political rule of General Noriega, Panama's military commander. Political unrest had erupted in mid-1987 when a high-ranking Panamanian military official alleged that Noriega was involved in murder, electoral fraud, and corruption, which prompted the formation of an opposition coalition that challenged his rule. The regime nullified the results of May 1989 national elections, which international observers maintain were won by the opposition by a 3-1 margin. It also harassed U.S. citizens in Panama, including the killing of a U.S. Marine lieutenant. President George H. W. Bush ultimately ordered U.S. forces into combat to safeguard the lives of Americans in Panama, to defend democracy, to combat drug trafficking, and to protect the operation of the Panama Canal.

In early January 1990, with the restoration of democracy and Noriega's arrest to face trial in the United States on drug charges, President Bush announced that the objectives of the U.S. intervention had been achieved. In terms of casualties, 23 U.S. soldiers and three U.S. civilians were killed, while on the Panamanian side, some 200 civilians and 300 Panamanian military were killed. While Congress was not in session during the intervention, in general, Members were strongly supportive of the action. In February 1990, the House overwhelmingly approved a resolution, H.Con.Res. 262, stating the President acted

Panama: Political and Economic Conditions and U.S. Relations 177

appropriately to intervene in Panama after substantial efforts to resolve the crisis by political, economic, and diplomatic means.

Status of Manuel Noriega

In the aftermath of the 1989 U.S. military intervention, General Manuel Noriega was arrested in January 1990 and brought to the United States to stand trial on drug charges. After a seven-month trial, Noriega was convicted on 8 out of 10 drug trafficking charges in U.S. federal court in Miami in 1992, and sentenced to 40 years in prison. That sentence was subsequently reduced to 30 years, and then to 20 years. With time off for "good behavior," Noriega was scheduled to be released from jail on September 9, 2007, but remained in U.S. custody pending appeals of his extradition to France. Noriega's defense filed a final appeal with the Supreme Court in July 2009 on the grounds that Noriega was granted "prisoner of war" status under the Geneva Convention in a 1992 U.S. court ruling and therefore was entitled to return to Panama. Noriega lost that appeal, and was extradited to France on April 26, 2010. In France, Noriega faced a 10-year prison sentence for his conviction in absentia in 1999 on money laundering charges. He was eligible for a new trial upon his extradition to France and in July 2010 was again convicted of drug money laundering and sentenced to seven years in prison.

When he was released from the United States, Noriega wanted to return to Panama in order to appeal his convictions in absentia, including for two murders: the brutal killing of vocal critic Hugo Spadafora in 1985; and the killing of Major Moisés Giroldi, the leader of a failed 1989 coup attempt. Panamanian courts sentenced Noriega to at least 60 years in prison, but the law only allows him to serve a maximum sentence of 20 years, and according to some reports, 18 years of Noriega's imprisonment in the United States could be subtracted from his sentence in Panama.[73] Nevertheless, there are additional outstanding cases against Noriega, including alleged responsibility for the deaths of several members of the Panamanian Defense Forces involved in the failed 1989 coup.[74]

Noriega's attorneys argued that since Noriega had been recognized as a prisoner of war in the U.S. courts, the United States should have repatriated him to his native Panama, insisting that this complies with the Geneva Conventions. U.S. officials argued that France's extradition should be honored because Panama by law does not extradite its nationals.[75] Panama had filed an extradition request for Noriega in 1991.

While Panamanian officials called for Noriega's extradition to Panama, they did not oppose the possibility of Noriega being extradited to France and stated that the government would respect the decision of the U.S. courts on this matter. Some observers maintained that Panamanian officials were reluctant to have Noriega return because of changes to Panama's penal code that could allow Noriega to serve little, if any, of his sentence.[76] In response to Noriega's extradition to France, Panama's Foreign Minister Juan Carlos Varela maintained that the Panamanian government respected the United States' sovereign decision, but that it would pursue legal and diplomatic means to return Noriega to Panama to serve sentences handed down by Panamanian courts.[77]

On January 12, 2011, Panama requested Noriega's extradition from France for the 1989 killing of Major Moisés Giroldi, the leader of a failed coup. According to Panama's Ministry of Foreign Affairs, Panama previously had requested Noriega's extradition from France for the 1985 killing of vocal critic Hugo Spadafora and is awaiting a response.[78]

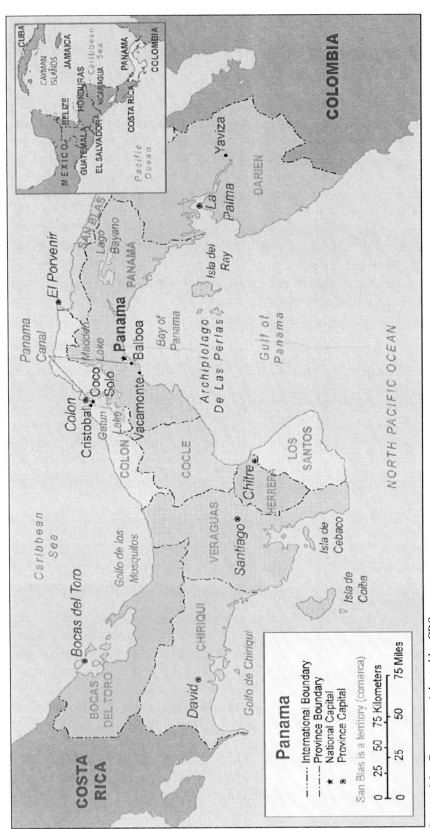

Source: Map Resources. Adapted by CRS.

Figure 1. Map of Panama.

APPENDIX A. LINKS TO U.S. GOVERNMENT REPORTS

Background Note, Panama
Date: September 16, 2010
Full Text: http://www.state

Congressional Budget Justification for Foreign Operations FY2011, Annex: Regional Perspectives (p. 745-749 of pdf)

Date: March 2010
Full Text: http://www.state

Country Reports on Human Rights Practices 2009, Panama

Date: March 11, 2010
Full Text: http://www.state

Country Reports on Terrorism 2009 (Western Hemisphere Overview)

Date: August 5, 2010
Full Text: http://www.state

International Religious Freedom Report 2010, Panama

Date: November 17, 2010
Full Text: http://www.state

International Narcotics Control Strategy Report 2010, Vol. I (Panama , pp. 506-509 of pdf)

Date: March 2010
Full Text: http://www.state

International Narcotics Control Strategy Report 2010, Vol. II (Panama, pp. 184-187 of pdf)

Date: March 2010
Full Text: http://www.state

Trafficking in Persons Report 2010 (Panama, pp. 265-266 of pdf link)

Date: June 14, 2010
Full Text: http://www.state

ACKNOWLEDGMENTS

Donald J. Marples, Specialist in Public Finance (ext. 7-3739), authored the section on Panama's "Tax Haven Status."

End Notes

[1] "Ex-Leader of Panama Linked to Visa Sales," *Washington Post*, November 27, 1999; Pablo Bachelet, "U.S. Uses Visas to Combat Corruption," *Miami Herald*, February 21, 2006.

[2] United States Trade Representative, *2006 National Trade Estimate Report on Foreign Trade Barriers*, p. 501.

[3] "Toss Up Between Torrijos and Endara," *Caribbean and Central America Report*, February 17, 2004.

[4] Frances Robles, "Ex-leader's Son Wins Presidency in Panama," *Miami Herald*, May 3, 2004.

[5] "Panama: Presidential Candidates Remark on FTA with US," *La Prensa* (Panama), January 24, 2004, translated by Foreign Broadcast Information Service.

[6] Marion Barbel, "Panamanian Congress Approves Modified Social Security Reform," *World Markets Research*, December 22, 2005.

[7] "Panama: Country Report," *Economist Intelligence Unit*, January 2008, p. 2.

[8] Richard Lapper, "Good Luck, Good Timing," *Financial Times*, July 24, 2007.

[9] "Panama: Torrijos to Undertake Security Reform by Decree," *Latin American Weekly Report*, July 3, 2008; "Torrijos Forges Ahead with Security Decrees," *Latin American Regional Report, Caribbean and Central America*, September 2008.

[10] "Panama: Torrijos Pushes Through Changes to Penal Code," *Latin American Weekly Report*, December 18, 2008.

[11] Marion Barbel, "President Unveils U.S. $1.1 billion Anti-Crisis Fund in Panama," *Global Insight*, January 23, 2009.

[12] "Panama: Martinelli's Presidential Prospects Strengthen," *Latin American Weekly Report*, January 15, 2009, "Panama Mogul Extends Lead in Election Race – Poll," *Reuters*, January 11, 2009.

[13] Tribunal Electoral de Panama, "Elecciones Generales del 3 de mayo de 2009."

[14] Asamblea Nacional de Panama, listing of deputies, available at: http://www.asamblea.gob.pa/diputados/index.html

[15] "Re-Election Motion Chucked Out in Panama," *LatinNews Daily*, January 6, 2011.

[16] "Country Report: Panama," *Economist Intelligence Unit (EIU)*, January 2011, p. 11.

[17] Ibid, p. 10; and "Re-Election Motion Chucked Out in Panama," *LatinNews Daily*, January 6, 2011.

[18] "Country Report: Panama," *EIU*, February 2011, p. 13.

[19] World Bank, *World Development Report 2010*.

[20] U.N. Economic Commission for Latin America and the Caribbean, *Social Panorama of Latin America 2010*.

[21] International Monetary Fund, "Panama: 2010 Article IV Consultation—Staff Report," October 2010, IMF Country Report No. 10/314.

[22] Inti Landauro, "Panama Approves Tax Bill to Boost Revenue, Cut Deficit," *Dow Jones Newswires*, March 16, 2010; Sean Mattson, "Panama: President Ricardo Martinelli Moves His Agenda Forward," *Noticen: Central American & Caribbean Affairs*, March 18, 2010; "Panama Unions Show New Signs of Life," *Latin American Regional Report: Caribbean & Central America*, April 2010.

[23] "Panama: Credit Update," *EIU – Business Latin America*, March 29, 2010.

[24] U.N. Development Program, *Informe Sobre Desarrollo Humano Para América Central 2009-2010: Abrir Espacios a la Seguridad Ciudadana y el Desarrollo Humano*, October 2009.

[25] "Panama: Drug-Fueled Violence on the Increase," *Noticen, Central American & Caribbean Affairs*, January 28, 2010.

[26] "Panama Politics: President's Popularity Slips," *EIU Views Wire*, March 23, 2010.

[27] "Panama, Colombia Build Police Stations on Border to Control Crime," *BBC Monitoring Americas*, December 28, 2010.

[28] "Country Report: Panama," *EIU*, January 2011, p. 9; "People Profile, José Eduardo Ayú Canals, Panama," *Latin NewsDaily*, January 25, 2011

[29] See the website of the Citizens Alliance for Justice at: http://www.alianzaprojusticia.org.pa/ ; The Washington, D.C.- based Due Process of Law Foundation has also done work on the issue of Panama's judicial system. For more information, see: http://www.dplf.org/index.php?c_ID=395&catID=1

[30] "Country Report: Panama," *EIU*, February 2011, p. 10.

[31] Sean Mattson, "Panamanian President Ricardo Martinelli Reverses Course on Controversial Legislation," *Noticen, Central & Caribbean Affairs*, November 11, 2010; "Panama: Martinelli Performs Major U-Turn," *Latin American Regional Report, Caribbean & Central America*, October 2010.

32 "Panama: Martinelli Hits Another Nerve," *Latin American Weekly Report*, February 24, 2010.

33 "Decree Fails to Resolve Panama Mining Row," *Agence France Presse*, February 23, 2011.

34 See the website of the Citizens Alliance for Justice at: http://www.alianzaprojusticia.org.pa/; The Washington, D.C.- based Due Process of Law Foundation has also done work on the issue of Panama's judicial system. For more information, see: http://www.dplf.org/index.php?c_ID=395&catID=1

35 "In Panama, Defamation Conviction Draws Outcry," Committee to Protect Journalists, October 7, 2010.

36 "Withdrawal of Proposal to Introduce Jail Terms for Insulting the President," Reporters Without Borders, January 12, 2011.

37 "UNHCR Welcomes New Panama Law," *UNHCR Briefing Notes*, April 1, 2008.

38 U.S. Department of State, "Trafficking in Persons Report," June 2010. Also see CRS Report RL3 3200, *Trafficking in Persons in Latin America and the Caribbean*, by Clare Ribando Seelke.

39 U.S. Department of State, Background Note: Panama, September 16, 2010.

40 In addition, see: United Nations Development Programme, *Human Development Report for Central America, 2009- 2010, Opening Spaces to Citizen Security and Human Development*, p. 12; and Louisa Reynolds, "Panama: Drug- Fueled Violence on the Increase," *Noticen: Central American & Caribbean Affairs*, January 28, 2010.

41 Information provided to CRS by the Department of State, February 15, 2011.

42 "Panamanian Minister Says Foreign Anti-Drugs Aid 'Nothing Substantial,'" *BBC Monitoring Americas*, September 30, 2009; and "Panama's Naval Air Stations Not Covert U.S. Military Bases – Minister," *BBC Monitoring Americas*, December 6, 2009.

43 Prepared by Donald J. Marples, Specialist in Public Finance, ext. 7-3739

44 A full discussion of the criteria can be viewed at http://www.oecd.org/document/23/0,3343,en_2649_33745_30575447_1_1_1_1,00.html and a broader discussion of tax havens can be found in CRS Report R40623, *Tax Havens: International Tax Avoidance and Evasion*, by Jane G. Gravelle.

45 For background, see as CRS Report R401 14, *The OECD Initiative on Tax Havens*, by James K. Jackson.

46 Organization for Economic Co-operation and Development, "A Progress Report on the Jurisdictions Surveyed by the OECD Global Forum in Implementing the Internationally Agreed Tax Standard," February 18, 2011, up-to date list available at: http://www.oecd.org/dataoecd/50/0/43606256.pdf.

47 The nine countries are Mexico, Barbados, Portugal, Qatar, Luxemburg, Netherlands, Singapore, South Korea, and Italy. Three additional double taxation agreements with France, Belgium, and Ireland are reportedly in the works. Information provided to CRS by the Embassy of Panama, February 7, 2011.

48 In September 2010, the OECD published a phase 1 peer review report that highlighted significant problems with Panama's legal and regulatory framework for transparency and exchange of information for tax purposes as of May 2010. See: Global Forum on Transparency and Exchange of Information for Tax Purposes, "Peer Review Report, Phase 1, Legal and Regulatory Framework: Panama," September 2010.

49 U.S. Government Accountability Office, *International Taxation: Large U.S. Corporations and Federal Contractors with Subsidiaries in Jurisdictions Listed as Tax Haven or Financial Privacy Jurisdictions*, GAO-09-157, December 18, 2008.

50 In 2012 the Panamanian corporate income tax rates is scheduled to fall to 25%. In addition, companies in the energy, telecommunication, financial, insurance, banking, and mining industries are currently taxes at a rate of 30%, falling to 27.5% in 2012, and 25% in 2014.

51 U.S. Congress, Senate Committee on Finance, *Offshore Tax Evasion: Stashing Cash Overseas*, 110th Cong., 1st sess., May 3, 2007.

52 Martin A. Sullivan, "Ah, Panama," *Tax Notes*, June 25, 2007, p. 1246.

53 Department of Commerce statistics, as presented by Global Trade Atlas.

54 U.S. Department of Commerce, Bureau of Economic Analysis, "U.S. Direct Investment Abroad Tables," *Survey of Current Business*, September 2010, p. 71.

55 Office of the United States Trade Representative, "Free Trade with Panama, Brief Summary of the Agreement," December 19, 2006.

56 Rosella Brevetti, "Panama, United States Conclude Negotiations on Free Trade Pact," but Labor Issues Remain," *International Trade Daily*, December 20, 2006.

57 Marc Lacey, "Fugitive from U.S. Justice Leads Panama's Assembly," *New York Times*, November 28, 2007.

58 "U.S. Presses on Panama, Colombia Deals," *Reuters News*, May 5, 2009.

59 Information provided to CRS by the Department of State, February 15, 2011.

60 "U.S. Focused on Labor Laws for New Panama Economic Zone," *Inside U.S. Trade*, February 17, 2011.

61 Information provided to CRS by the Department of State, February 15, 2011.

62 U.S. Department of the Treasury, Press Release, "U.S., Panama Sign New Tax Information Exchange Agreement," December 1, 2010. See the full text of the TIEA, available at: http://www.treasury.gov/resource-center/taxpolicy/treaties

63 U.S.-Panama Tax Information Exchange Agreement, Joint Declaration, November 30, 2010, available at: http://www.treasury.gov/resource-center/tax-policy

64 Information provided to CRS by the Department of State, February 15, 2011.

[65] See the witness testimony from the hearing, available at: http://waysandmeans.house.gov/Calendar/EventSingle.aspx?EventID=220430

[66] U. S. Congress, Senate Committee on Foreign Relations, *Losing Jobs and Alienating Friends: The Consequences of Falling Behind on Free Trade with Colombia and Panama*, committee print, 112th Cong., 1st sess., February 8, 2011, S. Prt. 112-?? (Washington: GPO, 2011), available at: http://lugar.senate.gov/issues

[67] Rainbow Nelson, "Canal Cash to Pay for Social Development," *Lloyd's List*, January 18, 2006.

[68] Autoridad del Canal de Panama (ACP), "Proposal for the Expansion of the Panama Canal, Third Set of Locks Project," April 24, 2006.

[69] "Torrijos Appeals for Approval of Canal Expansion," *Latinnews Daily*, September 1, 2006.

[70] "Panama: Torrijos Reveals Plans to Expand Canal," *Latinnews Daily*, April 25, 2006; Chris Kraul and Ronald D.White, "Panama is Preparing to Beef up the Canal," *Los Angeles Times*, April 24, 2006; John Lyons, "Panama Takes Step Toward Expanding the Canal," *Wall Street Journal*, April 24, 2006.

[71] "Panama: Groups Bid on Canal Expansion," *Economist Intelligence Unit, Business Latin America*, March 9, 2009.

[72] "Unidos por El Canal Virtual winner of ACP contract," *Business News Americas*, July 8, 2009; and "Panama Canal Announces 'Best Value' Proposal for New Set of Locks Expansion Contract," *States News Service*, July 9, 2009.

[73] Kathia Martinez, "A Homecoming for Noriega after Miami Release? Many Hope Not," *Associated Press Newswires*, August 12, 2007.

[74] "Torrijos on Edge over Noriega Release," *Latin American Regional Report, Caribbean and Central America*, August 2007.

[75] Carmen Gentile, "Noriega Court Bid Called a Charade; Aims to Avoid Extradition," *Washington Times*, August 14, 2007.

[76] Marc Lacey, "An Ambivalent Panama Weights Noriega's Debt and Threat," *New York Times*, July 29, 2007.

[77] "Panama's Noriega Extradited to France," *LatinNews Daily*, April 27, 2010.

[78] República de Panamá, Ministerio de Relaciones Exteriores, Comunicado de Prensa, "Extradición de Manuel Antonio Noriega por el caso Giroldi," January 12, 2011.

INDEX

#

20th century, 6, 22, 72

A

Abkhazia, 133
abolition, 14, 22, 172
Abraham, 63
abuse, 109, 162, 163
access, 5, 16, 17, 30, 41, 49, 67, 81, 82, 91, 92, 99, 111, 133, 135, 160, 165, 173, 176
accountability, 64, 67, 169
accounting, 80, 95
adaptation, 27
adult literacy, 24
adults, 58
advocacy, 17, 141
Afro-Caribbean origin, ix, 127
age, vii, 3, 12, 70, 91, 146, 150, 158
agencies, 43, 53, 72, 73, 134, 152, 159, 167
agricultural exports, 38, 90, 91, 172
agricultural sector, 6, 41, 90, 130, 139
agriculture, 6, 7, 13, 16, 42, 48, 58, 70, 72, 79, 127, 131, 146, 159
AIDS, 91
Air Force, 43
airports, 64, 161
alien smuggling, 135
ambassadors, 111
annual rate, 16
apparel industry, 7
apparel products, 95, 142
appropriations, 51, 52, 94, 117
Appropriations Act, 29, 51, 117, 124
aquifers, 17
arbitration, 8, 133
Argentina, 32, 33, 88, 90

armed forces, 15, 58, 65, 72, 73, 76, 79, 80, 112
armed groups, 103, 168
arms control, 43
arrest, viii, 55, 84, 105, 108, 118, 176
arrests, 141, 142, 143
Asia, 17, 175
assets, 149
asylum, 119
atmosphere, 89
authorities, 42, 54, 62, 98, 106, 117, 119, 139, 141, 149
authority, 71, 73, 77, 79, 109, 134, 162
autonomy, 37
awareness, 99

B

ban, 141
banking, 41, 151, 168, 181
banking sector, 168
banks, 3, 13, 24, 161
Barbados, 181
bargaining, 130, 173
barriers, 78, 80, 152
base, 48, 61, 76, 78, 85, 98, 118, 159, 167, 169
basic education, 134
basic needs, 114
beef, 13, 95, 127, 147
Belgium, 181
beneficiaries, 40, 95
benefits, 8, 9, 18, 30, 52, 66, 132, 139, 141, 171
bilateral relationship, 92, 140
biodiversity, 16, 66
births, 2, 126, 132, 146
black minority, ix, 127
blockades, 91
blueprint, 67
Bolivia, 33, 55, 121, 140

bonds, 5
border control, 77
border crossing, 50
border security, 168
Brazil, 24, 32, 48, 90, 114, 116, 119
breakdown, 58
Britain, 128
burn, 76
business education, 19
businesses, 26, 42, 52, 79, 93, 95, 132, 133, 141

C

Cabinet, 4, 12, 159, 175
cabinet members, 74
call centers, 37
candidates, 62, 72, 74, 85, 110, 113, 126, 149, 158, 159
cane sugar, 3, 7
capacity building, 41, 52, 115, 140
capital goods, 37, 171
capital markets, 49, 96
capital projects, 6
capitalism, 132
carbon, 16, 25, 26, 27
carbon emissions, 27
carbon neutral, 16, 25
Caribbean, viii, ix, 3, 4, 5, 7, 8, 12, 17, 30, 31, 32, 33, 42, 46, 54, 55, 56, 71, 80, 92, 95, 100, 102, 111, 121, 126, 127, 129, 137, 147, 169, 171, 180, 181, 182
Caribbean coast, ix, 42, 126, 127, 129
Caribbean countries, 80, 121
Caribbean Islands, 3
Caribbean nations, 5
cash, 24, 98, 161, 168, 169
cash flow, 98
casinos, 161
Catholic Church, 61, 108
cattle, 107, 127, 132, 146
caudillos (strongmen), ix, 137
Census, 31
challenges, viii, 16, 25, 45, 48, 78, 81, 86, 87, 91, 92, 98, 105, 133, 139, 159, 161
Chamber of Commerce, 4, 44
chaos, 109
checks and balances, 14
cheese, 142
chemical, 37, 59
chemicals, 3, 26, 71, 147
Chicago, 40, 63, 76
child labor, 141, 163, 165, 172
children, 15, 24, 90, 91, 96, 99, 146, 164, 165

Chile, 17, 32, 41, 101, 151
China, 3, 13, 17, 18, 23, 24, 25, 32, 59, 80, 147
cities, 1, 11, 17, 35, 57, 71, 75, 98, 125, 127, 145
citizens, vii, 19, 21, 24, 44, 67, 73, 78, 81, 91, 97, 134, 142, 152, 166, 176
citizenship, 44
City, vii, ix, 1, 3, 5, 6, 57, 59, 60, 62, 145, 146, 147, 150, 161, 167
civil liberties, 75, 85, 110, 119
civil society, 65, 87, 99, 101, 119, 140, 155, 160, 162, 163
civil war, viii, ix, 14, 18, 22, 37, 38, 39, 41, 45, 47, 49, 76, 128, 137
civilization, 3, 59
climate, 6, 16, 19, 42, 78, 89, 92, 132
closure, 6
clothing, 3, 37, 59
Coast Guard, 9, 15, 19, 29, 167
cocaine, 53, 97, 98, 141, 168
coffee, 13, 16, 36, 37, 41, 42, 54, 59, 64, 70, 71, 90, 95, 127, 131, 132, 142, 147, 158
collaboration, 133
collective bargaining, 172
colleges, 148
Colombia, 41, 50, 67, 89, 101, 128, 133, 140, 152, 164, 165, 167, 168, 173, 174, 180, 181, 182
colonization, 148
commerce, 2, 58, 64, 147
commercial, vii, 3, 5, 7, 22, 30, 42, 66, 71, 72, 76, 96, 99, 111, 133, 165, 168
commercial ties, 22
commodity, 7, 131
Common Market, 4, 37, 43, 59, 127
communication, 3, 98
communities, 42, 52, 127, 135, 163, 164
community, viii, 8, 17, 19, 44, 73, 74, 81, 82, 84, 85, 90, 91, 105, 111, 112, 113, 114, 146, 152, 169
compensation, 134, 142
competition, 15
competitiveness, 64, 73, 141, 166, 175
competitors, 21, 25
complement, 8, 24, 52
compliance, 39, 66, 95, 111, 116
composition, 54
conflict, 37, 47, 55, 60, 61, 62, 118, 128, 138, 164
Congo, 65
Congress, ix, 4, 29, 33, 46, 50, 52, 55, 58, 60, 61, 62, 63, 66, 70, 73, 74, 75, 81, 82, 84, 85, 86, 88, 91, 93, 94, 97, 98, 100, 102, 103, 105, 106, 107, 108, 109, 110, 112, 113, 114, 116, 117, 118, 120, 121, 122, 140, 143, 152, 156, 171, 172, 173, 176, 180, 181, 182
consensus, 31, 40, 74

consent, 174
conservation, 16, 18, 21, 26
Consolidated Appropriations Act, 29, 117
consolidation, 106, 117, 138
conspiracy, 89
Constitution, 2, 12, 14, 36, 58, 70, 109, 122, 126, 146, 160, 175
constitutional amendment, 65, 130, 149, 151
construction, 3, 9, 13, 16, 36, 50, 58, 59, 70, 98, 127, 132, 146, 147, 151, 159, 162, 176
consulting, 88
consumer goods, 3, 13, 37, 127, 171
Container Security Initiative, 78, 99, 167
containers, 99, 167, 168
Continental, 6
Continental Airlines, 6
control narcotics and crime, ix, 137
controversial, 31, 162
controversies, 73
conviction, 149, 164, 177
cooling, 17
cooperation, 5, 19, 55, 65, 77, 80, 92, 94, 98, 99, 115, 121, 152, 155, 166, 168
coordination, 98
copper, 147, 163
corruption, 22, 25, 31, 38, 39, 49, 50, 61, 62, 63, 66, 72, 73, 79, 80, 87, 92, 99, 100, 113, 120, 128, 129, 138, 141, 142, 157, 158, 159, 162, 163, 164, 176
cost, 6, 60, 73, 80, 91, 96, 159, 161, 170, 175
cost of living, 73, 161
Costa Rica, v, vii, viii, 11, 12, 13, 14, 15, 16, 17, 18, 19, 21, 22, 23, 24, 25, 26, 27, 28, 29, 30, 31, 32, 33, 41, 74, 78, 84, 101, 105, 108, 111, 115, 116, 118, 122, 123, 127, 133, 137, 147, 151, 176
counterterrorism, 73, 77, 166
country of origin, vii, 13
Coup, 32, 74, 100, 101, 112, 113, 120, 122, 123
credentials, 32, 152
credit rating, 161
crimes, 39, 53, 74, 87, 88, 89, 109, 111, 113, 135, 159
criminal activity, 67
criminal gangs, 50, 90
criminal investigations, 50, 99
criminal justice system, 53
criminals, 97, 98
crisis management, 79
critical infrastructure, 80
criticism, 110, 163
crops, 93
crown, 4
crude oil, 3, 59

CSS, 159
Cuba, 18, 24, 30, 32, 41, 48, 55, 60, 77, 121, 122, 132, 139
cultivation, 6, 13
culture, viii, ix, 55, 71, 97, 121, 127, 147
currency, 47, 49
Customs and Border Protection, 99, 167

D

damages, 48, 79
Daniel Ortega, ix, 126, 128, 129, 131, 133, 137, 138
death penalty, 98
deaths, 42, 48, 60, 85, 110, 126, 132, 146, 177
decision makers, 133
defamation, 164
deficit, 64, 151
deforestation, 21, 26
Delta, 6
democracy, viii, ix, 2, 4, 14, 15, 18, 22, 27, 45, 50, 61, 66, 78, 81, 90, 93, 106, 109, 114, 115, 117, 121, 130, 137, 138, 139, 140, 141, 146, 149, 150, 156, 166, 176
Democratic Change (CD) party, ix, 155, 156, 160
democratic elections, 138
Democratic Party, 2, 4, 36, 70, 75, 158
Democratic Revolutionary Party (PRD), ix, 147, 150, 155, 157
demonstrations, 85, 110
Denmark, 27
Department of Commerce, 181
Department of Energy, 99, 167
Department of Health and Human Services, 167
Department of Homeland Security, 56, 99, 103, 104, 167
deployments, 94
Deportations, 96
depository institutions, 171
deposits, 16
depression, 64
destiny, 148
detection, 53, 167
detention, 54, 85, 88, 110, 119, 163
detergents, 71
developed nations, 27
developing countries, 51
developing nations, 27
development assistance, 9, 18, 141, 166
DHS, 104
direct investment, 80, 147
disappointment, 116, 172
disaster, 22, 65, 78, 79, 80, 94
disaster assistance, 65

disaster relief, 78, 79, 80, 94
disbursement, 132
discrimination, 85, 110, 130, 163, 172
displaced persons, 62, 164
dissatisfaction, 73
distribution, 15, 16, 41, 126, 131
diversification, 41, 76
diversity, 26, 27, 167
doctors, 159
domestic demand, 48, 76
domestic investment, 131, 133
domestic labor, 95
domestic laws, 173
Dominican Republic, ix, 15, 17, 30, 31, 33, 41, 46, 50, 54, 64, 78, 84, 92, 95, 103, 121, 132, 137
donors, 40, 132
downsizing, 65
draft, 6, 50, 61, 88, 164
dream, 148
drought, 65
drug abuse, 168
drug smuggling, 53
drug trafficking, 29, 43, 49, 75, 97, 98, 149, 156, 162, 167, 168, 170, 176, 177
drugs, 52, 53, 140, 168

E

earnings, 23, 81, 91
earthquakes, 41, 42, 53, 59
economic activity, 6, 91
economic assistance, 8, 9, 79, 124
economic crisis, 6, 16, 64, 92
economic development, ix, 6, 25, 43, 72, 87, 132, 134, 137, 139, 152, 159, 175
economic downturn, 24, 76, 151
economic growth, vii, ix, 6, 8, 16, 18, 21, 23, 24, 26, 42, 49, 64, 66, 72, 78, 81, 83, 87, 91, 93, 135, 150, 155, 160, 161, 166
economic integration, 41, 65
economic migrants, 99
economic performance, 7, 158
economic policy, 16
economic problem, 91, 114
economic progress, ix, 155, 156
economic reform, viii, 45, 50, 60, 82, 92, 138, 150, 157
economic reforms, viii, 45, 50, 60, 82, 92, 138, 150
economic resources, 16
economics, 158
Ecuador, 41, 55, 90, 121
education, 18, 24, 42, 52, 55, 67, 77, 79, 91, 93, 115, 121, 148, 166

educational attainment, 24
educational opportunities, 15
El Salvador, v, vii, viii, 3, 17, 18, 28, 30, 35, 36, 37, 38, 39, 40, 41, 42, 43, 44, 45, 46, 47, 48, 49, 50, 51, 52, 53, 54, 55, 56, 66, 72, 76, 77, 78, 97, 99, 102, 103, 127, 133, 138, 151, 165
election, 14, 18, 31, 38, 45, 47, 51, 61, 62, 72, 73, 74, 77, 85, 90, 94, 98, 100, 105, 112, 113, 114, 120, 121, 123, 129, 130, 134, 140, 149, 150, 156, 157, 158, 159, 160, 172
election fraud, 129
electricity, 3, 6, 15, 16, 17, 132
e-mail, 76
embargo, 128
embassy, 5, 15, 24, 63, 76, 84, 112, 115, 119, 120, 121, 131, 151
emergency, 50, 51, 74, 115, 119, 167
emigration, 130
employees, 95
employment, 41, 52, 54, 76, 79, 95, 96, 172
employment growth, 41
employment opportunities, 41
encouragement, 148
enemies, 32, 33
energy, 6, 16, 26, 49, 66, 91, 95, 132, 139, 181
energy prices, 132
enforcement, 41, 61, 64, 98, 133, 152, 168
engineering, 78, 149
enrollment, 148
environment, 5, 17, 18, 21, 26, 27, 41, 65, 77, 78, 93
environmental degradation, 18, 21, 26
environmental issues, 52
environmental management, 79
environmental organizations, 176
environmental protection, 21, 26, 66, 78
environmental standards, 64, 163, 172
epidemic, 91
equipment, 3, 13, 23, 29, 40, 53, 59, 99, 127, 132, 140, 167, 169
ETA, 128
ethanol, 54, 132
ethyl alcohol, 37
EU, 7, 17, 56, 86, 113, 127
Europe, 7, 111, 168
European Union, 7, 17, 23, 41, 91, 111, 127, 152
evacuation, 42
evidence, 55, 89, 95, 97, 164, 165
evolution, 148, 149
exchange rate, 49, 70, 100, 121
exclusion, 108
executive branch, 108, 139
exercise, 14, 120, 121, 168
exile, viii, 84, 101, 105, 107, 108, 109

Index

187

expenditures, 6, 25, 132
expertise, 79
exploitation, 26, 99, 165
export market, 16, 64, 171
exporter, 16, 80
export-led growth, 41
exports, 7, 18, 23, 31, 48, 54, 64, 76, 80, 95, 114, 127, 131, 132, 137, 142, 147, 171, 172
expulsion, 75
external shocks, 49, 91
extraction, vii, 37
extradition, 62, 177
extreme poverty, 151, 161

F

faith, 73, 102
families, 24, 41, 44, 135, 161
family members, 96
Farabundo Marti National Liberation Front, viii, 18, 36, 38, 45
farmers, 52, 93, 115, 141
farms, 79
FBI, 43, 97
FDI, 22, 23, 64, 80, 142
FDI inflow, 64
fear, 87, 95, 159
Federal Bureau of Investigation, 43, 97
Federal Register, 96, 103
fiber, 80
financial, vii, ix, 3, 6, 21, 24, 27, 31, 41, 45, 49, 51, 52, 53, 64, 67, 81, 82, 83, 91, 92, 96, 111, 114, 127, 133, 146, 152, 155, 159, 160, 161, 169, 175, 181
financial crimes, 152, 169
financial crisis, vii, ix, 21, 24, 31, 45, 49, 51, 64, 81, 91, 96, 111, 114, 155, 159, 160, 161
financial institutions, 64, 83, 91, 96, 160
financial markets, 67
financial sector, 64
financial sector reforms, 64
financial support, 82, 92
financial system, 82
firearms, 49, 159
fiscal deficit, 49, 73, 91, 114
fiscal stimulus, vii, 21
fiscal surpluses, 16
fish, 171
fisheries, 13, 70, 127, 133
fishing, 2, 6, 19, 127, 131, 133, 168
fixed rate, 3
flexibility, 24
flights, 168

flooding, 6, 42, 48, 93, 176
floods, 59, 167
flowers, 59, 64
fluctuations, 7
folklore, 147
food, 3, 13, 37, 54, 59, 64, 65, 80, 95, 131, 140, 161, 172
food safety, 172
force, 2, 7, 9, 12, 17, 19, 25, 30, 36, 39, 42, 58, 64, 65, 70, 73, 75, 78, 79, 85, 88, 92, 95, 108, 109, 110, 118, 119, 126, 132, 135, 141, 146, 148, 150, 151, 153, 162, 166, 171, 174, 175
Ford, 149
foreign aid, 52, 93, 94, 115, 139, 140, 166, 167
foreign assistance, 52, 79, 82, 90, 92, 93, 102, 115, 117, 118, 119, 140, 141, 142
Foreign Broadcast Information Service, 180
foreign direct investment, 6, 22, 64, 95
foreign exchange, 27, 96
foreign firms, 31
foreign investment, 16, 18, 64, 80, 132, 139, 155, 161, 171
foreign language, 19
foreign policy, 23, 24, 46, 67, 133, 149
formation, 111, 116, 176
France, 32, 64, 100, 101, 102, 122, 123, 124, 149, 177, 181, 182
fraud, 47, 129, 135, 157, 176
free market economy, 134
free trade, 16, 17, 18, 22, 23, 25, 27, 41, 43, 54, 66, 131, 141, 150, 151, 156, 159, 166, 171, 172
free trade area, 41
Free Trade Area of the Americas, 17, 43, 55
freedom, 37, 67, 85, 89, 110, 118, 119, 130, 163, 164, 172
freezing, 149
friction, 19, 47
fruits, 13, 70, 142, 171
fuel distribution, 95
funding, 9, 24, 29, 50, 52, 53, 79, 93, 94, 135, 143, 156, 167, 169
funds, 8, 26, 28, 29, 33, 51, 52, 79, 93, 102, 115, 124, 132, 138, 140

G

gangs, 43, 49, 53, 55, 97, 98, 142, 156, 167
GAO, 181
GDP, 2, 3, 5, 12, 13, 16, 24, 25, 32, 36, 37, 41, 48, 59, 64, 65, 70, 71, 76, 91, 96, 127, 131, 139, 147, 151
general election, 4, 14, 72, 85, 107, 108, 109, 112, 115, 117, 150

188   Index

Geneva Convention, 177
Georgia, 133
Germany, 64
global economic conditions, vii, 21
good behavior, 177
goods and services, 152, 172
governance, viii, 48, 67, 83, 105, 109, 138
government failure, 101
government procurement, 30, 64
government spending, 49, 114
governments, ix, 7, 9, 22, 46, 50, 53, 60, 64, 67, 87, 118, 138, 155, 156
governor, ix, 2, 4, 13, 127
grades, 12, 36, 146, 148
grants, 24, 28
Great Britain, 4
Great Depression, 72
greenhouse, 27
gross domestic product, 24, 76, 90, 91, 131
Gross Domestic Product, 48
grouping, 111
growth, ix, 2, 7, 13, 16, 23, 24, 36, 41, 43, 48, 49, 59, 61, 64, 70, 76, 81, 82, 90, 91, 127, 131, 132, 138, 139, 142, 147, 151, 155, 161, 175
growth rate, ix, 2, 7, 13, 16, 36, 49, 70, 127, 138, 139, 147, 151, 155, 161
Guatemala, v, vii, viii, 5, 7, 8, 13, 17, 22, 28, 30, 41, 57, 58, 59, 60, 61, 62, 63, 64, 65, 66, 67, 71, 77, 78, 88, 97, 99, 127, 151
Guatemalan border, viii, 71
guidance, 73, 119
guilty, 50

H

habitat, 26
Haiti, ix, 65, 137
hardliners, 39
health, 16, 52, 55, 67, 73, 77, 79, 80, 91, 93, 121, 134, 141, 146, 147, 150, 152, 166, 167
health care, 16, 150
health care system, 150
health services, 67, 146
health status, 79
heart attack, 164
hegemony, 149
hemisphere, 29, 51, 53, 65, 76, 79, 86, 87, 92, 111, 113
heroin, 53, 141
high school, 36
higher education, 148, 152
highlands, 11, 57, 125, 127
highways, 6, 93

HIPC, 90, 102
history, 14, 18, 25, 37, 39, 42, 47, 73, 74, 95, 97, 128, 129, 133, 148, 166, 168
HIV, 5, 79, 91, 93, 94, 166
HIV/AIDS, 5, 79, 91, 93, 94, 166
homeland security, 99
homes, 26, 42, 79, 176
homicide, 82, 103, 162
homogeneity, 13
Honduran governmental institutions, viii, 84, 105
Honduran military, viii, 73, 78, 79, 84, 92, 94, 105, 108, 109, 115, 117, 118, 119, 120, 121, 122
Honduras, v, vii, viii, 4, 7, 17, 18, 24, 28, 30, 32, 33, 41, 42, 43, 51, 55, 60, 66, 69, 70, 71, 72, 73, 74, 75, 76, 77, 78, 79, 80, 81, 82, 83, 84, 85, 86, 87, 88, 89, 90, 91, 92, 93, 94, 95, 96, 97, 98, 99, 100, 101, 102, 103, 104, 106, 107, 108, 109, 110, 111, 112, 113, 114, 115, 116, 118, 119, 120, 121, 122, 123, 124, 133, 137, 151
horticultural crops, 41
host, 72
hotel, 132
hotels, 36, 127, 146
House, 4, 22, 29, 51, 56, 102, 103, 106, 116, 117, 122, 173, 176
House of Representatives, 4, 22
housing, 49, 70, 79, 160
human, viii, 15, 17, 18, 22, 24, 27, 29, 39, 53, 61, 62, 63, 66, 73, 75, 77, 78, 81, 82, 85, 86, 87, 88, 89, 92, 99, 100, 101, 110, 113, 122, 129, 134, 141, 163, 164, 165
human development, 24
Human Development Index, 132
Human Development Report, 24, 181
human right, viii, 15, 17, 18, 22, 27, 29, 39, 53, 61, 62, 63, 66, 73, 75, 77, 78, 81, 82, 85, 86, 87, 88, 89, 92, 100, 101, 110, 113, 122, 129, 134, 141, 163, 164, 165
human rights, viii, 15, 17, 18, 22, 27, 29, 39, 53, 61, 62, 63, 66, 73, 75, 77, 78, 81, 82, 85, 86, 87, 88, 89, 92, 100, 101, 110, 113, 122, 129, 134, 141, 163, 164, 165
humanitarian aid, 79, 106
hunting, 2, 146
hurricanes, 6, 41, 42, 91
husband, 158
hydroelectric power, 16

I

ICC, 77
ideal, 171
ideals, 132

Index

189

identification, 170, 173
identity, 148
illiteracy, 65
image, 47, 150
IMF, 31, 32, 45, 48, 49, 55, 70, 82, 90, 92, 102, 122, 132, 134, 139, 140, 180
immigrants, 54, 96, 97, 157
immigration, 78
imports, 7, 16, 18, 31, 54, 64, 80, 91, 95, 111, 127, 142, 147, 171
impotence, 89
imprisonment, 177
improvements, 87, 135
inauguration, 51, 61, 75, 84, 86, 88, 90, 91, 92, 102, 105, 106, 109, 121, 133, 158
income, 2, 13, 22, 36, 41, 49, 64, 65, 76, 79, 90, 135, 137, 141, 161, 166, 170, 181
income distribution, 65, 161
income inequality, 166
income tax, 41, 161, 170, 181
independence, 4, 8, 14, 22, 37, 59, 66, 72, 128, 130, 148, 162, 163, 174
Independence, 2, 12, 36, 58, 70, 72, 126, 146
indexing, 91
Indians, vii, ix, 3, 13, 37, 70, 147
indigenous peoples, 71
indirectly-elected governor, ix, 127
individuals, 97, 119, 152, 161
industries, 7, 15, 16, 41, 107, 128, 146, 181
industry, 6, 16, 36, 58, 76, 90, 168
ineffectiveness, 163
inefficiency, 63
inequality, 49, 92, 138
infant mortality, 65, 91, 132
infection, 91
inflation, 2, 16, 49, 61
informal sector, 131, 139, 165
information exchange, 170, 171, 173
infrastructure, 6, 15, 17, 24, 42, 48, 49, 52, 72, 79, 96, 139, 141, 160, 161, 169
inmates, 50
insecurity, 80
inspections, 172
institutions, viii, ix, 14, 15, 25, 27, 37, 39, 43, 52, 63, 73, 79, 84, 87, 96, 98, 105, 108, 118, 120, 129, 130, 132, 134, 137, 138, 141, 148, 151, 157, 166
insurgency, viii, 45, 50, 78
integrated circuits, 13, 23
integration, 67, 73, 77
integrity, 156
intellectual property, 30, 31, 41, 42, 64, 80, 134, 142, 152
intellectual property rights, 41, 42, 134, 152

intelligence, 39, 94, 98
Inter-American Development Bank, 49, 82, 90, 92, 102, 134, 152, 160
interest rates, 49
internally displaced, 165
international community, viii, 17, 74, 81, 82, 84, 85, 90, 91, 105, 111, 112, 113, 114
International Criminal Court, 29, 77
international financial institutions, 24, 31, 64, 79, 81, 90, 92, 111, 152
International Monetary Fund, 31, 45, 48, 55, 82, 90, 92, 102, 132, 134, 139, 152, 161, 180
International Narcotics Control, 28, 51, 56, 103, 142, 168, 169, 179
international terrorism, 38
intervention, ix, 27, 155, 156, 157, 166, 176, 177
intimidation, 63, 89, 119, 172
investment, 5, 6, 8, 16, 17, 19, 23, 24, 30, 42, 48, 52, 54, 55, 64, 67, 78, 91, 95, 99, 114, 121, 132, 133, 135, 141, 151, 152, 161, 163, 166, 171, 175
investments, 6, 16, 24, 42, 67, 78, 80, 95, 96, 107
investors, 9, 102, 128, 142
Iran, ix, 132, 133, 137, 139, 143
Iraq, 27, 38, 43, 50, 73, 77, 78
Ireland, 181
iron, 37
islands, 6, 140
isolation, viii, 13, 81, 122
Israel, 24
issues, 9, 15, 25, 42, 66, 75, 78, 82, 84, 87, 88, 92, 107, 133, 141, 171, 172, 173, 174, 182
Italy, 64, 181

J

Jamaica, 77
Japan, 7, 13, 64, 127, 147
job creation, 5, 159
jobless, 42
journalists, 75, 86, 88, 89, 163, 164
judicial branch, 62, 109, 150, 163
judiciary, 4, 38, 40, 63, 74, 100, 108, 121, 138, 141, 142, 150, 162, 163
jurisdiction, 17, 29, 74, 153

K

kidnapping, 167
Korea, 173

L

labor force, 13, 41, 130
labor market, 53
Ladinos, viii, 59
languages, viii, ix, 3, 58, 59, 71, 126, 127, 146
Latin America, viii, ix, 22, 24, 27, 28, 29, 31, 32, 33,
    43, 45, 46, 50, 55, 56, 64, 73, 74, 82, 86, 90, 91,
    100, 101, 102, 103, 111, 114, 121, 122, 123, 137,
    138, 143, 147, 152, 161, 168, 180, 181, 182
Latinos, 102
law enforcement, 5, 19, 29, 50, 53, 86, 98, 99, 142,
    159, 165, 169
laws, 16, 31, 61, 64, 95, 99, 109, 126, 159, 163, 165,
    168, 169, 171, 173
lead, 6, 27, 47, 71, 87, 95, 117, 151, 159, 160, 170,
    176
leadership, 15, 24, 32, 113, 128, 169
legality, 109, 143
legislation, 6, 14, 23, 25, 31, 49, 52, 55, 58, 94, 98,
    138, 155, 162, 163, 169, 170, 171, 172, 173, 174
lending, 72
letters of agreement, 43
liberalization, 157
Liberia, 11, 170
Libertarian, 12, 22
life expectancy, 24, 132
light, 7, 37, 64, 161
light rail, 161
liquid fuels, 16
literacy, 3
litigation, 133
livestock, 36, 70, 147
living conditions, 15, 79, 82, 96
loans, 24, 49, 79, 91, 111, 114, 151, 160
local government, 79, 141
logging, 3, 21, 26, 76
logistics, 78, 112
lubricants, 3
Luxemburg, 181

M

machinery, 3, 31, 59, 71, 95, 127, 142, 171
macroeconomic management, 64
majority, viii, ix, 4, 21, 24, 25, 30, 31, 38, 40, 49, 53,
    71, 73, 80, 85, 113, 114, 130, 131, 138, 147, 150,
    155, 156, 158, 160, 168
malnutrition, 65, 91
management, 18, 29, 41, 53, 93
manipulation, 163
manufactured goods, 147

manufacturing, 37, 64, 70, 80, 95, 130, 133, 147
marches, 61
marijuana, 53, 98
maritime security, 175
market access, 15, 30, 43, 141, 171
market-oriented economic policies, vii, 21, 22, 23,
    48
marketplace, 148
marriage, 25
materials, viii, 13, 37, 59, 99, 108, 118, 147, 167
matter, 17, 92, 115, 116, 120, 177
Mayan peoples, viii, 59
meat, 132
media, 30, 73, 75, 85, 89, 97, 110, 113, 119, 130,
    141
mediation, 115, 116
medical, 9, 13, 23, 24, 31, 78, 94, 140, 147, 151, 167
medical assistance, 9, 167
medical care, 24
membership, 55, 77, 98, 118, 152, 162
memory, 158
merchandise, 171
metals, 71
Mexico, ix, 3, 7, 13, 17, 24, 29, 33, 37, 41, 55, 59,
    62, 66, 67, 71, 80, 96, 99, 101, 102, 103, 120,
    123, 127, 137, 147, 152, 167, 181
Miami, 6, 32, 33, 40, 63, 76, 102, 122, 131, 143,
    149, 151, 177, 180, 182
middle class, 15
Middle East, 3
migrants, 9, 53, 54, 96, 140
migration, 51, 54, 78, 82, 92
militarization, 85, 110, 159
military, viii, ix, 7, 9, 13, 14, 15, 22, 25, 29, 37, 38,
    39, 50, 55, 59, 60, 61, 62, 65, 66, 72, 73, 77, 78,
    79, 80, 82, 83, 84, 88, 92, 93, 94, 98, 102, 105,
    107, 108, 109, 110, 111, 115, 117, 118, 119, 120,
    121, 122, 124, 130, 134, 140, 149, 150, 151, 155,
    156, 157, 164, 166, 167, 174, 175, 176, 177
military aid, 9, 50, 93, 111
military dictatorship, 150
military exercises, 167, 174
military government, 88, 149
military junta, 60
military-to-military, 80
Millennium Challenge Account (MCA), ix, 79, 137,
    141
mineral resources, 76
minimum wage, 84, 91, 100, 107, 121
Minneapolis, 63
minorities, viii, 71, 108
mission, 28, 65, 72, 78, 119, 167
missions, 19, 78, 80, 86, 113

mixed economy, 132

mixed Ibero-European and indigenous heritage, ix, 127

modernization, 73, 169

molasses, 3

monetary policy, 16

money laundering, 49, 53, 66, 78, 135, 149, 152, 168, 169, 177

monopoly, 15, 17

Montenegro, 60

mortality, 2, 12, 36, 58, 70, 126, 146

mortality rate, 2, 12, 36, 58, 70, 126, 146

motivation, 170

multilateral aid, 114

murals, 148

murder, 28, 49, 50, 60, 67, 98, 103, 164, 168, 172, 176

music, 147

N

NAFTA, 95, 171

narcotics, ix, 9, 19, 43, 53, 66, 78, 82, 87, 92, 97, 135, 137, 168

national debt, 5

National Defense Authorization Act, 29

National Liberation Party, vii, 12, 15, 21, 22

national origin, 130

National Party, viii, 2, 70, 72, 73, 75, 81, 85, 87, 112, 113, 120

National Public Radio, 103

national security, 75

National Security Council, 120

national strategy, 159

nationalism, 148

nationality, 130, 152

natural disaster, 22, 52, 65, 80, 91, 93, 167

natural disasters, 22, 52, 65, 80, 91, 93, 167

natural resources, 18, 70

negotiating, 17, 41

Netherlands, 13, 147, 181

neutral, 27

Nicaragua, v, vii, ix, 14, 17, 18, 30, 32, 41, 42, 55, 72, 76, 77, 78, 92, 121, 125, 126, 128, 129, 130, 131, 132, 133, 134, 135, 137, 138, 139, 140, 141, 142, 143, 151, 165

nickel, 59

nominee, 85, 100, 112

North America, 3, 9

Norway, 67

NPR, 103

NRP, 2

nucleus, 60

null, 122

O

OAS, 5, 8, 40, 43, 63, 66, 74, 77, 85, 86, 90, 101, 111, 113, 118, 119, 120, 122, 123, 134

Obama, 28, 29, 32, 51, 52, 93, 106, 115, 116, 166, 167, 172

Obama Administration, 28, 29, 51, 52, 93, 106, 115, 116, 166, 167, 172

obstacles, 58

oceans, 174

offenders, 99

Office of the United States Trade Representative, 181

Official exchange rate, 3

officials, 14, 43, 49, 50, 51, 53, 54, 55, 56, 84, 86, 87, 89, 90, 95, 97, 98, 99, 107, 110, 115, 116, 120, 130, 133, 141, 157, 162, 163, 169, 173, 174, 175, 177

oil, 16, 26, 31, 84, 91, 102, 111, 121, 122, 138, 139, 142, 147, 171

open economy, 78, 82

Operation Iraqi Freedom, 43, 77

operations, 6, 28, 29, 42, 50, 52, 55, 60, 65, 93, 94, 98, 133, 135, 166, 168, 174, 175

opinion polls, 158, 160

opportunities, 16, 42, 76, 80, 94, 98, 133, 151

ores, 151

organ, 4, 110

Organization of American States, 8, 15, 43, 66, 74, 77, 85, 100, 110, 111, 118, 122, 131, 134, 150, 152

organize, 165

organs, 109

ornamental plants, 13

Oscar Arias, vii, 17, 21, 22, 32, 33, 74, 111, 115, 116, 118

outreach, 98

Overseas Private Investment Corporation, 152

oversight, 12, 14

ozone, 27, 32

P

Pacific, 17, 41, 42, 43, 53, 125, 127, 137, 142, 148, 169, 174, 175, 176

PACs, 60

Pakistan, 104

palm oil, 71

PAN, 58, 62

Panama, v, vi, vii, ix, 17, 23, 33, 41, 71, 145, 146, 147, 148, 149, 150, 151, 152, 153, 155, 156, 157, 158, 159, 160, 161, 162, 163, 164, 165, 166, 167, 168, 169, 170, 171, 172, 173, 174, 175, 176, 177, 178, 179, 180, 181, 182
paranoia, 149
parents, 96
Parliament, 43, 66, 77, 152
pasture, 36
PCM, 101
peace, viii, 17, 27, 37, 38, 39, 40, 41, 45, 47, 50, 59, 61, 62, 63, 64, 65, 66, 67, 77, 78, 80, 118
peace accord, viii, 37, 39, 40, 41, 45, 47, 50, 59, 62, 63, 64, 65, 66, 67
peace accords, viii, 37, 39, 40, 41, 45, 50, 59, 62, 64, 65, 66, 67
peace plan, 17, 27
peace process, 62, 67
peacekeeping, 65, 78, 80
peer review, 170, 181
penalties, 55, 159
per capita income, 16, 22, 36, 90, 131, 137, 161, 166
permit, 65, 73, 173
Peru, 41
petroleum, 6, 13, 15, 37, 71, 80, 91, 95, 111, 127
pharmaceuticals, 3, 59, 142
Philadelphia, 63, 151
piracy, 3
plants, 16, 59
plastic products, 13
plastics, 142
platform, 15, 41, 73, 80
playing, 14, 39, 133
polarization, viii, 30, 81, 84, 86, 87, 88, 105, 113
police, 15, 25, 29, 43, 48, 50, 52, 53, 55, 58, 65, 73, 79, 88, 98, 103, 110, 117, 119, 130, 141, 150, 157, 159, 161, 162, 168, 169
policy, viii, 6, 16, 18, 21, 25, 65, 78, 81, 92, 98, 181
policy reform, 18
policymakers, 96
political crisis, viii, 24, 28, 32, 33, 76, 79, 81, 82, 85, 86, 87, 91, 92, 95, 98, 100, 102, 105, 106, 111, 112, 114, 116, 117, 118, 120, 149
political enemies, 132
political force, 134
political instability, 114
political opposition, 85, 162
political participation, 119, 135
political parties, 30, 58, 60, 83, 87, 88, 107, 108, 113, 123, 126, 130, 131, 150
political party, viii, 4, 22, 25, 38, 45, 47, 61
political power, 45, 156
political problems, 81

political system, 15, 47, 152
politics, 22, 25, 72, 124, 138, 158
polling, 25, 58, 73, 108
pollutants, 26
pollution, 26, 27
popular support, 61, 98
popular vote, 14, 74, 126
population, vii, viii, ix, 2, 3, 12, 13, 16, 17, 36, 37, 45, 47, 52, 53, 58, 59, 65, 71, 76, 79, 88, 91, 113, 126, 127, 132, 137, 146, 147
population growth, 2, 12, 36, 58, 126, 146
populist policies, 84, 107, 157
Portugal, 164, 181
poultry, 36, 95
poverty, vii, 5, 13, 21, 24, 32, 33, 41, 42, 45, 49, 52, 55, 67, 76, 77, 81, 82, 84, 90, 91, 92, 97, 107, 114, 132, 135, 138, 139, 140, 141, 151, 158, 159, 160, 161
poverty alleviation, 5, 91
poverty line, 81, 82, 91, 114
poverty reduction, 55, 82, 90, 92, 139, 140, 151
preferential treatment, 162
preparation, 131
preparedness, 22
preservation, 118, 134
presidency, 8, 25, 38, 60, 73, 75, 85, 109, 112, 120, 121, 126, 128, 129, 138, 150, 157, 158
President Obama, 46, 51, 56, 106, 115, 117, 120
presidential campaign, 161
presidential veto, 130
prevention, 50, 93, 98, 115, 165
primary school, 146
principles, 170, 172
prisoners, 50
prisons, 50, 97
private enterprises, 67
private investment, 48
privatization, 41, 42, 157, 158, 159
producers, 42, 54
professionalism, 39
professionalization, 79
professionals, ix, 60, 147
program administration, 56
progressive income tax, 15
project, ix, 18, 19, 47, 63, 64, 79, 93, 150, 151, 155, 156, 159, 161, 162, 163, 170, 175, 176
proliferation, 51
property rights, 133, 135, 141
prosperity, 7, 15, 46
protection, vii, 16, 18, 21, 24, 25, 26, 27, 61, 64, 80, 150, 159, 165, 170
public administration, 147
public debt, 91

public finance, 64, 81, 91
public health, 24, 64, 159
public officials, 130, 163
public opinion, 159
public pension, 41
public safety, 130
public sector, 5, 14, 16, 91, 130, 169
public service, 42, 52, 160
public support, 25, 73
public welfare, 165
Puerto Rico, 76
purchasing power, 147
purchasing power parity, 147

Q

quality of life, 175
quotas, 54

R

race, 38, 130, 157, 158, 161
radiation, 99, 167
radio, 47, 82, 85, 89, 110
rainfall, 16, 145
rape, 67
ratification, 22, 23, 25, 30, 66, 174
raw materials, 13, 127
real estate, 127, 133, 146
reality, 60
recession, vii, ix, 21, 24, 31, 45, 48, 49, 54, 72, 96, 111, 114, 155, 159, 161
recognition, viii, 27, 28, 81, 86, 90, 105, 112, 133, 172
recommendations, 39, 87, 101, 134, 139
reconciliation, viii, 43, 81, 86, 87, 92, 111, 114, 120, 129, 134
reconstruction, 38, 41, 43, 51, 52, 94
recovery, vii, 21, 24, 32, 41, 45, 54, 114, 135, 140
recurrence, 164
reelection, 14, 31, 157
reform, viii, 14, 16, 31, 39, 43, 49, 50, 52, 58, 62, 65, 72, 73, 81, 86, 91, 111, 121, 130, 140, 141, 150, 157, 159, 161, 162, 163, 165, 169
Reform, 2, 82, 88, 180
reforms, 31, 40, 41, 42, 54, 55, 60, 61, 62, 64, 81, 82, 84, 87, 88, 89, 91, 110, 142, 152, 159, 164, 176
refugee status, 112, 120
refugees, 3, 18, 164, 165
regional integration, 52, 77, 78
regulations, 67, 170
regulatory framework, 181

rehabilitation, 50
rehabilitation program, 50
rejection, 73, 86, 112, 113
relief, 73, 78, 79, 90, 94, 135
religion, viii, 59, 127, 130
remediation, 79
remittances, 41, 48, 49, 53, 81, 91, 96, 97, 114, 131, 139
renewable energy, 16
repair, 17, 48, 79
repression, 100, 122, 149
requirements, 14, 76
resentment, 174
reserves, 26, 163
resettlement, 62
resistance, 61, 71, 89, 101, 128, 129
resolution, ix, 8, 22, 42, 64, 66, 67, 74, 84, 93, 94, 105, 106, 115, 116, 118, 122, 133, 176
resources, 2, 5, 13, 17, 18, 25, 27, 59, 70, 79, 91, 98, 102, 122, 127, 147, 168, 169
response, 33, 49, 52, 60, 65, 79, 82, 93, 108, 122, 129, 135, 140, 149, 162, 169, 177
restaurants, 3, 13, 36, 127, 146
restitution, 112, 116, 120, 164
restoration, 18, 74, 120, 148, 176
restrictions, 29, 85, 89, 110
retail, 36, 41, 127, 146
retirement, 159
retirement age, 159
revenue, 91, 114, 161, 170
rhetoric, 73, 132, 140
rhythm, 147
rights, 29, 39, 50, 62, 64, 66, 75, 78, 80, 85, 86, 87, 88, 89, 92, 95, 110, 113, 118, 130, 133, 134, 141, 148, 163, 164, 165, 172, 174
risk, 89, 98, 99, 132, 141, 167
risk factors, 99
roots, 150
rotations, 43
routes, 43, 176
rubber, 59
rule of law, 29, 43, 61, 66, 77, 78, 79, 81, 106, 116, 118, 141, 166
rules, 64, 80, 133
rules of origin, 80
runoff, 25, 38, 61, 62
rural areas, vii, viii, 3, 36, 37, 41, 58, 67, 99, 138, 159, 165
rural development, 93, 141
rural population, 139
Russia, 133

S

sabotage, 60
safe haven, 167
safety, 8, 166, 175
salmon, 147
San Salvador, vii, 6, 35, 37, 38, 42, 47
sanctions, 29, 33, 84, 91, 105, 111, 112, 114, 171, 176
scarcity, 6
school, 9, 24, 29, 62, 79, 107, 132, 175
school enrollment, 107, 132
science, 158
scope, 41
seafood, 2, 6, 95, 147, 171
sea-level, 148
second language, ix, 3, 147
Secretary of Homeland Security, 96
security, 15, 21, 25, 28, 29, 39, 40, 48, 50, 52, 55, 60, 65, 73, 75, 79, 80, 82, 84, 85, 87, 88, 92, 93, 98, 99, 102, 110, 115, 117, 120, 124, 134, 140, 141, 152, 155, 159, 162, 165, 166, 167, 168, 169, 175
security assistance, 79, 80, 102, 115, 124, 166
security forces, 15, 29, 39, 40, 60, 75, 85, 88, 110, 117, 134, 141
security services, 159, 169
seizure, 106, 116, 143, 164
Senate, 4, 33, 116, 171, 173, 174, 181, 182
Senate Foreign Relations Committee, 173
senses, 22
services, 13, 15, 16, 24, 29, 30, 36, 44, 52, 64, 67, 78, 82, 99, 115, 119, 127, 133, 146, 147, 151, 165
settlements, 3, 128
sewage, 15, 17, 26
sex, 99, 165
shelter, 99
showing, 38, 47, 85, 160
shrimp, 6, 70, 71, 90, 95, 127, 147
signals, 55, 103
signs, 24, 32, 100, 121
silver, 148
Singapore, 17, 23, 25, 151, 163, 181
slaves, 91
smuggling, 66, 140, 169
social activities, 146
social change, 67
social development, 65, 102, 115, 141, 152
social expenditure, 32, 161
social indicator, 15, 67, 81, 139
social movements, 30
social organization, 123
social problems, 96

social programs, 150
social protection plan, vii, 21, 24
social security, 139, 159, 176
Social Security, 180
social support, 161
social welfare, vii, 21, 23, 24, 25, 48
social welfare programs, vii, 21, 23, 24, 25, 48
socialism, 132
society, 13, 46, 61, 81, 84, 85, 87, 88, 96, 98, 105, 107, 108, 110, 113, 148
Solicitor General, 14
solidarity, 51
solution, 103, 111, 115, 118, 170
South America, 5, 16, 90, 97, 111, 141, 145, 148, 168, 175
South Korea, 163, 173, 181
South Ossetia, 133
sovereignty, 8, 61, 133, 140
Spain, vii, 7, 13, 14, 22, 33, 37, 59, 64, 67, 72, 89, 102, 128, 147, 148, 151
species, 26
speculation, 6
speech, 130, 140, 163, 164
spending, 25, 28, 48, 54, 64, 91, 114, 131, 132, 157
stability, 8, 37, 49, 64, 73, 81, 82, 91
stabilization, 78
standard of living, vii, 16, 21, 24
state, vii, 2, 4, 12, 15, 17, 21, 22, 23, 24, 25, 27, 31, 37, 49, 63, 75, 85, 89, 90, 94, 101, 109, 110, 114, 119, 129, 131, 132, 137, 138, 146, 157, 158, 179
state enterprises, 158
state of emergency, 75, 85, 110
state-owned enterprises, 31, 49, 129, 157
states, 7, 8, 11, 37, 55, 90, 100, 101, 111, 124, 133, 174
statistics, 50, 56, 98, 181
steel, 37
stimulus, vii, 21, 24, 131
storage, 146
structural adjustment, 31
structure, 65
subsistence, 58, 76
subsistence farming, 76
substitution, 109
succession, 15, 84, 105
sugarcane, 41, 147
supervision, 112
suppliers, 3, 13, 37, 59
suppression, 85, 110, 113
Supreme Court, viii, 2, 4, 12, 14, 25, 31, 36, 38, 40, 58, 61, 62, 70, 74, 84, 105, 108, 109, 112, 117, 118, 120, 121, 122, 126, 130, 143, 146, 150, 162, 163, 164, 177

Index 195

surplus, 171
survival, 93, 166
sustainability, 175
sustainable development, 5, 8, 18, 26, 66
sustainable economic growth, 81, 134, 141, 166
sustainable growth, 78, 135
Sweden, 147

T

tactics, 30, 50
Taiwan, 7, 18, 24, 41, 147, 151
takeover, 61
target, 48, 65, 91, 159
tariff, 30, 95, 171
tax base, 64, 161
tax collection, 64
tax evasion, 49, 161, 170, 171
tax increase, 92
tax policy, 170
tax rates, 161
tax reform, 91, 161
tax system, 161
taxation, 170, 181
taxes, 41, 161, 169, 173, 181
teachers, 91, 107, 159
technical assistance, 18, 22, 52, 89
techniques, 98
technology, 23, 147
telecommunications, 6, 15, 31, 41, 42, 53, 72, 80, 95, 127, 132, 147
telephone, 6, 76
tension, 140
tensions, 138
tenure, 62
territorial, 5, 8, 43, 66, 67, 133
territory, 4, 7, 18, 26, 37, 43, 60, 71, 77, 85, 110, 133
terrorism, 43, 51, 78, 98, 99, 129, 167
terrorists, 128
textiles, 7, 13, 37, 54, 59, 64, 70, 127, 133, 137
third country fabric, 142
threats, 65, 76, 88, 89, 95
Title I, 30, 171
Title II, 30, 171
tobacco, 3, 71, 137
tourism, 6, 9, 13, 16, 18, 24, 48, 64, 81, 91, 95, 114, 133, 147, 151
TPA, 152
trade, 3, 5, 7, 16, 17, 18, 23, 28, 30, 31, 41, 43, 46, 52, 54, 55, 65, 66, 67, 77, 78, 80, 84, 91, 93, 95, 110, 115, 121, 127, 128, 133, 139, 140, 142, 152, 157, 158, 161, 165, 166, 169, 171, 172, 175
trade agreement, 17, 23, 41, 54

trade benefits, 41, 171
trade deficit, 41, 171
trade liberalization, 17, 18, 158
trade preference, 7, 30
trade union, 165
trading partners, 7
traditions, vii, 37, 147
trafficking, 9, 43, 49, 66, 78, 80, 82, 92, 97, 99, 135, 142, 157, 163, 165, 168
trafficking in persons, 78, 82, 92, 135, 163
trainees, 19
training, 29, 30, 40, 43, 52, 53, 79, 93, 94, 98, 99, 152, 167, 168, 169
training programs, 29, 94
trajectory, 28, 48
transformation, 65
translation, viii, 59
transparency, 53, 64, 67, 73, 132, 135, 141, 156, 169, 170, 171, 172, 173, 181
transport, 3, 49, 59, 79, 97, 168
transportation, 3, 15, 42, 58, 91, 93, 115, 119, 127, 135, 141, 146, 147, 151
transportation infrastructure, 42
transshipment, 141, 168
Treasury, 39, 173
treaties, 150, 153, 174, 175, 181
treatment, 17, 26, 85, 95, 110
trial, ix, 84, 105, 109, 157, 164, 172, 176, 177
Trinidad, 32, 33
Trinidad and Tobago, 32, 33
tropical forests, 18, 26, 28
turnout, 30, 38, 86, 113
turnover, 157

U

U.S. assistance, ix, 18, 28, 29, 67, 93, 134, 137, 166, 167
U.S. Department of Commerce, 33, 42, 56, 80, 103, 143, 181
U.S. Department of the Treasury, 181
U.S. economy, 76
U.S. policy, 27, 43, 66, 78, 81, 82, 92, 134, 168
U.S.-Dominican Republic-Central America Free Trade Agreement (CAFTA-DR), ix, 137
UN, 17, 39, 40, 41, 63, 65, 67, 77, 78, 134, 152
unemployment rate, 16, 139
UNESCO, 134
UNHCR, 165, 181
unions, 23, 30, 48, 101, 108, 113, 130, 165, 173
United Kingdom, 6, 7, 8, 66, 104

Index

United Nations, 5, 15, 17, 24, 27, 43, 62, 63, 74, 75, 77, 90, 97, 103, 111, 118, 119, 131, 132, 134, 140, 151, 181
United Nations Development Programme, 181
universities, 27
urban, 6, 19, 99, 100, 121, 127, 146, 149
urban youth, 19
urbanization, viii, 59
Uruguay, 32, 33

V

value added tax, 41
VAT, 41
vegetables, 13, 59, 64, 132, 137, 142, 147
vehicles, 59, 71, 142
Venezuela, ix, 13, 30, 33, 48, 55, 67, 90, 91, 102, 111, 121, 122, 127, 132, 133, 137, 138, 139, 148
vessels, 99, 151, 167, 168
veto, 130, 164
Vice President, 15, 21, 25, 28, 30, 33, 40, 48, 63, 75, 85, 87, 100, 112, 131, 149, 150, 173
victims, 25, 89, 99, 165
violence, 5, 28, 47, 49, 61, 63, 85, 89, 95, 97, 98, 103, 113, 134, 163, 164, 168
violent crime, 45, 63, 65, 67, 84, 87, 97, 103, 107
Volunteers, 79
vote, 5, 22, 25, 30, 33, 38, 39, 45, 47, 55, 61, 62, 72, 73, 85, 108, 109, 112, 116, 122, 129, 130, 138, 150, 157, 158, 160, 172, 174, 175, 176
voters, 47, 73, 159
voting, viii, 4, 38, 47, 58, 59, 121, 126, 139, 175

W

wage increases, 92
wages, 91, 96, 135
waiver, 134, 142
walking, 122
war, viii, 18, 22, 37, 39, 40, 41, 45, 72, 128, 177
Washington, 5, 15, 32, 40, 54, 55, 56, 63, 76, 100, 103, 115, 118, 123, 124, 131, 143, 151, 173, 180, 181, 182
wastewater, 32
water, viii, 3, 6, 15, 17, 26, 27, 71, 79, 93, 127, 131, 132

water resources, 131
water shortages, 132
water supplies, 17
watershed, 47
waterways, 26
wealth, 13
weapons, 97
web, 76
welfare, 22, 24, 150
welfare state, 22
well-being, 78
White House, 46, 51, 56, 124
wholesale, 146
wildlife, 6
withdrawal, 39
witnesses, 25
wood, 70
wood products, 70
worker rights, 141, 156, 165
workers, vii, 13, 24, 53, 72, 76, 89, 92, 95, 96, 130, 131, 139, 152, 155, 159, 162, 165, 167
workforce, 75, 76
World Bank, 17, 22, 31, 46, 49, 65, 82, 90, 91, 92, 101, 102, 134, 137, 139, 143, 152, 161, 180
World Development Report, 31, 143, 180
World Health Organization, 134
World Health Organization (WHO), 134
World Trade Center, 44
World Trade Organization, 17, 43, 77, 134, 158
worldwide, 16, 76, 170
WTO, 77, 134

Y

yarn, 71, 80

Z

Zelaya, viii, ix, 18, 24, 73, 74, 75, 76, 81, 83, 84, 85, 87, 88, 89, 90, 91, 92, 94, 98, 100, 101, 102, 105, 106, 107, 108, 109, 110, 111, 112, 113, 114, 115, 116, 117, 118, 119, 120, 121, 122, 123, 124, 127, 128, 133
zinc, 71